'*The Psychology of Political Communicators* provides a timely and strong set of comparative research studies that analyze how rhetorical political appeals to reason and emotion are challenging liberal democratic societies. The contributors seek to explain a variety of current topics including the rise of populism, Donald Trump's victory, gender discrimination in media, media ownership and trust. Tackling these controversial political and social trends, the volume is organized around three elements of political communication: political discourse and its cultural contexts, politicians in their roles as communicators, and the changing media environment. The chapters help us to understand the crucial and dynamic role of political communicators in shaping preferences and making meaning of the disruptive political world.'

—*Ann Crigler, University of Southern California*

THE PSYCHOLOGY OF POLITICAL COMMUNICATORS

In this timely study, Ofer Feldman, Sonja Zmerli, and their team of experts shed light on the multiple ways communication affects political behavior and attitudes. Written for students and scholars alike, *The Psychology of Political Communicators* uses examples from the US, Europe, Asia, and the Middle East to examine the nature, characteristics, content, and reception of communication in three major areas of discourse:

- The style and nature of language used by political actors in the national and international arenas
- The discourse used in nationalist populist movements and during negative campaigns
- The rhetoric of the media as it tries to frame politics, political events, and political actors

Collectively, the chapters form a solid foundation on which to understand the different roles language plays in the conduct of politics, the way in which these roles are performed in various situations in different societies and cultures, and the political outcomes of verbal behavior. This book will be of interest to scholars and students of political psychology and communication studies.

Ofer Feldman is Professor of Political Psychology and Behavior at the Faculty of Policy Studies, Doshisha University, Kyoto, Japan. He is the author of more than 90 journal articles and book chapters, and more than 100 encyclopedia items, in the fields of political psychology/behavior, communication studies, and Japanese politics, and the sole author, sole editor, and co-editor of 15 books and monographs, including *Talking Politics in Japan Today* (2004), *Seiji shinrigaku* [*Political Psychology*] (in Japanese, 2006), and the *Politische Psychologie: Handbuch für Studium und Wissenschaft* [*Political Psychology: Handbook for Study and Science*] (in German, 2015, with Sonja Zmerli).

Sonja Zmerli is Professor of Political Science at the Institut d'Études Politiques de Grenoble, France. Her research interests revolve around social capital, civil society, political support, income inequality, and welfare regimes. Her articles have appeared in *Public Opinion Quarterly*, *European Political Science Review*, *American Behavioral Scientist*, and *Social Science Research*. Most recently, she has co-edited the *Handbook on Political Trust* (2017, with Tom van der Meer).

Routledge Studies in Political Psychology
Edited by Howard Lavine
University of Minnesota

Advisory Board
Ted Brader, *University of Michigan*; Eugene Borgida, *University of Minnesota*; Marc Ross, *Bryn Mawr College*, and Linda Skitka, *University of Illinois, Chicago*

Routledge Studies in Political Psychology was developed to publish books representing the widest range of theoretical, methodological and epistemological approaches in political psychology. The series is intended to expand awareness of the creative application of psychological theory within the domain of politics and foster deeper appreciation of the psychological roots of political behavior.

1 **The Many Faces of Tolerance**
 Attitudes towards Diversity in Poland
 Ewa A. Golebiowska

2 **Emotions in Conflict**
 Inhibitors and Facilitators of Peace Making
 Eran Halperin

3 **Fox News and American Politics**
 How Television News Shapes Political Views and Behaviors
 Dan Cassino

4 **The Political Psychology of Women in U.S. Politics**
 Edited by *Angela L. Bos and Monica C. Schneider*

5 **The Feeling, Thinking Citizen**
 Essays in Honor of Milton Lodge
 Edited by *Howard Lavine and Charles S. Taber*

6 **The Psychology of Political Communicators**
 How Politicians, Culture, and the Media Construct and Shape Public Discourse
 Edited by *Ofer Feldman and Sonja Zmerli*

THE PSYCHOLOGY OF POLITICAL COMUNICATORS

How Politicians, Culture, and the Media Construct and Shape Public Discourse

Edited by
Ofer Feldman and Sonja Zmerli

NEW YORK AND LONDON

First published 2019
by Routledge
711 Third Avenue, New York, NY 10017

and by Routledge
2 Park Square, Milton Park, Abingdon, Oxon, OX14 4RN

Routledge is an imprint of the Taylor & Francis Group, an informa business

© 2019 Taylor & Francis

The right of Ofer Feldman and Sonja Zmerli to be identified as the authors of the editorial matter, and of the authors for their individual chapters, has been asserted in accordance with sections 77 and 78 of the Copyright, Designs and Patents Act 1988.

All rights reserved. No part of this book may be reprinted or reproduced or utilized in any form or by any electronic, mechanical, or other means, now known or hereafter invented, including photocopying and recording, or in any information storage or retrieval system, without permission in writing from the publishers.

Trademark notice: Product or corporate names may be trademarks or registered trademarks, and are used only for identification and explanation without intent to infringe.

Library of Congress Cataloging-in-Publication Data
Names: Feldman, Ofer, 1954– editor. | Zmerli, Sonja, 1966– editor.
Title: The psychology of political communicators : how politicians, culture, and the media construct and shape public discourse / edited by Ofer Feldman and Sonja Zmerli.
Description: New York, NY : Routledge, [2018] | Series: Routledge studies in political psychology ; 6 | Includes bibliographical references and index.
Identifiers: LCCN 2018026204 | ISBN 9781138596184 (hardback) | ISBN 9781138596191 (pbk.) | ISBN 9780429947292 (epub) | ISBN 9780429947285 (mobipocket/kindle)
Subjects: LCSH: Communication in politics. | Mass media–Political aspects. | Political psychology.
Classification: LCC JA85 .P79 2018 | DDC 320.01/4–dc23
LC record available at https://lccn.loc.gov/2018026204

ISBN: 978-1-138-59618-4 (hbk)
ISBN: 978-1-138-59619-1 (pbk)
ISBN: 978-0-429-48789-7 (ebk)

Typeset in Bembo
by Wearset Ltd, Boldon, Tyne and Wear

CONTENTS

List of Figures	*ix*
List of Tables	*x*
Notes on Contributors	*xii*

1 Introduction: Liberal Democracies and the Study of Political Communicators
 Ofer Feldman and Sonja Zmerli — 1

PART I
Political Leaders' Discourse — 11

2 The New American Electoral Politics: How Invited Behavior and Reality TV Explain Donald Trump's Victory — 13
 Michael Alan Krasner

3 Political Communicators and Control in Political Interviews in Japanese Television: A Comparative Study and the Effect of Culture — 31
 Ofer Feldman and Ken Kinoshita

4 Comparing Japanese and US Leaders' Communication: The Construction of Meaning in Addresses to the United Nations General Assembly — 56
 Sarah Tanke

PART II
Populist Communication and Negative Campaigning — 77

5 *They* Caused our Crisis! The Contents and Effects of Populist Communication: Evidence from the Netherlands — 79
   Michael Hameleers

6 Populism in Self-Directed and Mediated Communication: The Case of the Five Star Movement in the 2013 Italian Electoral Campaign — 99
   Cristina Cremonesi

7 Fighting With Fire: Negative Campaigning in the 2015 UK General Election Campaign as Reported by the Print Media — 123
   Annemarie Walter

PART III
Media Discourse — 143

8 Representations of Televised Debates in the Press and Their Influence on Political Candidates: The Cases of Spain, the UK, and the US — 145
   Laura Pérez Rastrilla

9 Non-Systemic Factors Underlying Rapid Change in Gender-Biased Media Framing of Female Politicians: 2009 and 2013 Israeli Newspaper Election Coverage — 165
   Gilad Greenwald and Sam Lehman-Wilzig

10 Old Traps and New Prospects: Gendered Media Images of Leading Female Politicians in Germany as Evidence for a Contested Modernization of Gender Knowledge — 185
   Dorothee Beck

11 "Men Prefer Redheads": Media Framing of Polls and its Effect on Trust in Media — 204
   Pazit Ben-Nun Bloom and Marie Courtemanche

12 Media Ownership: Propositions for an Extended Research Agenda — 225
   Sonja Zmerli

Index — 234

FIGURES

3.1	Proportions of direct replies to questions by politicians from different groups	49
5.1	The presence of populist ideas in Dutch media outlets	85
5.2	Comparing the presence of populist ideas in the media across outlets and journalistic routines	86
5.3	The direct effects of populist blame exposure on blame perceptions	92
5.4	The crucial role of source support in the effects of populist communication	93
5.5	Marginal effect plots for interaction attitudinal congruence and populist blame attribution in forced and selective exposure conditions	94
7.1	Use of negative campaigning in the 2015 UK general election campaign in print media	132
7.2	Use of negative and positive campaigning per party in the 2015 UK general election campaign in the print media	133
7.3	Overall pattern of attack behavior in the 2015 UK parliamentary election campaign in the print media	134
7.4	Party origin of attacks on parties in the 2015 UK parliamentary election campaign in the print media	135
7.5	Reported attack behavior per newspaper	136
9.1	Cartoon by Eran Wolkovsky, January 2, 2009	174
9.2	Cartoon by Amos Biderman, January 10, 2013	175
9.3	Percentage of total reports with gender coverage: Livni (2009) compared to Livni and Yachimovich (2013) – *Yedioth Ahronoth* and *Haaretz*	178
11.1	Article placement by meta-frame	215
11.2	Article size by meta-frame	217

TABLES

3.1	Types of questions posed to the different groups of interviewees	39
3.2	Cross-national comparison on the types of questions asked by interviewers and subsequent responses from interviewed politicians	41
3.3	Subjects of inquiries posed to the different groups of interviewees	42
3.4	The required perspective of replies, and the manner and style of questions from the different groups of interviewees	43
3.5	Distribution of the threat to face and the target of threat	45
3.6	Interviewers' reactions to replies of interviewees from different groups	47
3.7	Cross-national comparison on the reaction to questions and replies	48
4.1	List of examined addresses to the UNGA, 2006–2015	61
4.2	Frequent words in the Japanese and US corpora (AntConc)	62
4.3	Comparison of keywords in the Japanese and US corpora (AntConc)	65
4.4	Comparison of keywords between individual leaders (AntConc)	66
5.1	Exploring the appeal of populist ideas	90
6.1	Main characteristics of the press outlets analyzed	105
6.2	Information on the analyzed data (time frame: February 16–23, 2013)	106
6.3	Operationalization of populism "as a thin-centered ideology"	108
6.4	Operationalization of populism as a communication style	109
6.5	Reference to the elements of populism as a "thin-centered ideology" by communication channel	110

6.6	Reference to the elements of populism as a communication style by communication channel	111
6.7	Articles containing a reference to elements of populism as a "thin-centered ideology" by newspaper	113
6.8	Connotations given to the elements of populism as a "thin-centered ideology" by newspaper	114
6.9	Articles containing reference to the elements of populism as a communication style by newspaper	115
6.10	Connotations given to the elements of populism as communication style by newspaper	116
6.11	References to the elements of populism as a populist "thin-centered ideology" by type of communication and media outlet	117
7.1	Characteristics of selected newspapers in the 2015 general election campaign	130
7.2	Who attacks the most, as portrayed in the print media	137
7.3	Who used positive campaigning the most, as portrayed in the print media	138
9.1	Percentage and number of news reports with gender coverage frames: Livni (2009) vs. Livni and Yachimovich (2013) in *Haaretz* and *Yedioth Ahronoth*	174
11.1	Frames' characteristics hypotheses	211
11.2	Summary of content analysis findings	216
11.3	Trust in media and trust in poll by experimental condition	219

CONTRIBUTORS

Dorothee Beck is a Research Associate in the project entitled " 'Genderism' in Media Debate. Thematic Cycles from 2006 to 2016" at Philipps-University Marburg, which is funded by the Hessen State Ministry of Higher Education, Research and the Arts. Her research interests cover the relation of politics, gender, and the media. She is also a freelance consultant in personal and organizational communication and the coordinator of the Global Media Monitoring Project (GMMP) in Germany (http://whomakesthenews.org/gmmp).

Pazit Ben-Nun Bloom is an Associate Professor and the Gillon Chair in Political Science at the Hebrew University of Jerusalem, specializing in comparative political behavior and political psychology. She is the recipient of several awards and grants (e.g., ERC, ISF, NSF). Her academic work appeared in such venues as *The American Political Science Review*, *British Journal of Political Science*, *Comparative Political Studies*, *Journal of Public Administration Research and Theory*, *PLoS One*, *Political Psychology*, and *Political Behavior*.

Marie Courtemanche is an Associate Professor in the Department of Political Science at Thiel College. She has received grants from the Greenville Neuromodulation Center (GNC) to conduct her research (2015 and 2016) and is the co-author of a number of academic works appearing in such journals as *The American Political Science Review* (2015), *Political Behavior* (2012), and *Social Sciences* (2017).

Cristina Cremonesi obtained a Ph.D. in Political Science at the University of Pavia in 2017. Currently she is a Post Doc Researcher at the Department of Cultures, Politics and Society of the University of Turin. Her research interests concern populism, political communication, political attitudes, and electoral behavior. She is part of the Cost Action IS 1308 – Populist Political Communication in Europe.

Ofer Feldman is a Professor of Political Psychology and Behavior at the Faculty of Policy Studies, Doshisha University, Kyoto, Japan. He is the author of more than 90 journal articles and book chapters, and more than 100 encyclopedia items, in the fields of political psychology/behavior, communication studies, and Japanese politics, and the sole author, sole editor, and co-editor of 15 books and monographs, including *Talking Politics in Japan Today* (2004), *Seiji shinrigaku [Political Psychology]* (in Japanese, 2006), and the *Politische Psychologie: Handbuch für Studium und Wissenschaft [Political Psychology: Handbook for Study and Science]* (in German, 2015, with Sonja Zmerli).

Gilad Greenwald is a Lecturer in the School of Communication at Bar-Ilan University, Israel. His co-authored chapter is based, in part, on his recently granted Ph.D. dissertation. He is interested in cultural, historical, and political conceptions of gender, as they are reflected in female leaders' media framing during election campaigns. For the past five years, he has lectured in the fields of Mass Communication, International Relations, and Government and Politics.

Michael Hameleers is an Assistant Professor in Political Communication at the Amsterdam School of Communication Research (ASCoR), Amsterdam, The Netherlands. His research focuses on the intersections between populism and the media. Specifically, his research aims to provide in-depth insights into the presence, prominence, and effects of populist blame attribution in the media. In the midst of the global rise of populist parties, this research agenda aims to offer new insights into the role of the media in the persuasiveness and electoral success of populism.

Ken Kinoshita is an Assistant Professor at the Faculty of Social and Environmental Studies, Fukuoka Institute of Technology, Fukuoka, Japan. He has published several articles and books related to the working of parliament and political communication, including "Niinsei-ron" [Bicameral Theory] (in Japanese, 2015).

Michael Alan Krasner is an Associate Professor of Political Science at Queens College, CUNY, and also co-directs the Taft Institute, which promotes political participation. His articles have appeared in the *Journal of Peace Research*, *New German Critique*, *Social Policy*, *New York Affairs*, and *Urban Education*, and he is the co-editor of and a contributor to the forthcoming book *Immigrant Crossroads: Globalization, Incorporation, and Placemaking in Queens NY*.

Sam Lehman-Wilzig (Ph.D., Harvard University, 1976) served as Chair, Department of Political Studies (2004–2007) and the School of Communication (2014–2016) at Bar-Ilan University (Israel), and also as Chair, Israel Political Science Association (1997–1999). His fields of expertise are Political Communication; New

Media and Journalism; Extra-Parliamentary Activity; and The Information Society – authoring 57 academic articles and book chapters, plus three books in those fields.

Laura Pérez Rastrilla is a Fellow at the Department of Global Journalism at the Complutense University of Madrid. She was the recipient of a predoctoral grant from UCM. Her research focuses on strategic communication in international organizations and media coverage of armed conflicts. She has held visiting fellowships at the University of Rijeka, RANEPA (Moscow), the Free University of Brussels, and the University of Ljubljana.

Sarah Tanke is a Ph.D. candidate in political science/international relations at Sciences Po, Center for International Studies (CERI), CNRS, Paris, and her dissertation deals with Japanese multilateral diplomacy. She has recently published "Une diplomatie du respect: le Japon et le multilatéralisme" (*L'Harmattan*, 2017) and conducted research stays at the University of Cambridge, the German Institute for Japanese Studies (DIJ) in Tokyo, and Columbia University.

Annemarie Walter is Assistant Professor at the School of Politics and International Relations at the University of Nottingham. Her unique expertise is negative campaigning in comparative perspective; on this theme she has written her dissertation and published numerous articles in international peer-reviewed journals. Her research interests include election campaigns, political psychology, party strategy, and electoral behavior. Recently she published with Alessandro Nai an edited volume with ECPR Press entitled *New Perspectives on Negative Campaigning: Why Attack Politics Matters*.

Sonja Zmerli is Professor of Political Science at the Institut d'Études Politiques de Grenoble, France. Her research interests revolve around social capital, civil society, political support, income inequality, and welfare regimes. Her articles have appeared in *Public Opinion Quarterly*, *European Political Science Review*, *American Behavioral Scientist*, and *Social Science Research*. Most recently, she has co-edited the *Handbook on Political Trust* (2017, with Tom van der Meer).

1

INTRODUCTION

Liberal Democracies and the Study of Political Communicators

Ofer Feldman and Sonja Zmerli

Understanding Political Discourse: The Effect of Culture, Politicians, and the Media

Public discourse, as an essential ingredient of liberal democracies, is constituted in the public sphere where interests are articulated, opinions expressed and formed, arguments and counterarguments exchanged, and information circulated. Ideally, different types of actors are granted equal access to this discursive space: citizens as much as civil society organizations, businesses, scientists or experts, politicians, decision-makers, and the mass media. Irrespective of their specific interests, all types of communicators strive to place their issues on the public agenda and influence the way they are represented in public discourse.

As a hallmark of liberal democracies, public discourse is essential to solidifying the relationship between citizens and the state, as it contributes to enhancing political actors' responsiveness to citizens' political or economic preferences and to holding them accountable.

As a matter of fact, communication in the public sphere flows along several paths: downward from elected representatives to the general public, horizontally among political actors, including the news media, and upward from the general public and citizens' groups to decision-makers. And yet, the major goal of *political* communicators is to influence citizens' political opinions, attitudes, and behavior. By virtue of communicators' use of rhetoric, that is, the art of persuasive speaking or writing, citizens' beliefs, value orientations, or attitudes may be either reinforced or transformed and actions initiated. *Political* rhetoric is then the use of persuasion in the political process, i.e., the strategies used by decision-makers, members of various political groups, media reporters and editors, and other actors who are involved in public affairs.

The impact of political rhetoric can be encompassing as it appeals both to *reason* by creating political knowledge, framing a political situation to favor a particular "way of seeing" it, generating perceptions of political realities, or defining uncertain circumstances about which people must make political judgments; and to *emotions* by arousing a sense of compassion, solidarity, anger, fear, or even hatred, all of which affect people's political attitudes and behavior. As such, political rhetoric lies at the heart of political psychology (Feldman, 2015).

In recent years, consolidating as well as established liberal democracies around the globe have been experiencing a substantive emotive reorientation of public discourse with far-reaching political consequences. Most notably, mushrooming populist movements, Britain's EU referendum campaign, or Donald J. Trump's primary and US presidential campaign are illustrative examples of the use of communication strategies that greatly appeal to citizens' emotions. Their apparent effectiveness has made public discourse more polarizing, and increasingly difficult to reach political compromise and preserve social cohesion. Consequently, scholarly interest in the underlying causes and mechanisms has gained momentum.

Related to these developments yet conceptually distinct are political communicators' intentions and available resources to determine the social representations of issues, individuals, or groups of actors by framing them according to the political communicators' ideological dispositions or self-interests. In this constant contest over the social and political meaning of the world, politicians and the mass media both play a pivotal role. Of course, both types of political communicators work interdependently, although the intensity and the direction of dependency might vary. In recent years, though, the media, and in particular privately owned news media, have incrementally transformed their basic concept from that of information broker committed to the spreading of facts to that of broadcaster of networks' opinions or ideological frames, with at times rather "loose" connections to reality. Certainly, the newly coined term of "fake news," which is frequently used by so-called conspiracy theorists, some of which are renowned TV or radio show hosts, is a reflection of this trend.

While these so-called *opinionated* news media, which provide a fertile ground for the rise of populism, have hit the scene in numerous liberal democracies, no other better exemplifies this trend than Rupert Murdoch's conservative Fox News Channel, which was launched in the US in 1996 following the liberalization of the media landscape (Hopkins & Ladd, 2014). And yet, its uncontested success with conservative voters and considerable impact on their knowledge acquisition and opinion formation can surely partly be attributed to the specific cultural, religious, political, and economic environment characteristic of the US.

As a consequence, to fully be able to understand and reflect on the current challenges to liberal democratic societies, a profound assessment of *three* pivotal elements and how they are interrelated is indispensable.

There is, as the first element, the cultural context in which political discourse is embedded, or in other words, in which messages are produced, transmitted, perceived, decoded, and interpreted. Cultural features also greatly determine what it is possible to say or not in a given place or at a particular time, and thus have great bearing on the meaning of political messages. What is more, political rhetoric varies across different political settings: Political communicators in liberal democracies, for example, use different rhetorical styles than their counterparts in authoritarian regimes (Abdul-Latif, 2011; Anderson, 1998; Bayram, 2010; Marinelli, 2013), including different rhetorical devices such as slogans or metaphors (Beer & De Landtsheer, 2004; Charteris-Black, 2011; Feldman, 2004; Hülsse & Spencer, 2008; Taran, 2000). Yet, cultural characteristics affect not only political rhetoric but the entire communication that takes place in a given society. As a consequence, language that deals with political issues cannot be seen in isolation from everyday language. In fact, all language has the potential to become *political* language, that is, language used by political communicators with regard to political matters and for political purposes.

The second element focuses on politicians as political communicators. Apart from their leadership qualities, negotiation skills, and ability to build and preserve effective working relationships with colleagues, bureaucrats or the media, politicians have to demonstrate sufficient rhetorical skills to communicate effectively in the public sphere. They must cajole, convince, and persuade their constituents in order to achieve their political goals, which is to either maintain the status quo or initiate political change. When rhetoric is skillfully employed, savvy politicians can effectively mobilize voters to support their policies (Grube, 2013). For this matter, political actors undoubtedly possess a variety of reasons and motives for their choice of certain rhetorical styles which they vary according to the audience, time, and place. By the same token, they tend to focus their speeches, appeals, and declarations on issues they are familiar with, and to refrain from those that might adversely affect their political agenda or public image (Shenhav, Rahat, & Sheafer, 2012). Their language might be clear with direct appeals, revealing their real thoughts and intentions (Feldman, 2004), or they may, conversely, resort to equivocation as a communication style and thus appear ambiguous, contradictory, obscure, or even evasive (Feldman, Kinoshita, & Bull, 2017). Politicians' ability (or lack of) to choose the "right" words for the "right" public can make or break a political career (Feldman, 2004).

The third element is the media. In contemporary politics, the media are of central importance, as politicians and other officials mostly communicate indirectly with the electorate via print media, television, or radio, and also increasingly directly via social network services such as Twitter or Facebook. At the same time as the primary sources of political and social information for the general public, the media select and exclude issues to report on and thus define the news, frame particular aspects of the perceived reality, and "set the tone" for how the news is to be interpreted. As a consequence, the media affect citizens' political attitudes and behavior by influencing the way they construct images and perceptions of the political world and decision-makers (Bull & Feldman, 2012). The emergence of opinionated news media, frequently associated with the concentration of private media ownership, further exacerbates the impact of the media as a communicator with a genuine political agenda (Boukes, Boomgaarden, Moorman, & de Vreese, 2014). To counteract these significant trends, other political communicators try to control the scope and nature of the information spread this way. For this matter, political actors often tend to filter the information they volunteer to journalists, to prohibit them from publishing information which they wish to keep under wraps and to exploit their relationship with media representatives to their own advantage. Attempts to develop cozy relationships with reporters and editors, which, ideally, should result in favorable media coverage through which they seek the public's sympathy, understanding, and support for their political visions and activities, have proven quite fruitful (Feldman, 2011).

The empirical studies, comprised in this volume, all aim to unravel how these three elements interact to shape public discourse with a major interest in their impact on recent disruptive political and societal trends in liberal democracies. Employing a variety of conceptual and methodological approaches, these studies, individually and collectively, highlight the multiple roles political communicators play in various societies from the East to the West, including the US, the UK, Spain, the Netherlands, Germany, Italy, Israel, and Japan. The ensuing chapters thus aim to further our understanding of communicators' roles from a comparative and cross-cultural perspective.

Structure of the Book

Within the broad conceptual framework of political psychology, behavior, and linguistics, the contributions to this volume examine the nature, characteristics, content, and reception of political communication in the public sphere in three major areas of discourse analysis which guide the volume's structure:

1. The style and nature of the language used by *political figures* when addressing the public either directly, such as at rallies or the United Nations, or indirectly via the media through political interviews.
2. The language, frames, and tools used to promote populist communication.
3. The various communication strategies employed by *the media* as they try to frame politics, political events, political actors, and the polity for citizens as well as for decision-makers.

In accordance with these three analytical fields, the chapter contributions are organized into three thematic sections: Part I "Political Leaders' Discourse"; Part II "Populist Communication and Negative Campaigning"; and Part III "Media Discourse."

The first chapter of this volume, by Michael Alan Krasner, addresses in an up-front manner the presumably most unexpected and most consequential electoral victory in 2016: the election of Donald J. Trump as president of the United States. In his contribution, "The New American Electoral Politics: How Invited Behavior and Reality TV Explain Donald Trump's Victory," Krasner uses the concept of invited behavior to explore how Donald Trump adapted methods from Reality TV to connect to his voters, engaging with their anxiety and alienation and offering himself as their "voice" and their "winner." The techniques Trump employed echo earlier forms of "invited behavior," in which candidates invite their potential voters to feel a personal connection with the politician, but the novelty was that Trump's techniques were rooted in the paradigm of Reality TV, in which contestants win by being aggressive and by having the most outsized personality. This shift in approach and Trump's victory raise a fundamental question: Will the politics of the United States now be based on earlier political norms or on the new pseudo-reality created by the Reality TV methods?

The complex nature of interrelationships between the media and politicians in Japan is at the center of Ofer Feldman and Ken Kinoshita's following contribution, "Political Communicators and Control in Political Interviews in Japanese Television: A Comparative Study and the Effect of Culture." More specifically, this quantitative study analyzes, from a broad cross-national and cross-cultural perspective, the interpersonal interactions between interviewers and national and local politicians during broadcast political interviews and the extent to which each of the communicators succeeds in controlling the content of the televised interview, that is, the frame of the dialogue, the issues raised and discussed, and the scope and nature of the information the public receives. It further examines how changes in government affect the behavior of politicians from different political parties as they switch from opposition to ruling coalition and vice versa.

The third contribution to this first section focuses on how political leaders frame their understanding of international political issues. In her study "Comparing Japanese and US Leaders' Communication: The Construction of Meaning in Addresses to the United Nations General Assembly," Sarah Tanke draws on quantitative and qualitative discourse analysis to compare Japanese prime ministers' and American presidents' addresses to the United Nations General Assembly between 2006 and 2015. The comparative study demonstrates to what extent international status as well as socio-cultural, domestic, and individual factors contribute to differences in political discourse. Given that Japan continues to consider the United States as its most important bilateral ally, differences in the way international issues are framed supposedly play a crucial role in their diplomatic relations too.

The second section of this volume revolves around the theme of populist communication and its occurrences in three different cultural contexts. As the three contributions to this section forcefully demonstrate, populist communication is promoted by different types of communicators and via different types of communicative channels.

In his study "*They* Caused our Crisis! The Contents and Effects of Populist Communication: Evidence from the Netherlands," Michael Hameleers takes us to the Dutch context of highly salient and electorally successful populism and explores how populist messages are framed in media discourse and public opinion, and how such messages affect voters' opinions. Interestingly, populist communication is still a rare event in the traditional Dutch media, but highly salient in online communication. Yet populist messages are effective: They have an impact on voting behavior, populist attitudes, and perceptions of blame. This chapter thus provides systematic insight into how the central elements of populist communication can affect the opinions of citizens in an era of rising populism.

As the first study of its kind, the following chapter, "Populism in Self-Directed and Mediated Communication: The Case of the Five Star Movement in the 2013 Italian Electoral Campaign," by Cristina Cremonesi, investigates the causes of the renewed political success of populist parties in Italy by tracing the electoral communication of populist parties and their coverage in the print media. More specifically, it focuses on the rise of the Five Star Movement, an Italian populist party led by the former comedian Beppe Grillo, which was in its insurgent phase during the 2013 Italian electoral campaign. As the chapter reconstructs the full image of the movement as it was conveyed to Italian voters by analyzing both direct party-initiated communication and its newspaper coverage, it unveils the genuine role of some print media in setting up their own populist communication agenda.

In a similar vein, the final study of this second section, Annemarie Walter's "Fighting With Fire: Negative Campaigning in the 2015 UK General Election Campaign as Reported by the Print Media," highlights an under-researched topic, namely how negative campaigning through uncontrolled means of communication, such as newspapers, unfolds. Starting from the assumption that the way the media report electoral campaigns has an impact on voters' perceptions of the campaign and their voting decisions, the fact that the media are often criticized for painting a distorted picture of reality by over-representing negative campaigning and thereby amplifying its negative effects becomes all the more relevant. Walter's systematic and comprehensive study demonstrates that different newspapers indeed selected different positive and negative campaign statements to report on. In general, this selection process reflected the openly partisan nature of the newspaper.

With a distinct focus on the media as a political communicator but covering a wider array of topics, the third section particularly emphasizes the media's representations of political events as well as political actors and reporting more generally.

For instance, Laura Pérez Rastrilla's comparative study, "Representations of Televised Debates in the Press and Their Influence on Political Candidates: The Cases of Spain, the UK, and the US," focuses on the representations of televised electoral debates. By means of qualitative content analysis, she compares across three countries and numerous print media the representations of televised debates in order to examine whether and how different meanings are assigned to them and whether media representations of these events have an impact on candidates' subsequent TV performances. Rastrilla's empirical evidence suggests that televised debates are not associated with a universal meaning spread by the press, yet that prior newspaper representations of TV debates influence candidates' performances.

The causes and consequences of gender-biased framing of female politicians by the print media in Israel and in Germany and the ensuing trends are at the core of scholarly interest in the two following contributions.

Contrary to the "common wisdom" that biased media representations of female politicians are an indication of deep socio-cultural and historical conceptions of gender, Gilad Greenwald and Sam Lehman-Wilzig's study, "Non-Systemic Factors Underlying Rapid Change in Gender-Biased Media Framing of Female Politicians: 2009 and 2013 Israeli Newspaper Election Coverage," offers an alternative explanation. Based on quantitative content analysis of news items from two Israeli newspapers, they provide conclusive evidence that essential changes in media portrayals of female politicians might also be the result of circumstantial and election-specific developments. For instance, the findings reveal that the 2009 campaign coverage of Tzipi Livni was much more gender-biased than in 2013 during which the "novelty" factor of female candidates running for the office of prime minister was weaker. Moreover, in 2013 Livni was campaigning for the second time and was therefore presented as an experienced leader.

Similarly, Dorothee Beck examines change in and persistence of gendered media images of female political leadership and political masculinity in the German press. In her study, "Old Traps and New Prospects: Gendered Media Images of Leading Female Politicians in Germany as Evidence for a Contested Modernization of Gender Knowledge," she demonstrates that the media's perspective is that femininity remains the second gender in the political field. Yet, traits like motherly care, traditionally attributed to female politicians, have shifted from a criterion for exclusion from the political field to an aspect of feminine political capabilities. Political masculinity, though, is still the norm, and this no longer remains unspoken.

Different types of reporting and their impact on the perceived trustworthiness of the media have come under close scrutiny in Pazit Ben-Nun Bloom and Marie Courtemanche's study. In "'Men Prefer Redheads': Media Framing of Polls and its Effect on Trust in Media," they examine how the Israeli media present different types of polls and how this presentation affects trust in the media. Whereas publishing surveys and translating scientific results can promote an image of precision and neutrality, the media publish polls of varying methodological quality. The same newspaper may publish rigorous (apparently "objective") election studies at the same time as unrepresentative polls on people's sexual habits conducted by condom companies ("subjective" polls). The authors' line of argument is that the media create different frames for different types of surveys, each characterized by a distinctive pattern of presentation, in order to communicate the differences in the surveys to media consumers. Four types of frames are examined using a content analysis of a sample of survey-presenting articles published in the Israeli daily *Yedioth Ahronot* and confirmed using a validating experiment which also suggests that "subjective" polls reinforce readers' perception that the media are unprofessional and inaccurate, which leads to cynicism and distrust.

In conclusion, the final contribution by Sonja Zmerli asks which general inferences might be drawn from the studies presented in this volume and how the research agenda addressing today's threat of political and societal polarization exacerbated by populist communicators could be extended. In her essay, "Media Ownership: Propositions for an Extended Research Agenda," she proposes to consider whether and to what extent powerful media owners might pursue their own ideological, political, or economic agenda, which feed into populism, via their often opinionated news channels, broadsheets, or tabloids.

Finally, we hope this edited volume provides scholars interested in the field of political communication, political behavior, media, or cultural studies important insights as it addresses an array of questions which are at the heart of contemporary politics. For each of the chapters, it is possible to identify a range of issues with which students and researchers studying political behavior and psychology might be concerned, including political leaders' verbal behavior and its effect, and the news media's changing role within the political system. The book can thus be a useful and stimulating source for further research into the role played by political communicators in and across societies and cultures and a valuable guide for deepening our understanding of political rhetoric and communication around the world.

Words of thanks are due to many who helped bring this project to completion. The contributors to this volume graciously considered the ideas of the two editors and more than once, patiently and thoughtfully, revised and refined their contributions. For this, we both are most appreciative. We also appreciate the interest and support of Howard Lavine, the editor of the book series *Routledge Studies in Political Psychology*, for this publication project, and are grateful to Natalja Mortensen and Maria Landschoot, our editors at Routledge, who were very responsive and helpful during the progress of our collective efforts. Last, we owe a debt of gratitude to Kate Short for her careful copy-editing job and for her perceptive comments throughout, contributing greatly to the final quality of print.

References

Abdul-Latif, E. (2011). Interdiscursivity between political and religious discourses in a speech by Sadat: Combining CDA and addressee rhetoric. *Journal of Language and Politics*, 10, 50–67.

Anderson, R. D. (1998). Pragmatic ambiguity and partisanship in Russia's emerging democracy. In O. Feldman, & C. De Landtsheer (Eds.), *Politically speaking: A worldwide examination of language used in the public sphere* (pp. 64–75). Westport, CT: Greenwood Press.

Bayram, F. (2010). Ideology and political discourse: A critical discourse analysis of Erdogan's political speech. *ARECLS*, 7, 23–40.

Beer, F. A., & De Landtsheer, C. (2004). Metaphors, politics, and world politics. In F. A. Beer, & C. De Landtsheer (Eds.), *Metaphorical world politics* (pp. 5–52). East Lansing, MI: Michigan State University Press.

Boukes, M., Boomgaarden, H. G., Moorman, M., & de Vreese, C. H. (2014). News with an attitude: Assessing the mechanisms underlying the effects of opinionated news. *Mass Communication and Society*, 17(3), 354–378.

Bull, P., & Feldman, O. (2012). Theory and practice in political discourse research. In R. Sun (Ed.), *Grounding social sciences in cognitive sciences* (pp. 331–357), Cambridge, MA: MIT Press.

Charteris-Black, J. (2011). *Politicians and rhetoric: The persuasive power of metaphor* (2nd ed.). Basingstoke: Palgrave Macmillan.

Feldman, O. (2004). *Talking politics in Japan today*. Brighton: Sussex Academic Press.

Feldman, O. (2011). Reporting with wolves: Pack journalism and the dissemination of political information. In T. Inoguchi, & P. Jain (Eds.), *Japanese politics today: From Karaoke to Kabuki democracy* (pp. 331–357). New York: Palgrave Macmillan.

Feldman, O. (2015). Politische Rhetorik. In S. Zmerli, & O. Feldman (Eds.), *Politische Psychologie: Handbuch für Studium und Wissenschaft* (pp. 201–217). Baden-Baden: Nomos Verlagsgesellschaft. [in German].

Feldman, O., Kinoshita, K., & Bull, P. (2017). Failures in leadership: How and why wishy-washy politicians equivocate on Japanese political interviews. *Journal of Language and Politics*, 16(2), 285–312.

Grube, D. (2013). *Prime ministers and rhetorical governance*. London: Palgrave Macmillan.

Hopkins, D. J., & Ladd, J. M. (2014). The consequences of broader media choice: Evidence from the expansion of Fox News. *Quarterly Journal of Political Science*, 9(1), 115–135.

Hülsse, R., & Spencer, A. (2008). The metaphor of terror: Terrorism studies and the constructivist turn. *Security Dialogue*, 39, 571–592.

Marinelli, M. (2013). Jiang Zemin's discourse on intellectuals: The political use of formalised language and the conundrum of stability. *Journal of Current Chinese Affairs*, 42, 111–140.

Shenhav, S. R., Rahat, G., & Sheafer, T. (2012). Testing the language-power assumption of critical discourse analysis: The case of Israeli's legislative discourse. *Canadian Journal of Political Science*, 45, 207–222.

Taran, S. (2000). Mythical thinking, Arestotelian logic, and metaphors in the parliament of Ukraine. In C. De Landtsheer, & O. Feldman (Eds.), *Beyond public speech and symbols: Explorations in the rhetoric of politicians and the media* (pp. 120–143). Westport, CT: Praeger.

PART I
Political Leaders' Discourse

2

THE NEW AMERICAN ELECTORAL POLITICS

How Invited Behavior and Reality TV Explain Donald Trump's Victory

Michael Alan Krasner

Introduction

By traditional American political standards, Donald Trump's campaign for president should have ended quickly and ignominiously because he was spectacularly unqualified – ignorant of the issues and without political experience – and because he violated every relevant norm (Wayne, 2016). He insulted his party's elders, engaged in juvenile name-calling, and attacked the media. Yet Trump flourished, winning the Republican nomination handily and coming close enough in the popular vote to defeat Hillary Clinton in the Electoral College and become president of the United States.

This chapter argues that using the concept of invited behavior to analyze the methods and the effects of Reality TV explains not only this particular result, but also illuminates a new general pattern in American electoral politics. In section two of this chapter, invited behavior is adumbrated and a brief overview of the main idea is offered based on one example. Sections three and four of this chapter provide in-depth analysis of Reality TV as a genre and of the Reality TV devices Trump used in his campaigning. Section five identifies media coverage as the main benefit of Trump's behavior and a crucial cause of his success. Section six discusses the crucial political and analytical questions that have emerged, and section seven offers a brief conclusion.

Invited Behavior

Invited behavior (Krasner, 2012, 2014) refers to the process by which political leaders exploit existing social norms to gain support. Examples include signaling for applause in a speech (Atkinson, 1984; Bull, 2006; Bull & Feldman, 2011), and (in American politics) telling a joke (inviting laughter), extending a hand (inviting a handshake) or both hands to hold a baby (inviting trust), or confessing a transgression (inviting forgiveness) (Krasner, 2012). Most Americans learn early in life to laugh at a joke or sympathize with a confession. Politicians rely on these learned responses to defuse threats or encourage allegiance.

For example, John F. Kennedy, while campaigning for president, used a joke to defuse the accusation that his father was buying the election for him. He pretended to read a telegram from his father, which supposedly said, "Dear Jack, Don't buy a single vote more than is necessary. I'll be damned if I'm going to pay for any landslide" (Kennedy, 1958). The audience, including attending journalists, laughed and thus Kennedy re-established his control of the immediate situation. Instead of being the spoiled, undeserving son of an ambitious oligarch, Kennedy reframed himself as the leader who rises above a threat by demonstrating grace under pressure. By telling the joke, Kennedy invited both the journalists and the public to join him in the laughter that dismissed as unimportant the accusations against him and that re-established him as a worthy leader. More specifically, Kennedy re-established himself as someone who was worthy to take over the respected institution of the presidency (Krasner, 2002).

By contrast, Donald Trump has responded to media criticism by using the methods of Reality TV – aggression, belligerence, crudeness (Deery, 2015). He has hit back, for example, by calling the media "scum" (Hensch, 2015). Later, he accused them of "lying ... cheating ... stealing" (Hessler, 2017, p. 23). Instead of defusing the threat by inviting laughter from all concerned, Trump was inviting the audience to take sides, to join him vicariously in attacking the media. More broadly, he was inviting the audience to see him and to support him as their champion against a corrupt system that included a corrupt media.

The dynamic is the same – an invitation is being issued and accepted – but the content of the invitation and the demeanor of the candidate are sharply different. When major American political institutions enjoyed support and esteem, a candidate had to be respectful of those institutions and deemed worthy of leading them. That meant being knowledgeable, commanding, competent, dignified, serious, and consistent.

But currently support for all the major institutions of American politics has eroded sharply. Most Americans don't have much confidence in the media, the presidency, the Congress, or the Supreme Court. Only the military, the police, and small business enjoyed rankings above 50% in 2016. The overall rankings are substantially lower now than they were ten years ago (Gallup, 2017a). Similarly, most Americans are dissatisfied with how the country is governed (Gallup, 2017b). Further, most Americans feel and have felt that the country is headed in the wrong direction (RealClearPolitics, 2017). In this situation, as Trump is the first presidential candidate to demonstrate, attacking previously respected institutions is good politics. Inviting supporters to join in an attack on established politicians, the media, and the Congress works in this context of disillusion and alienation.

It also works on an electorate primed by binge-watching the winner-take-all, no-holds-barred forms of Reality TV that have come to the fore in America in the last two decades (Deery, 2015). This form, which Donald Trump dominated long before he turned his attention to the presidency (Associated Press, 2004), is particularly well-suited to his bellicose and self-aggrandizing style, and to a political moment defined by mistrust, anxiety, and resentment (Albertson & Gadarian, 2015; Cramer, 2016; Pew Research Center, 2017).

In this system, the old leadership virtues come under question: If the institutions don't work and the country is headed in the wrong direction, why trust the sort of people who have led in the past? Why do we want somebody who is experienced in the "bad old" system? Why do we want somebody dignified, knowledgeable, serious, etc., if they have done a bad job? Doesn't it make more sense to look for someone who is different both in background and in manner? Shouldn't we support someone who will aggressively challenge the system? And don't we want a winner because we feel our country has been losing? (Two thirds of Trump voters saw the 2016 election as the last chance to stop America's decline [Bump, 2016]). For voters with such attitudes, turning away from "old" systems accompanied a turn toward a new model based on Reality TV, which, as the next two sections discuss in detail, provided a blueprint for how to be a winner.

Reality TV: The New Paradigm

Reality TV expanded from a relatively small niche genre of the 1950s and 1960s to become a dominant format in contemporary television (Deery, 2015). Shows such as *Big Brother* and *Survivor*, and, more recently, *Keeping Up with the Kardashians*, have ranked among the most popular of their eras. In particular, Trump's show, *The Apprentice*, attracted an average of over 20 million viewers in its first season (2004) and ranked fifth overall (Associated Press, 2004).

Reality TV differs from other genres by supposedly being an unscripted, spontaneous expression of the feelings of the participants, whether they be contestants in a structured talent competition such as *American Idol*, or competitors in a more extended game in the fashion of *Survivor* or *Big Brother*.

In the latter cases, ubiquitous 24-hour videotaping removes the fourth wall that ordinarily denotes a fictional program. The audience sees the contestants as they "really are" – in good moments and bad – polite or rude, fractious or tranquil, controlled or explosive. Instead of being aware that they are an audience watching a work of fiction – a play or a movie – the viewers are invited to be part of the situation and to develop personal relationships with the players (Parashar, 2015; Russell & Puto, 1999).

Although Reality TV contestants were not candidates for political office, the shows sometimes echoed democratic processes (as in the case of *American Idol*, incorporating viewer votes to determine who should be eliminated), and established new norms of competition that could be applied to the political sphere. Thus, participants (who may be potential political leaders) may be seen in starkly informal settings where speech and behavior are governed by sharply different norms from those that have usually been applied to candidates for high office. Instead of the formality and social distance of debates or speeches, we have the casualness of the kitchen table. Vulgarity, crudity, and aggression occur frequently and therefore become normalized and legitimized, especially as they often "work" in the context of the show. As one of the most insightful theorists of Reality TV puts the point: "[o]ver time, the sheer prevalence of Reality TV content on our screens may function to normalize certain values and behavior, some of which were previously disreputable or taboo" (Deery, 2015, p. 11).

Thus, some of the most successful contestants on Reality TV were those who deceived or abused other contestants, including their allies. On *Survivor*, Russell Hands, who became one of its most famous players, burned the socks and poured out the drinking water of his own teammates. Omarosa Manigault, an African-American contestant on Trump's show, *The Apprentice*, who until recently occupied a post in Trump's White House (Haberman & Alcindor, 2017), falsely accused other contestants of racist acts. Dr. Will Kirby, arguably the most successful contestant on the pioneering show *Big Brother*, announced his intentions to deceive and betray his fellow contestants, and proceeded to do exactly that (Patrick, 2016; author's observations).

Of course, in *The Apprentice*, Trump was not competing. He judged competing teams of would-be entrepreneurs who undertook economic contests in order to win a place in his organization. Though Trump was not a contestant, like any Reality TV performer he offered himself to the audience – his judgments, his style, his personality were all on display; they were central to the program and its appeal (Kranish & Fisher, 2016). As the person whose monologue began each show and as the unique decision-maker, he was inviting the audience to be impressed by him, to agree with his decisions, to admire his accomplishments, his riches, his status, his expensive clothing, his decisive manner. In short, he was asking the audience to accept him as a worthy leader.

Making Politics Into Reality TV: Eight Strategies in Search of a Candidate

This section draws on the work of several sources (Deery, 2015, cited in Goldhill 2016; Field, 2017; Patrick, 2016) as well as the author's analysis, to show how Donald Trump used the strategic methods of Reality TV in his campaigns. In so doing, Trump was establishing new norms of political campaigning and a new definition of good leadership, substituting the values and techniques of Reality TV for the traditional values, techniques, and models of American politics.

Like many Reality TV shows, the contest for the Republican nomination in 2016 began with a plethora of candidates – 17 at the outset – thus putting a premium on the ability to (1) distinguish oneself in a crowded field; (2) make the strongest possible connection to the audience; and (3) be the most successful exploiter of the removal of the fourth wall. Trump did so by employing eight strategies, which are detailed below: Create a clear persona; stick to a simple, quick message; connect emotionally; connect personally (talk regular); create drama; break the rules to stay one step ahead; challenge the facts to blur reality; and keep the spotlight on you. Put in the language of our main concept, the contest turned on which candidate could issue the most compelling invitation. Thus, the first strategy for success on Reality TV:

Create a Clear Persona

The logic is obvious: If the scene is crowded, one must stand out to succeed. If the audience's attention span is limited, as the attention span for politics of most Americans is notoriously limited (Achen & Bartels, 2017), then one must make a strong first impression.

Donald Trump began with a distinct advantage: He was already famous. He had an outsized public presence based first on his years as a flamboyant celebrity (and self-branding) billionaire real estate developer in New York City, the media capital of the United States, though that image had been severely tarnished by the year 2000.[1] From this limbo, he was rescued by Reality TV: "*The Apprentice* turned Trump from a blowhard Richie Rich … [to a] symbol of straight talk, an evangelist for the American gospel of success … supremely competent and confident, dispensing his authority and getting immediate results" (Kranish & Fisher, 2016, p. 218). Keeping in mind that Trump's show at its peak attracted millions of viewers and that Reality TV has been shown to create a strong sense of connection between audiences and performers (Parashar, 2015; Russell & Puto, 1999), one can conclude that Trump began the campaign with a core group of supporters who were convinced of his leadership abilities.

Trump's self-presentation included braggadocious assertions about his business success. Before his formal announcement, he asserted, "I'm the most successful person ever to run for the presidency, by far" (Hafner, 2015). At the formal announcement of his running for president in June 2015, he said, "I'm very rich" (Trump, 2015). Just after his announcement in a televised interview, Trump asserted:

> I was a great student. … I go out, I make a tremendous fortune. I write … the No. 1 selling business book of all time … I do *The Apprentice*, a tremendous success … I've employed tens of thousands of people over the years.
>
> (CNN, 2015)

In American culture, the successful businessman is not only admired, but is seen to be universally capable, hence the oft-heard mantra that the government should be run like a business (Newport & Saad, 2016). Thus, the carefully crafted public profile that Trump brought with him into the contest put him several steps ahead of the other candidates. He was already a highly public "brand." "No candidate since Ronald Reagan had entered politics as well-known as Trump" (Tanenhaus, 2017).

To this advantage he added an unprecedented degree of outspokenness that included vulgarity, crudeness, bullying, and lying. As noted above, he did not play by the previous rules of presidential nomination contests (Wayne, 2016). Instead, he made up schoolyard names for his opponents – "Low Energy Jeb" (ex-governor Jeb Bush), "Little Marco" (Senator Marco Rubio), "Lying Ted" (Senator Ted Cruz) – engaging in personal attacks that would have been considered far beyond the pale in any other year and from any other candidate, and exhibited little regard for the truth.

A few more examples will suffice to make the point: When Trump made his formal announcement for president, he labeled the Mexicans who came to the United States without documentation as "rapists … and drug dealers" (*Washington Post*, 2015). In a salvo against Megyn Kelley, the Fox News anchor with whom he was engaged in verbal combat, Trump said she had "blood coming out of her eyes, her whatever" (Rucker, 2015). In March 2016, when Ted Cruz was Trump's most threatening rival, Trump posted a tweet with an unattractive picture of Cruz's wife, Heidi, next to an alluring photo of his wife, Melania, with the caption: "A picture is worth a thousand words" (Trump, 2016a).

On May 3, 2016, the eve of the Indiana primary that would eliminate Ted Cruz from the Republican contest, Trump said in an interview on Fox News that, shortly before the assassination of President John F. Kennedy, Cruz's father had been distributing leaflets together with Lee Harvey Oswald (who was the assassin according to the Warren Commission) (Fox News, 2016). Like so many of Trump's statements, this assertion was an outright lie.

Many viewers recoiled from the vulgarity, immaturity, xenophobia, misogyny, and simple dishonesty that they perceived in such statements, but for others they were more virtue than vice. They established that Trump was not an ordinary politician. He was not careful. He was not "politically correct." He would say whatever he felt. What came into his mind would come out of his mouth. He would not calculate. He would not trim his sails or alter his views to fit the fashion. Surveys indicated that 71% of Republican voters believed that Trump "told it like it was" (Marist Poll, 2015).

Crucially, then, he was seen by his supporters as honest, genuine, and trustworthy precisely because he was "rough around the edges." He was as different as he could be from the detested conventional, mealy mouthed, calculating politicians who constantly promised and never delivered, who said one thing and turned around after the election and did something else (Hochschild, 2016).

Thus, the invitation that Trump put forward for support was based on a much more distinct and powerful personal image than that projected by any other candidate. The response generated is exemplified in the reaction of one man at a Louisiana rally as described by Hochschild (2016, p. 224): "I see a middle-aged man, arms uplifted, as in the rapture, saying to those around him and no one in particular, 'To be in the *presence* of *such a* man!'" (italics in original).

The next strategy element is:

Stick to a Simple, Quick Message

Here Trump also stood out. He said again and again, loudly, that the United States was in crisis, that the US was declining, that the US didn't win any more, that other countries took terrible advantage of the US, that the American military was weak, that the US was threatened by ISIS, that the US had no good leaders or plans, that the US government made terrible deals, that immigrants were stealing jobs and murdering good citizens, and that only he could save the country. He offered few details of how he would do so. Instead he offered himself as the all-purpose solution.

Here are illustrative passages from Trump's acceptance speech to the Republican National Convention (Trump, 2016b):

> I have visited the ... communities crushed by our horrible and unfair trade deals. These are the forgotten men and women of our country ... but they will not be forgotten long. ... I am your voice ... Not only have our citizens endured domestic disaster, but they have lived through one international humiliation after another. ... our sailors being forced to their knees by their Iranian captors at gunpoint ... [the Iran agreement] one of the worst deals ever negotiated ... In Libya, our consulate brought down in flames ... I'm going to make our country rich again. ... I'm going to turn our bad trade agreements into great trade agreements. ... I am going to bring our jobs back ...

And he added, in a powerful phrase that touched both the chords of nationalism and the chords of the fading American Dream – individualist salvation – that "We will make America great again" (Trump, 2016b).

With the exception of Bernie Sanders, no other 2016 candidate came close to offering a message that rivaled Trump's for simplicity and directness and Trump's message had far more emotional appeal than Sanders'. Thus, Trump's invitation and its premise were plainer, more direct, more resonant, and simpler than those of any other candidate:

> Join me in recognizing that we are in trouble because our leaders are rotten. And accept me as your leader because I am different (in part because I am telling you this hard truth). I can make us great again if you will only support me.

Connect Emotionally

This dimension is captured by Hochschild's vivid and insightful analysis of a Trump rally (2016, p. 225): "Trump is … [focused on] emotional responses … rather than on detailed policy prescriptions. … His supporters … yearn to feel pride but instead have felt shame. Joined together with others like themselves, they now feel hopeful, joyous, elated…" Hochschild goes on to invoke Durkheim's concept of collective effervescence, felt by those who, "gather to affirm their unity," (Hochschild, 2016, p. 225) and to suggest that a charismatic leader such as Trump can become the unifying totem, but that "[t]he source of the awe and excitement isn't simply Trump himself; it is the unity of the great crowd of strangers gathered around him. If the rally itself could speak, it would say, 'We are a majority' " (Hochschild, 2016, pp. 225–226).

Thus people are invited to join the like-minded group that releases and validates previously suppressed feelings and opinions and which coalesces around the totemic leader. Potential supporters are invited to express openly their true feelings, to overcome political correctness, and to speak their minds and hearts as the candidate does. They are also invited to join with fellow sufferers, to be thus liberated, and to feel powerful as a result. They are invited to use this power to oust the deceitful politicians who have promised and failed to deliver for the people. And they are invited to accept and support Donald Trump as a new sort of leader whose vulgarity and aggression demonstrate his authenticity and the fact that he is different from the old leaders, and further to accept him as *in himself* the answer to America's problems. As an additional inducement, they are invited to participate either directly or vicariously in verbal abuse or physical attacks against enemies.

Thus, in general the invitation is to indulge primitive urges – to violence both verbal and physical, to domination, to crude language, to threats and intimidation. Trump offered to pay the legal fees of anyone who would beat up hecklers at his rally: "If you see someone getting ready to throw a tomato, knock the crap out of them … I'll pay the legal fees" (*Daily Mail*, 2016).

In some important way, the invitation being offered is to join in a process of emotional expression as much as it is to engage in an action that will change policy. The invitation does include the idea that a supremely good leader will replace the bad ones and reform American politics, but the question of how much actual results matter as opposed to the emotional satisfaction of first having one's feelings expressed and legitimated and then having one's champion win the White House is an open one. I will return to this point at the conclusion of the chapter.

Connect Personally, Talk Regular

By engaging in personal conflict with his opponents and the media and by connecting emotionally, Trump imitated the qualities most prized in Reality TV.

As Deery explains, "You don't have to back it up with anything. That kind of self-validating authenticity is enough. People say they're being authentic or unfiltered" (Deery, 2015, quoted in Goldhill, 2016). This echoes Hochschild's point about Trump being the "emotions" candidate, but, crucially, it is a commonplace about Reality TV, where Trump starred for 14 seasons.

In Reality TV, pretty much everyone does "talk regular," meaning that they use commonplace vocabulary and relatively simple sentence structures, but this is not necessarily the case with politicians. Trump brought the simple, common language of Reality TV to politics. In fact, several formal linguistic analyses demonstrated that Trump's language was much simpler than that of the other candidates. In October 2015, *The Boston Globe* newspaper used a linguistic test (the Flesch Kincaid readability test) to analyze candidates' announcement speeches. Bernie Sanders' speech was rated at a tenth-grade level, Hillary Clinton's at 7.7 and Trump's at 4.1, meaning that it could be understood by a fourth grader (Viser, 2015).

Similarly, researchers from the Language Technology Institute at Carnegie Mellon University found that the vocabulary in Trump's speeches was at a seventh-grade level, the lowest among the four main contenders (Clinton was at 9, Sanders over 10 and Cruz over 8) and that Trump's grammar score was fifth-grade plus, while the others were all at seventh-grade level (Spice, 2016).

A third analysis (Liberman, 2015) of selected speeches and press conference responses based on most often used words discovered very interesting differences between Trump and Jeb Bush. Bush's favorite 13 words focused on policy and included "strategy," "government," and "president." His most used word was "the." Only six of his favorite 13 words were one syllable.

By contrast, eight of Trump's favorite 13 words were one syllable. His most used word was "I" and his fourth most used word was "Trump." None of his favorite words referred to an institution, an official, an office, or an abstraction. It seems fair to say that Bush represented standard political rhetoric, while Trump was using the kind of common-speech self-promotion that is most effective on Reality TV.

This discussion reinforces the conclusion that Trump's invitation was the simplest, but also suggests that the simple language reinforced the idea that Trump was a regular person, not part of the political elite, not one to endlessly qualify and complicate the issues, but to present them in simple, dramatic, emotional terms and to offer himself as the simple, all-purpose solution. The implicit invitation is to join Trump in rejecting the frustrating, overly complicated view of the world presented by standard politicians and to accept Trump as the simple solution to all the world's problems. Further, and perhaps even more importantly, the invitation comes from the candidate who is seen to be sincere and most like the ordinary voter is his ordinary speech and emotional directness. Deery's comment is relevant here: "Reality TV is supposedly about amateurs, not professional actors. Being an amateur has a lot of validation and I think you see that in contemporary American politics" (quoted in Goldhill, 2016).

Create Drama

Drama brings attention; drama also conveys strength by presenting the protagonist as a winner in a stressful situation with high stakes. Inevitably, she/he who survives heated conflict will be seen as a strong leader.

Thus, all of the conflicts Trump's insults generated, all of the controversy that came from his crude attacks either on his rivals or their policies served his purpose by creating such drama, putting him at the center of situations that would command attention and give him the opportunity to gain support.

One former Reality TV producer says: "[We] look for larger-than-life personalities who speak their mind and don't shy away from conflict. Self-awareness is a liability. They reveal their character through conflict, and the bigger the character, the deeper the conflict, the better the show" (Grossman, 2015).

The invitation thus implied is: Join me (Trump) at the center of the action. Join the person around whom the world revolves. Join the man who makes things happen. Be part of the strongest side that is bound to win. Be part of this version of the political world, which is indistinguishable from the melodrama of Reality TV.

Break the Rules, Stay One Step Ahead

Breaking the rules and making unpredictable moves keep opponents off balance and draw the attention of the media and the audience. Insulting rivals and party elders flagrantly breaks the rules. So does refusing a loyalty oath. In the very first Republican debate on August 6, 2015, Trump was the only candidate to refuse to pledge his support to the eventual Republican nominee (Fox News, 2015). A second striking example is Trump's decision to pull out of the last debate in Iowa, which took place on January 28, 2016. By doing so he avoided a situation in which the other candidates would likely have joined forces to attack him (Patrick, 2016). The effect is to keep rivals guessing and again to keep one's self at the center of attention.

Trump also followed this strategy during the second televised debate with Hillary Clinton. He paced throughout the debate, often appearing in the camera frame directly behind his opponent or marching through the frame as she spoke. The actions were rude and perhaps menacing – he is a large man, after all, and she is a small woman – but perhaps most important, they were unprecedented. Nobody had ever done that before during a modern American presidential debate (author's observation), and thus the action commanded attention, functioned as a distraction from Clinton's responses, and was clearly an attempt to weaken his opponent's performance.

Trump also delighted his supporters and captured media attention by saying new and outrageous things at nearly every opportunity. One reporter for a well-regarded publication commented that Trump deserved his coverage because he said new things, while the other candidates only repeated their stump speeches (Ball, 2017).

This dimension extends the invitation to include: Join the man who will defy convention and shake up the system. Join the man who's always a step ahead of the opposition; who will always surprise you. Join the man who will break the rules to win and who will break the rules to help our country win and to help you and your family win.

Challenge the Facts, Blur Reality

By treating the facts as malleable or ignoring them altogether, Trump gained the widest possible latitude for all the other strategies. He could literally say anything, leaving the audience to puzzle out what was real and what was not, a pattern that, Deery reminds us, is typical of Reality TV. "Part of the game is to watch the show and discuss with friends the extent to which something may or may not be 'real' or 'true.' It's radical subjectivism: You decide what's real, what's a fact, what's not" (quoted in Goldhill, 2016). Or he could, as Anderson (2017) says in his extended analysis of why reality no longer applies to American society in general and politics in particular, count on his supporters to accept him as the ultimate expression of "fantasyland," a world in which feelings and wishes counted for more than facts.

Keep the Spotlight on You

All of the devices and examples previously mentioned serve this end, which is critical for successful competition. If the spotlight is on you, it's not on anyone else. No one else is becoming better known and better liked. No one else is getting the chance to put forward a policy, or make a claim or an attack that might damage you or gain support for them. It is in this sense that the saying, "There's no such thing as bad publicity," may be true. Moreover, if you are the center, you must, in the minds of the politically unsophisticated, have something going for you. You will come first to their minds when they are deciding for whom to vote.

The invitation here is identical to that for the element of drama. Potential supporters are invited to join the person who makes things happen, the one who is always at the heart of the action, the one who seems by the sheer force of personality to dominate others and carry all before him. The invitation epitomizes the personalized, simplified, and melodramatic world of Reality TV.

Summary: Donald Trump's Invitation

Donald Trump was the first presidential candidate to ignore the old presidential campaign norms that called for courtesy, dignity, self-control, maturity, and knowledge and instead to campaign by the norms of Reality TV – aggression, bombast, manipulation, crudeness and vulgarity, and a simplistic narrative based, in Trump's case, on fear mongering, racism, xenophobia, and sexism. Trump invited Americans to join him in the open excoriation of immigrants, women, and minorities and to further join him in open support for violence.

Trump's invitation combined nationalist right-wing populism with authoritarianism, as though he were saying: I invite you to trust and support me as the leader who will restore the greatness of our country and the social order that elevates the white working people who have for years been betrayed by the elites who privileged feminist women, blacks, Hispanics, and immigrants instead of those who have worked hard, played by the rules, and who built this country in the first place.

The Results

Reaping a Bonanza: How Following a Reality TV Strategy Produced Media Domination

The observant reader will have noted the remarkable coincidence between the rules for becoming a Reality TV star and the elements that attract American mainstream media news coverage. For its news stories, the American mainstream media crave drama, simplification, and personal conflict. This tendency, insightfully critiqued many years ago as "soap opera news" (Nimmo & Combs, 1983), has been discussed by numerous other media analysts (Bennett, 2016; Patterson, 1994).

In the 2016 nomination campaign, Trump's mastery of media brought unprecedented results as he garnered nearly two billion dollars' worth of free news coverage (so-called "earned media"), and outpaced his nearest rival, Ted Cruz, by a ratio of six to one (Confessore & Yourish, 2016). There seems little doubt that the practices and qualities just discussed produced this dramatic difference. Nor is there much doubt that this pattern of media domination was a key element in Trump's victory (Confessore & Yourish, 2016; Yglesias, Zarracina, & Frostenson, 2016), especially given the very small amounts Trump spent on advertising (Confessore & Yourish, 2016). Earned media was, along with social media, Trump's main connection to voters.

Mainstream media leaders conceded their proclivities, albeit with differing effects. Les Moonves, chairman of the board, president, and chief executive officer of CBS, famously said: "It may not be good for America, but it's damn good for CBS" (Bond, 2016). His evaluation of Trump's candidacy's effect on the network was largely positive:

> Moonves called the campaign for president a "circus" full of "bomb throwing," and he hopes it continues… "Man, who would have expected the ride we're all having right now? … The money's rolling in and this is fun," he said. "I've never seen anything like this, and this is going to be a

very good year for us. Sorry. It's a terrible thing to say. But, bring it on, Donald. Keep going," said Moonves. "Donald's place in this election is a good thing," he said.

(Bond, 2016)

In the aftermath of the election, Jeff Zucker, president of CNN, conceded one flaw in his network's coverage, which had included running Trump campaign rallies in their entirety without comment, while defending it overall. "We probably did put on too many of the campaign rallies in the early months unedited," Zucker said. "In hindsight we probably shouldn't have done that as much" (Gold, 2016).

Whatever the attitudes of the mainstream media leadership may have been, the hugely disproportionate coverage that Trump received remains a decisive factor in his gaining the Republican nomination. He was the first candidate to exploit fully the mainstream media's standard operating procedures.

This was no accident. Trump's starring role in *The Apprentice* gave him precisely the training and inclinations that he needed to exploit maximally these mainstream media norms. His victory was the triumph of Reality TV over actual reality. He repeatedly used the techniques of Reality TV to shape the mainstream media's coverage of the campaign. Thus, not surprisingly, the coverage shaped by the methods of Reality TV became the political reality of 2016 for much of the American public.

This inversion marks a truly remarkable turn of events. Instead of the sober and serious virtues traditionally associated with would-be presidents, a whole new set of traits came to the fore. Instead of the command of complexity, for example, the ability to make simplified emotional appeals took center stage. Instead of considered judgment, self-indulgent shooting from the hip produced support. Flamboyance challenged knowledge, while the ability to manipulate feelings took precedence over the command of policy. Dignity was replaced by comfort in front of a television camera.

Trump used the techniques of Reality TV to present himself as the people's champion – the one truly independent figure who was not a politician, not bound to the system – the one strong man who would fight anybody, who would never back down, who meant what he said and said what he meant. He might sometimes be crude, even ugly, but in a world where ruthless enemies cut the heads off American journalists, wouldn't putting up with a little crudity make sense for the sake of getting a strong, decisive leader? And he might seem sexist sometimes, but didn't all men talk that way? Hadn't he just been caught saying what all men said in locker rooms? What about Kennedy when he was president? And if Trump sounded racist or anti-immigrant sometimes, well, there were real problems there, weren't there? Maybe he went a little too far, but at least he was talking about the right things. As noted earlier, surveys indicated that a strong majority of Republicans believed that Trump "told it like it is" (MSNBC/Telemundo/Marist Poll, 2015).

The Crucial Question: Will Reality or Reality TV Dominate American Politics?

At this point in the discussion, the analytical and the political converge. The dynamics revealed by the concept of invited behavior explain the power of the connection made between Trump and his supporters and underscore the possibility that Reality TV may win out over reality as the dominant force in American politics.

The counterargument has been that Donald Trump's appeal would drop sharply once he became president because the people who voted for him in expectation of a leader who would help them materially would be disappointed. Yet many Trump supporters have remained loyal to Trump even when they learned he proposes to cut the very programs that have helped them personally. For example, a woman whose life was profoundly helped by a program for rape victims said in response to President Trump's proposed cuts in that program: "We have to look at what we spend money on," adding, "I will stand behind my president" (Kristof, 2017).

The crucial part of that statement is the last sentence and all that is implied by the word "my." The analysis of the dynamics of the relation between Trump and his supporters, based on the concept of invited behavior and the "rules" of Reality TV, illuminates the implied relation. Most importantly, it illuminates the mutual validation between Trump and his followers and the emotional and symbolic satisfaction gained by Trump's supporters from his campaign, his surprise election, and his continued aggressive behavior as president, all of which make him "my president," meaning the president who speaks for and represents people like me.

Of course, political science has always recognized that politics is the realm of emotional displacement as well as the realm of the rational pursuit of self-interest (Edelman, 1985, 1988; Lasswell, 1948). The political question is therefore one of balance. Will most Americans, most of the time, be manipulated by the techniques of Reality TV in particular and propaganda in general, or will they respond in terms of what serves their material and existential self-interest? For political scientists, the analytical question is, what are the factors that affect the answer to this political question? What are the factors that incline the system toward rationality and what are the factors that incline the system toward irrationality (and how do we define and measure these key variables)?

Conclusion

This chapter has, it is hoped, illuminated the process by which one candidate gained the presidency by issuing a successful invitation to the American people based on the techniques of Reality TV and also indicated how this process produces two results antithetical to democratic politics.

First, it invites and persuades the people to accept and become actors in a melodramatic pseudo reality – a world of looming threats, black-and-white conflicts, and heroic, rescuing leaders. Second, it creates a pseudo leader – a demagogue on a small screen who will save the beleaguered victims of the current corrupt system and protect them from existential threats at home and abroad. In practice, this leader proceeds to savage the interests of the very people who elected him by serving the same elites against whom he railed during the election campaign, as the recently passed tax bill demonstrates (Gleckman, 2017; Krugman, 2017; Tackett & Tankersly, 2017). All the while Trump bemoans the continuing transgressions of the media and officialdom and the threats of illegal immigrants and terrorists. Baker (2017) quotes a political science professor to this effect:

> "His appeal was definitely populist and his rhetoric remains so, but the reality of how he's governed has been more of a rich-person conservative with feints toward his populist base," said Sheri Berman, … "There's this split between rhetoric and reality for those who are paying attention to the details, which of course most voters have neither the time nor the energy to do."

If this sort of reality and this sort of leader prevail, American democracy as we have known it will perish. While the forms and rituals of campaigns and elections may persist, the substance of democratic politics will have been replaced by the nether world of Reality TV.

Note

1. The events that tarnished Trump's public image included the failure of his airline, The Trump Shuttle, and bankruptcies that involved several of his Atlantic City, New Jersey casinos and his flagship property, the Plaza Hotel in New York City, as well as his crumbling marriages (Kranish & Fisher, 2016).

References

Achen, C., & Bartels, L. (2017). *Democracy for realists*. Princeton, NJ: Princeton University Press.
Albertson, B., & Gadarian, S. K. (2015). *Anxious politics*. New York: Cambridge University Press.
Anderson, K. (2017). *Fantasyland*. New York: Random House.
Associated Press (2004, April 6). The Apprentice soars among TV viewers. Retrieved from https://usatoday30.usatoday.com/life/television/news/2004-04-06-apprentice-soars_x.htm.
Atkinson, J. M. (1984). *Our masters' voices*. London, New York: Methuen.
Baker, P. (2017, April 18). As Trump drifts away from populism, his supporters grow watchful. *New York Times*. Retrieved from www.nytimes.com/2017/04/18/us/politics/populism-donald-trump-administration.html.
Ball, M. (2017, April 7). *Comments in a roundtable presentation to the Midwest Political Science Association*. Author's observation.
Bennett, W. L. (2016). *News: The politics of illusion* (10th ed.). Chicago, IL: University of Chicago Press.

Bond, P. (2016, February 29). Leslie Moonves on Donald Trump: "It may not be good for America, but it's damn good for CBS." Retrieved from www.hollywoodreporter.com/news/leslie-moonves-donald-trump-may-871464.

Bull, P. (2006). Invited and uninvited applause in political speeches. *British Journal of Social Psychology*, 45, 563–578.

Bull, P., & Feldman, O. (2011). Invitations to affiliative audience responses in Japanese political speeches. *Journal of Language and Social Psychology*, 30, 158–176.

Bump, P. (2016, December 2). Two-thirds of Trump voters viewed the election as America's last chance. *Washington Post*. Retrieved from www.washingtonpost.com/news/the-fix/wp/2016/12/02/two-thirds-of-trump-voters-viewed-the-election-as-americas-last-chance/?utm_term=.bf18c7569ffd.

Catoline, A. J. (2016, October 12). Editing Trump: The making of a reality TV star who would be president. *Cinemontage*. Retrieved from http://cinemontage.org/2016/10/editing-trump-reality-tv-star-who-would-be-president/.

CNN (2015, July 1). Donald Trump: GOP takes me seriously. *CNN interview with Don Lemon* [Video File]. Retrieved from www.youtube.com/watch?v=AbdE1GNy7pQ&feature=youtu.be.

Confessore, N., & Yourish, K. (2016, March 15). $2 billion worth of free media for Donald Trump. *New York Times*. Retrieved from www.nytimes.com/2016/03/16/upshot/measuring-donald-trumps-mammoth-advantage-in-free-media.html.

Cramer, K. J. (2016). *The politics of resentment*. Chicago, IL: University of Chicago Press.

Daily Mail (2016, February 1). Trump warns audience at final pre-caucus rally that TOMATO-throwing protesters might interrupt his speech – and says fans should "knock the c**p out of 'em!" *Daily Mail*, Retrieved from www.dailymail.co.uk/news/article-3427111/Trump-warns-audience-final-pre-caucus-rally-TOMATO-throwing-protesters-interrupt-speech-says-fans-knock-c-p-em.html.

Deery, J. (2015). *Reality TV*. Malden, MA: Polity Press.

Edelman, M. J. (1985). *The symbolic uses of politics*. Urbana, IL: University of Illinois Press.

Edelman, M. J. (1988). *Constructing the political spectacle*. Chicago, IL: University of Chicago Press.

Field, K. (2017, February 15). What reality TV taught Trump, according to professors who study it. *Chronicle of Higher Education*. Retrieved from www.chronicle.com/article/What-Reality-TV-Taught-Trump/239200.

Fox News [JanRhett Ster] (2015, August 7). First republican primary debate 8.6.15 [Video File]. Retrieved from www.youtube.com/watch?v=mL3WKWMnytk.

Fox News (2016, May 3). WATCH: Trump connects Cruz's father to Lee Harvey Oswald. Retrieved from http://insider.foxnews.com/2016/05/03/watch-trump-calls-out-cruzs-father-old-photo-lee-harvey-oswald.

Gallup News (2017a, June 26). Americans' confidence in institutions edges up. Retrieved from http://news.gallup.com/poll/212840/americans-confidence-institutions-edges.aspx.

Gallup News (2017b, November 1). How Americans perceive government in 2017. Retrieved from http://news.gallup.com/opinion/polling-matters/221171/americans-perceive-government-2017.aspx?g_source=Polling+Matters&g_medium=sidebottom&g_campaign=tiles.

Gleckman, H. (2017, December 13). The Senate's tax bill would cut taxes three times more for business owners than workers. *Tax Policy Institute*. Retrieved from www.taxpolicycenter.org/taxvox/senates-tax-bill-would-cut-taxes-three-times-more-business-owners-workers.

Gold, H. (2016, October 14). Jeff Zucker has no regrets. *Politico*. Retrieved from www.politico.com/blogs/on-media/2016/10/jeff-zucker-cnn-no-regrets-229820.

Goldhill, O. (2016, November 6). Five reality TV show strategies Donald Trump has used throughout his campaign. *Quartz*. Retrieved from https://qz.com/828700/2016-presidential-election-donald-trump-has-used-reality-tv-strategies-throughout-his-campaign.

Grossman, S. (2015, September 26). Donald Trump, our reality TV candidate. *New York Times*. Retrieved from www.nytimes.com/2015/09/27/opinion/donald-trump-our-reality-tv-candidate.html?_r=0.

Haberman, M., & Alcindor, Y. (2017, December 13). Omarosa Manigault Newman to leave White House job next month. *New York Times*. Retrieved from www.nytimes.com/2017/12/13/us/politics/omarosa-manigault-newman-leaves-white-house.html?_r=0.

Hafner, J. (2015, June 1). Trump: I won't do straw poll if everyone backs out. *Des Moines Register*. Retrieved from www.desmoinesregister.com/story/news/elections/presidential/caucus/2015/06/01/donald-trump-straw-poll-mitt-romney-gucci-store/28313569/.

Hensch, M. (2015, October 26). Trump calls media "scum." *The Hill*. Retrieved from http://thehill.com/blogs/ballot-box/presidential-races/258057-trump-the-media-is-scum.

Hessler, P. (2017, July 24). How Trump is transforming rural America. *The New Yorker*. Retrieved from www.newyorker.com/magazine/2017/07/24/how-trump-is-transforming-rural-america.

Hochschild, A. (2016). *Strangers in their own land*. New York: The New Press.

Kennedy, J. F. (1958, March 15). Address before the Gridiron Club, Washington, DC. *John F. Kennedy Presidential Library and Museum*. Retrieved from www.jfklibrary.org/Asset-Viewer/Archives/JFKSEN-0900-009.aspx.

Kranish, M., & Fisher, M. (2016). *Trump revealed*. New York: Simon and Schuster.

Krasner, M. A. (2002). *Jokes and politics: The power of humor*. Paper presented to the 26th Annual Scientific Meeting of the International Society of Political Psychology, Berlin, July 16–19.

Krasner, M. A. (2012). *Invited behavior: A theoretical derivation and proposed experiment*. Paper presented to the 22nd IPSA World Congress, Madrid. July 8–12.

Krasner, M. A. (2014). *Invited behavior: Theory and attempted investigation*. Paper presented to the 23rd IPSA World Congress, Montreal, July 19–23.

Kristof, N. (2017, April 1). In Trump country, shock at Trump budget cuts, but still loyalty. *New York Times*. Retrieved from www.nytimes.com/2017/04/01/opinion/sunday/in-trump-country-shock-at-trump-budget-cuts-but-still-loyalty.html?_r=0.

Krugman, P. (2017, December 14). Republicans despise the working class. *New York Times*. Retrieved from www.nytimes.com/2017/12/14/opinion/republicans-working-class-taxes.html.

Lasswell, H. (1948). *Power and personality*. New York: Viking Press.

Liberman, M. (2015, September 5). The most Trumpish (and Bushish) words. *Language Log*. Retrieved from http://languagelog.ldc.upenn.edu/nll/?p=21068.

Marist Poll (2015, December 8). National Questionnaire. *MSNBC*, Retrieved from http://maristpoll.marist.edu/128-clinton-leads-trump-and-cruz-competitive-against-bush-rubio-and-carson/.

Newport, F., & Saad, L. (2016, March 2). Economic issues are Trump's strong suit among Republicans. *Gallup News*. Retrieved from http://news.gallup.com/poll/189731/economic-issues-trump-strong-suit-among-republicans.aspx?g_source=Election%202016&g_medium=newsfeed&g_campaign=tiles.

Nimmo, J., & Combs, D. (1983). *Mediated political realities*. London: Longman.
Parashar, S. (2015). Television connectedness: A comparative study of television programs. *International Journal of Applied Services Marketing Perspectives*, 4(3), 1737–1746.
Patrick, M. (2016, February 24). How Trump is winning with Reality TV. *Film Theory*. Retrieved from www.youtube.com/watch?v=n6PcQ1Be5ak&t=9s.
Patterson, T. (1994). *Out of order*. New York: Vintage.
Pew Research Center (2017, May 3). Public trust in government, 1958–2017. *Pew Research Center*. Retrieved from www.people-press.org/2017/05/03/public-trust-in-government-1958-2017/.
RealClearPolitics (2017). Direction of country. *RealClearPolitics*. Retrieved from www.realclearpolitics.com/epolls/other/direction_of_country-902.html.
Rucker, P. (2015, August 7). Trump says Fox's Megyn Kelly had "blood coming out of her wherever." *Washington Post*. Retrieved from www.washingtonpost.com/news/post-politics/wp/2015/08/07/trump-says-foxs-megyn-kelly-had-blood-coming-out-of-her-wherever/?utm_term=.ddceed09b5dd.
Russell, C., & Puto, C. (1999). Rethinking television audience measures: An exploration into the construct of audience connectedness. *Marketing Letters*, 10(4), 393–407.
Spice, B. (2016, March 16). *Most presidential candidates speak at grade 6–8 level*. Retrieved from www.cmu.edu/news/stories/archives/2016/march/speechifying.html.
Tackett, M., & Tankersly, J. (2017, December 18). Champion of the "little guy"? Trump's actions tell another story. *New York Times*. Retrieved from www.nytimes.com/2017/12/17/us/politics/trump-working-class.html?hp&action=click&pgtype=Homepage&clickSource=story-heading&module=first-column-region&region=top-news&WT.nav=top-news.
Tanenhaus, S. (2017). The making of the tabloid presidency. *Devil's bargain: Steve Bannon, Donald Trump, and the storming of the presidency* by Joshua Green. *New York Review of Books*, LXIV, 13. Retrieved from www.nybooks.com/articles/2017/08/17/steve-bannon-donald-trump-tabloid-presidency/.
Trump, D. (2015, June 16). Donald Trump presidential campaign announcement full speech. *C-SPAN* [Video File] Retrieved from www.youtube.com/watch?v=apjNfkysjbM.
Trump, D. (2016a). March 23 tweet. Retrieved from https://twitter.com/realdonaldtrump/status/712850174838771712?lang=en.
Trump, D. (2016b). *Acceptance Speech*. Republican National Convention. Retrieved from www.vox.com/2016/7/21/12253426/donald-trump-acceptance-speech-transcript-republican-nomination-transcript.
Viser, M. (2015, October 20). For presidential hopefuls, simpler language resonates. *Boston Globe*. Retrieved from www.bostonglobe.com/news/politics/2015/10/20/donald-trump-and-ben-carson-speak-grade-school-level-that-today-voters-can-quickly-grasp/LUCBY6uwQAxiLvvXbVTSUN/story.html.
Washington Post (2015, June 16). Full text: Donald Trump announces a presidential bid. *Washington Post*. Retrieved from www.washingtonpost.com/news/post-politics/wp/2015/06/16/full-text-donald-trump-announces-a-presidential-bid/?utm_term=.ff895a8f56cb.
Wayne, S. J. (2016). *The road to the White House, 2016*. Boston, MA: Cengage.
Yglesias, M., Zarracina, J., & Frostenson, S. (2016, July 18). How Donald Trump won. *Vox*. Retrieved from www.vox.com/2016/7/18/12184728/how-donald-trump-won.

3

POLITICAL COMMUNICATORS AND CONTROL IN POLITICAL INTERVIEWS IN JAPANESE TELEVISION

A Comparative Study and the Effect of Culture

Ofer Feldman and Ken Kinoshita

Introduction

Televised political interviews are organized media performances that aim to probe public officials and subject-matter experts on policy issues and questions of concern to the general public, including policy developments, stances of competing political candidates and groups, and political alternatives. These interviews offer interviewers—journalists, social critics, and scholars and researchers from different fields the opportunity to ask questions and challenge answers while allowing the interviewee to present their views to a large audience outside the television studio.

Such media events often resemble a battleground or struggle, as one or multiple participants try to dominate the direction of the discourse and the topics discussed. Interviewers try to obtain information through their questioning, request clarifications, and express disagreement to earlier utterances, and they argue against, criticize, or confront the stances and opinions of interviewees. Interviewees endeavor to affect the content of information conveyed to the public and to influence the way their viewers perceive their policies' orientations and relevant events that have taken place in the public domain. They tend to screen and mask their opinions and views, focusing their discourse on issues that make them feel most comfortable and competent and that are likely to garner public support, while avoiding issues with which they are unfamiliar or that might adversely affect their political agenda or public image. Savvy interviewees utilize various techniques to hedge and avoid answering tough questions (Feldman, Kinoshita, & Bull, 2015).

The distinctive setting of the interviews, in which interviewers and officials meet face to face in front of a large televised audience, enables viewers and researchers to monitor their communicative style when presenting or answering questions, that is, to follow the strategies employed by the participants to pursue their goals and watch how the players interact with each other.

This chapter focuses on these aspects of interviews, detailing interpersonal interactions during broadcast political interviews in Japan. It examines communicative patterns, focusing on the questions asked by interviewers and the responses of high-echelon members of the Japanese National Parliament (Diet) as well as local political leaders. It further compares Japanese interviewees' reactions to questions with those of their counterparts in two Western countries, the United Kingdom and the Netherlands. Throughout, special attention is paid to the extent to which each of the participants succeeds in controlling one key resource at stake in the interview: the content. Controlling the content of a televised interview determines the frame of the dialogue and the issues raised and discussed during these media shows. More importantly, it also controls the scope and nature of the information disseminated to the public.

Based on data collected over 14 months from three televised interview programs in Japan, the chapter first provides criteria to analyze questions and responses. From a cross-national, cross-cultural comparative perspective, the ensuing discussion details the types of questions posed during interviews and the corresponding types of answers interviewees provided. It further describes the reactions of interviewers to the interviewees' replies and the feedback of interviewees to the questions posted at them. Finally, the chapter discusses two important aspects at the center of the interaction between politicians and interviewers in Japan: the extent to which these aspects are affected by Japanese culture and their effect on the rhetorical culture in this country.

In addition, during the course of this study (2012 through 2013), two different political groups held political power in Japan and dominated the administration: (1) in the period before the December 16, 2012 general election for the Lower House of the National Diet, the Democratic Party of Japan and its coalition partner, the People's New Party, were in power; and (2) after the general election, the Liberal Democratic Party and the *Kōmei* Party regained control over Japan and maintained it through the end of the study (June 30, 2013). This change in government enabled us to follow the behavior of politicians from different political parties as they switched roles from opposition to ruling coalition and vice versa during the course of the study.

Methodology

The Interviews

The study is based on 145 live interviews with politicians broadcast over a period of 14 months (May 2012–June 2013)[1] on three nationally broadcast television programs: *Puraimu Nyūsu*[2] (Prime News; 111 interviews), *Shin Hōdō*

2001 (New Broadcast 2001; 13 interviews), and *Gekiron Kurosufaya* (Gekiron Crossfire; 21 interviews).[3]

The sample of 145 interviews consisted of 133 interviews with national politicians from all of the political parties represented in the Diet[4] and of 12 interviews with local politicians (e.g., the governors of *Tōkyō* and *Ōsaka*). Questions were usually posed by prominent journalists, who also functioned as moderators of the wider discussion. Scholars or experts in areas such as public policy or economics (referred to as *komenteitā* or "commentators") often participated in the interviews and contributed their own questions. Interviews were not scripted, but interviewees had a general idea of what was going to be asked. Only questions asked by the moderators or commentators were included in the analysis.

Procedure

Interviews from the three programs were recorded using a DVD recorder. A verbatim transcript was made of each selected interview. Criteria for identifying questions and responses were determined as detailed below. Two coding sheets were devised for analyzing the structure and verbal content of the interviews: the first for interviewer questions and the second for interviewee responses.

Examining Interviewers' Questions

"Questions" were regarded as utterances made by interviewers to elicit information from interviewees. The total number of identified and analyzed questions was 3,748: 1,977 posed to Diet members who belonged to the ruling coalition at the time, 1,365 to opposition party members, and 406 questions to local politicians.

The coding sheet first considered several features to analyze the questions (for details, see Feldman & Kinoshita, 2017a). It classified interview questions into two groups or types according to their syntactic expression: The first consisted of *prefaced questions*, including queries such as "What do you think?," "What do you feel?," and "Can I ask you…?" The second group, *non-prefaced questions*, included (1) yes/no questions; (2) disjunctive or alternative questions; (3) interrogative-word questions (or the *WH-questions*, i.e., questions that start with *what, why, who, when, where,* or *how*); and (4) declaratives, imperatives, or *moodless* questions (i.e., those that lack a finite verb) that may or may not be accompanied by a rising intonation even though the expression clearly functions to elicit information.

In this chapter, the prefaced questions are regarded as *open questions*; the non-prefaced questions (excluding the interrogative-word questions) are considered *closed questions*; and the WH-questions are categorized as *limited choice questions*.

Second, the coding sheet included two queries to identify the key topics at the core of the interview and the issues at stake in each question–response pair:

(1) "What is the main subject of the question?" and (2) "What is the main subject of the response?" Each of these two questions was sub-divided (and coded) with respect to six mutually exclusive criteria based on the content of the questions and answers (e.g., Feldman, Kinoshita, & Bull, 2016): (1) *knowledge* of a certain topic or fact or lack thereof; (2) *human affairs/significant others* (i.e., others' performance at work, impressions of their activities, etc.); (3) *political and social institutions* (e.g., impressions of and opinions on the activities and ideas within political parties and party factions); (4) *political process* (e.g., decision-making procedures, courses of action in the government, and political parties); (5) *political commitment* (e.g., pledges regarding courses of action); and (6) *issues* (e.g., opinions and views on policy issues and the public agenda). If category 6 was selected, the issues at the focus of the discussion were noted and were later clustered in related categories as detailed in the Results.

Third, the coding sheet assessed interviewers' questions in terms of their toughness and neutrality – two dimensions in which interviewers could be seen to vary. Interviewers' questions may be framed in such a way that will pose a threat to an interviewee's "face," that is, their reputation, dignity, and honor, and interviewees constantly run the risk of making *face-damaging responses* that make themselves and their political partners look bad, and may constrain their future freedom of action. "Face" is thus a prime issue in the interaction between interviewers and interviewees that often determines whether or not politicians *directly* reply to a question. This notion is particularly relevant in Japan where its meaning encompasses not only an individual's performance and abilities but also their standing and reputation within a given group. The concept of face is of extreme importance in maintaining interpersonal relationships, and the instinct to preserve "face" is deeply rooted in the culture. To disagree with, criticize, or offend someone in public would result in public embarrassment and the "loss of face," which means the loss of self-respect, self-worth, and dignity that the Japanese value very highly for both the speaker and listener. Examining the toughness of questions posed during televised programs enables us to weight the extent of threat to face of the interviewees and the questions' effects (Feldman & Kinoshita, 2017b).

To measure the toughness of questions, the coding sheet included two related questions. The first rated the question in terms of toughness (threat) on a six-point scale from 1 ("not threatening at all") to 6 ("highly or extremely threatening/tough"). "Not threatening" questions allowed at least one type of response that essentially posed no threat to face, and "tough" questions were defined as those where each of the possible responses presented at least some type or amount of threat to face. The second rated the question in terms of whom the threat was aimed at: (1) the interviewee, (2) the political party, (3) the government (e.g., the administration, the cabinet), (4) a group the interviewee belonged to, and (5) other.

The fourth feature included in the coding sheet tried to identify the interviewers' attitudes in terms of the cohesive ties that exist between questions and the answers preceding them. During interviews, interviewers assess the responses given by interviewees to determine whether they have answered the question or hedged. If interviewers consider the response (1) to be an answer, they can either expand on the same topic, for example, by raising a minor implication of a prior statement to encourage an interviewee to reconfirm or expand on prior remarks (termed "topic extension"), or they can shift to a new topic, that is, bring up a new aspect of the general topic under discussion rather than relating back to the preceding answer (a "topical shift"). Conversely, an interviewer who views the response as (2) a non-answer can either "reformulate" or restate an interviewee's declared position with the implication that the preceding answer was not sufficient and needs clarification or expansion (termed "reformulation"), or they can follow up by directly challenging the answer through making explicit the possible implications or presumptions of the answer, with the goal of testing some aspect of the interviewee's intentions, actions, or attitudes (termed "challenge").

Finally, the coding sheet included parameters to assess the *manner* in which questions were asked, the *required perspective* needed to answer, and the *style* in which questions were presented.

The *manner* in which questions were asked, especially the pragmatic means of weight reduction, was determined by examining the two ways in which interviewers challenged an interviewee's point of view either through questions accompanied by accounts (i.e., the interviewers provide their own logic or opinions as the basis for challenging questions) or quotation of critics (i.e., interviewers based their questions on actual or hypothetical critiques by an interviewee's opponents or cited other actual or potential challengers).

The *required perspective*, either the personal perspective or that of a social or political group interviewees were asked to provide, was assessed by distinguishing questions that explicitly sought from interviewees (1) personal or private information, such as their own opinions and feelings, as opposed to questions that sought (2) information, ideas, or views prevalent in the groups that interviewees belonged to (e.g., political parties). The *style* in which questions were presented was examined by differentiating between grammatically complete and incomplete questions. Questions categorized as grammatically complete follow the syntactic Japanese rule that the question particle *ka* must be attached to the end of the sentence accompanied by a rising intonation. Grammatically incomplete questions (i.e., those that lack the particle *ka*) are considered less formal, less direct, and friendlier, yet they still project turn-yielding despite their incomplete structure.

Examining Interviewee Responses

The second coding sheet focused on the interviewees' responses. To analyze these responses, the study utilized the equivocation theory. According to this theory, equivocation is a form of indirect communication that is ambiguous, contradictory, and tangential and that may also be incongruent, obscure, or even evasive (Bavelas, Black, Chovil, & Mullett, 1990, p. 28). Individuals typically equivocate when they are placed in an "avoidance-avoidance conflict" (or a communicative conflict), wherein all possible responses to a question have potentially negative consequences for the respondent, but a response is still expected by interlocutors and the audience. Here, the fundamental proposal is that equivocation does not occur without a situational precedent. In other words, although it is individuals who equivocate, such responses must always be understood in the situational context in which they occur. This is known as the *Situational Theory of Communicative Conflict* (STCC). Such conflicts are especially prevalent in interviews with politicians because of the nature of the interview situation. Under these conditions, interviewers may have an interest in pursuing controversial, sensitive, and divisive issues, and therefore put pressure on politicians to choose among undesirable alternatives in which all potential responses may damage the image of the politicians or alienate part of the electorate (Bavelas et al., 1990, pp. 246–249).

Bavelas et al. (1990) further theorized that equivocation can be conceptualized in terms of four dimensions, namely, *sender*, *receiver*, *content*, and *context*. In this chapter, only the context dimension was considered, with certain modifications (Feldman et al., 2015), to analyze interviewees' response attitudes. The question used in the coding sheet was, "To what extent is the interviewee's reply a direct answer to the question?" This was evaluated on a six-point Likert-type scale ranging from (1) "This is a direct answer to the question asked" through (6) "Totally unrelated to the question." Only (1) was regarded as a full reply; 2–6 were coded as equivocation to different degrees. Furthermore, if the answer was not (1), that is, the interviewee failed to reply to the question, then the response was coded in terms of 12 categories of non-reply (based on Bull & Mayer, 1993; e.g., intentionally ignores the question, acknowledges the question without answering it, and deflects a question back to the interviewer).

Coding

Each question identified in this study was coded and examined in light of the various categories explained above. The coding on the questions and replies was conducted initially by well-trained graduate and undergraduate students. Any problem that arose during the coding was resolved immediately through discussion with the authors. An inter-coder reliability study of a sample of 300 questions was conducted with another undergraduate student regarding each of the parameters examined. His analysis was performed independently of the main coders and resulted in a high level of agreement: The sample showed a Cohen's (1960) kappa of 0.87 for interview questions based on syntactic expression, 0.85

for the syntactic structure of the questions, 0.97 for quotation of critics/questions accompanied by accounts, 0.96 for questions that seek individual opinion/views as the representative of a group, 0.97 for grammatically complete/incomplete questions, 0.72 for the subjects of inquiry/response, 0.79 for the 19 issue types (see below), 0.87 for the threat level, and 0.85 for the context dimension.

Cross-National, Cross-Cultural Comparison

To understand the significance of the data gathered in Japan regarding the control over political interviews, that is, the power of the interviewers or the interviewees to impose their agenda or their preferred framing of the discussed matters on their partners to the dialogue, the ensuing discussion compares related data from the UK and the Netherlands (Voltmer & Brants, 2011).

There are obvious differences in sample size and research goals between the two studies. In comparison to our sample of 145 interviews aired during 14 months (May 2012–June 2013) in Japan, the data from the European countries consist of only 24 interviews, 10 from the Netherlands and 14 from the UK, broadcast over a period of four months (September–December 2009). The Japanese data include 3,748 questions and answers, in comparison to 281 questions collected together in the Netherlands (154 questions) and the UK (127 questions). Whereas the sample from the Netherlands and the UK was drawn from daily and weekly news or current affairs programs and political talk shows, the Japanese data were gathered explicitly from interview programs broadcast on a daily or weekly basis. Furthermore, the longest interview in the European countries lasted about 16 minutes, and the mean duration was about 5 minutes; the figures for Japan were 45 minutes and 44 seconds, and 24 minutes and 36 seconds, respectively. Lastly, the study of the Netherlands and the UK focused mainly on the control of content and time during interviews, while our research in Japan examined a wide range of issues from which we were able to draw data to analyze aspects related also to the control over content.

Although these two studies are not definitely similar with their research goals and the samples' size, the study from the European countries offers, in the limited empirical information available in the field, useful cross-national, cross-cultural data to compare with data gathered in Japan.

Results

The discussion of the results centers on two aspects associated with the control of the interview in terms of content: (1) the type of question and the corresponding type of answer, and (2) the reactions of interviewers to the interviewees' replies and the feedback from interviewees to the questions posed.

Type of Question and Corresponding Type of Answer

The type of question determines the degree of freedom interviewees are given to form their response and to choose the perspective and reasons they use to support their answer. Open questions, such as "What do you think?" and "What do you feel?," allow interviewees to reply in their own words, carry less risk of biased responses, and enable interviewees to disclose their real views and intentions. With open questions, interviewees can reveal what is more relevant and important to them with fewer limitations, without having desirable answers suggested to them in the question itself, as may happen with closed questions. The latter, as a whole, aim to control the nature and direction of responses and to obtain specific, focused information on a given issue. These questions often limit the interviewees' choices to clear-cut options such as "yes" or "no" or make them choose between two or three possible alternatives. Most interviewees prefer to articulate their own arguments, so they understandably favor open questions. Limited choice questions (who, what, etc.) lie between the open and closed types and enable more freedom in answers yet put some boundaries on the choices the interviewees can make in their replies.

Table 3.1 presents the distribution of the types of questions posed to the sample of national and local politicians on selected TV interview shows in Japan. The most frequently employed interrogative formats to all interviewed politicians were open questions (58.1%), followed by closed questions (36.5%, dominated by yes/no interrogatives, 32%, Feldman & Kinoshita, 2017a), and limited choice questions (5.4%).

Table 3.1 reveals slight differences in these proportions across the level of interviewed politicians. Whereas the proportion of open questions posed to politicians from the different levels is nearly identical, national politicians were challenged with more closed questions and fewer limited choice questions as compared with local politicians. Members of the ruling coalition and members of the opposition parties had an almost identical proportion of closed questions and only a slightly different proportion of open and limited choice questions. This demonstrates a general uniformity in the type of questions posed to national level politicians, regardless of their position in the Diet.

Different patterns are apparent in the distribution of question types and response patterns of Japanese politicians and those from the UK and the Netherlands (Table 3.2). In Japan, the majority of the questions posed to politicians were *open questions* (58%), implying that interviewers in this country asked questions that allowed interviewees flexibility in describing and explaining events and issues more than they did in the UK (26%) and the Netherlands (about 9%). The share of *closed questions*, on the other hand, was 36% in Japan, which is slightly higher than in the Netherlands (about 32%), but much lower than in the UK (66%). The data regarding the UK are supported by Bull's (1994) earlier findings that most questions (71.5%) directed at British

TABLE 3.1 Types of questions posed to the different groups of interviewees ($n = 3{,}748$)

		Politicians			Local level	Total
		Diet members				
		Coalition members	Opposition members	Total		
1. Open	Count	1,146	797	1,943	236	2,179
	% within question	52.6%	36.6%	89.2%	10.8%	100%
	% within interviewees	58.0%	58.4%	58.1%	58.1%	58.1%
2. Closed	Count	733	505	1,238	129	1,367
	% within question	53.6%	36.9%	90.6%	9.4%	100%
	% within interviewees	37.1%	37.0%	37.0%	31.8%	36.5%
3. Limited choice	Count	98	63	161	41	202
	% within question	48.5%	31.2%	79.7%	20.3%	100%
	% within interviewees	5.0%	4.6%	4.8%	10.1%	5.4%
Total	Count	1,977	1,365	3,342	406	3,748
	% within question	52.7%	36.4%	89.2%	10.8%	100%
	% within interviewees	100%	100%	100%	100%	100%

politicians by interviewers were either closed yes/no or declarative questions. Bull's results, which reported only 23.2% of the questions to be open-ended, suggest that televised interviews in the UK transmit political information through a conflictual communication style, probably because interviewers in the UK, arguably more so than in the Netherlands and Japan, perceive themselves as playing primarily a watchdog role over the administration (Voltmer & Brants, 2011). Finally, in Japan, only about 5% of the questions interviewers posed to politicians were *limited choice questions*, compared to 8% in the UK (8%) and the much greater 60% in the Netherlands.

The responses rates (type of answer) in Table 3.2 reveal that Dutch interviewers are extremely successful in controlling the content of the interview, because the overwhelming majority of the responses (93%) provide the asked-for information, whereas about one-quarter of the responses of British politicians were evasive. These results are completely in contrast with those of Japan, where interviewers appear the least able to control the content of the interview. Including the responses to open questions, which were also coded for their replies, Japanese interviewees gave evasive replies to almost 60% of questions.

Topic, Perspective and Style, and Threat to Face of Questions

To put the above findings in perspective, further details are offered on: (1) the subjects at the core of the questions; (2) the perspective from which interviewees were required to reply and the manner and style in which these questions were asked; and (3) the questions' mood (or threat to face).

(1) Subjects of inquiry: The data were initially divided into general categories of issues (1,945 of the 3,748 questions, 51.9%) and non-issues (1,803, 48.1%) (Feldman et al., 2016). The specific issues and non-issues are listed in Table 3.3.

Interviewers were most interested in hearing politicians' views on selected topics from the political, economic, and social agenda. Additionally, politicians were asked to share their thoughts on and assessments of non-issues, e.g., the evaluation of the performance of other politicians and officials and their reasoning on the working of the administration and other political institutions. As expected, because of their knowledge of and involvement in decision-making processes on the national level, members of the ruling coalition parties were presented with questions related to political issues more frequently than their counterparts from the opposition camp (62% and 37%, respectively). Conversely, opposition parties' members were more frequently asked about non-issues (63% and 38%, respectively), including their assessment of the government's performance.

(2) The perspective of inquiry and the manner and style in which the questions were asked: Table 3.4 details the perspective of inquiry and the manner and style in which the questions were asked. In a large majority of the questions

TABLE 3.2 Cross-national comparison on the types of questions asked by interviewers and subsequent responses from interviewed politicians (in percentages)

	Japan (n = 3,748)			UK (n = 127)				Netherlands (n = 154)			
	Type of question			Type of question				Type of question			
	Open	Closed	Limited choice	Total	Open	Closed	Limited choice	Total	Open	Closed	Limited choice	Total
Type of answer
Provides information	37.3	49.2	39.6	41.8	–	69.5	60.0	52.4	–	93.8	92.3	92.8
Evades information	62.7	50.8	60.4	58.2	–	30.5	40.0	23.0	–	6.2	7.7	6.5
Open answer	–	–	–	–	100.0	–	–	24.8	100.0	–	–	0.7
Total	58.1	36.5	5.4	100.0	26.2	65.8	7.9	100.0	8.6	31.6	59.9	100.0

Notes

n indicates the number of exchanges (question–reply pairs). In Japan, open questions were also coded as either a full reply or not. In the samples of the UK and the Netherlands, four cases are missing (uncodable) (based on Voltmer & Brants, 2011).

TABLE 3.3 Subjects of inquiries posed to the different groups of interviewees (n = 3,748)

		Politicians			Local level	Total
		Diet members				
		Coalition members	Opposition members	Total		
Non-issues	Count	753	859	1,612	191	1,803
	% within questions	41.8%	47.6%	89.4%	10.6%	100%
	% within interviewees	38.1%	62.9%	48.2%	47.0%	48.1%
Issues	Count	1,224	506	1,730	215	1,945
	% within questions	63.0%	26.0%	89.0%	11.0%	100%
	% within interviewees	61.9%	37.1%	51.8%	53.0%	51.9%
Total	Count	1,977	1,365	3,342	406	3,748
	% within questions	52.8%	36.4%	89.2%	10.8%	100%
	% within interviewees	100%	100%	100%	100%	100%

Issues:

(1) Government Bureaucracy (e.g., functioning of officials in the different government ministries) (684 questions); (2) Foreign Policy and Diplomacy (e.g., relations with the USA, China, and Korea) (456); (3) Economy (286); (4) Energy and Nuclear Power (261); (5) National Security (e.g., USA bases in Okinawa Islands, disputed islands with South Korea and China, tension with North Korea) (193); (6) Earthquake- and Tsunami-Affected Fukushima's (and other areas) Reconstruction Efforts (165); (7) Campaign Strategies (e.g., nomination of candidates, electorates' mobilization) (124); (8) TPP (Trans-Pacific Partnership) (97); (9) Constitution (e.g., revision, interpretation) (88); (10) Intra-Party Politics (e.g., strategy within a political party) (70); (11) Local Autonomy (65); (12) Diet Affairs Management (65); (13) Consumption Tax and Financial Affairs (61); (14) Cabinet and Government Performance (e.g., appointment of ministers, functioning of the cabinet) (52); (15) Interparty Cooperation (e.g., building grand coalition) (26); (16) Parties' Policy Beliefs and Preferences (e.g., objective of political parties) (21); (17) Public Opinion (opinion polls, support for political parties or issues) (16); (18) Diet's Dissolution (13); (19) *Yasukuni* Shrine [Shintō shrine in central Tōkyō, commemoration to war dead who served the Emperor during wars from 1867–1951. Since 1975 visits by Japanese prime ministers and ministers to the shrine have been causing concerns regarding a violation of the principle of separation of church and state] (10).

Non-issues:

(1) Knowledge of/familiarity with a certain topic/fact or lack of it (537, 10.6%); (2) Human affairs (382, 7.5%); (3) Political and social institutions (742, 14.6%); (4) Political process (547, 10.8%); (5) Political commitment (123, 2.4%).

These topics are mutually exclusive.

TABLE 3.4 The required perspective of replies, and the manner and style of questions from the different groups of interviewees ($n = 3{,}748$)

		Politicians				Local level	Total
		Diet members					
		Coalition members	Opposition members	Total			
Personal views, ideas, or opinion	Count	16	22	38		88	126
	% within questions	12.7%	17.5%	30.2%		69.8%	100%
	% within interviewees	0.8%	1.6%	1.1%		21.7%	3.4%
Affiliated group's views, ideas, or opinion	Count	1,961	1,343	3,304		318	3,622
	% within questions	54.1%	37.1%	91.2%		8.8%	100%
	% within interviewees	99.2%	98.4%	98.9%		78.3%	96.6%
Quotation of critics	Count	127	67	194		33	227
	% within questions	56.0%	29.5%	85.5%		14.5%	100%
	% within interviewees	6.4%	4.9%	5.8%		8.1%	6.1%
Account	Count	1,850	1,298	3,148		373	3,521
	% within questions	52.5%	36.9%	89.4%		10.6%	100%
	% within interviewees	93.6%	95.1%	94.2%		91.9%	93.9%
Grammatically completed	Count	1,027	579	1,606		201	1,807
	% within questions	56.9%	32.0%	88.9%		11.1%	100%
	% within interviewees	51.9%	42.4%	48.1%		49.5%	48.2%
Grammatically uncompleted	Count	950	786	1,736		205	1,941
	% within questions	48.9%	40.5%	89.4%		10.6%	100%
	% within interviewees	48.1%	57.6%	51.9%		50.5%	51.8%
Total	Count	1,977	1,365	3,342		406	3,748
	% within questions	52.8%	36.4%	89.2%		10.8%	100%
	% within interviewees	100%	100%	100%		100%	100%

(96.6%), interviewers sought information and views that were prevalent in the groups the interviewed politicians belonged to, including political parties and party factions, rather than personal views (3.4%). And local politicians were asked about their personal opinion much more often than national politicians (21.7% versus 1.1%), but these questions still represented a small minority of all questions asked.

Interviewers relied more on their own perceptions of events, providing their own logic or opinions (*questions accompanied by accounts*, 93.9%), and tended not to quote third parties, including interviewees' opponents or the news media (*quotation of critics*, only 6.1%), as the basis for their questions (Table 3.4). Politicians from the national level were asked more questions based on the interviewers' perceptions of reality as compared to local politicians, but the difference was quite small (94.2% versus 91.9%).

Finally, the table shows that Japanese interviews contained a slightly higher percentage (51.8%) of *grammatically incomplete questions* (those that lack the Japanese particle *ka* at the end of the sentence) as compared with *grammatically complete questions*. This indicates the tendency of interviewers to be less formal and to carry on in a cordial communication style with politicians at both the national and local levels.

(3) The questions' mood (threat to face): As noted previously, the interviewees' reputation, dignity, and honor (i.e., face) is a prime issue in the interaction between interviewers and interviewees. The questions' level of toughness determines whether the interviewee's face is threatened and thus affects the responses. Table 3.5 details the distribution of the threat to face along the threat-level scale and the target of the threat – either the face of the interviewees or that of the different groups they represented.

The "no threat at all" category contained 279 questions (7.4% of the questions), indicating that the remaining 3,469 questions (92.6%) contained varying degrees of toughness or threat to face. The most frequent type was level 2 ("slightly threatening"; 1,572 questions or 42%). Only about 12.8% (479) of all the questions were "very threatening" and "extremely threatening" (5 and 6 on the scale); therefore, those categories were combined in Table 3.5.

The majority of the questions asked during political interviews did not involve a great deal of threat to the interviewees – only 1.5% of the questions fall into this category. Furthermore, at every level of the scale, tough questions most often posed a threat to the face of the interviewees' affiliated groups, most notably political parties (e.g., criticizing contradictions in parties' political commitments and course of action, passing judgments on leaders' integrity, etc.) and the government (e.g., condemning contacts between officials or disapproving of procedures in public policy), rather than threatening the face of individual interviewees by directly objecting to, criticizing, or disapproving of their opinions, ideas, or activities.

TABLE 3.5 Distribution of the threat to face and the target of threat ($n = 3,748$)

	1. No threat at all: 279 questions	2. Slightly threatening: 1,572 questions	3. Somewhat threatening: 618 questions	4. Moderately threatening: 800 questions	5. and 6. Very and extremely threatening: 479 questions	Total: 3,748 questions
No threat at all	279	0	0	0	0	279 (7.4%)
Individual	0	36	11	8	1	56 (1.5%)
Political party	0	867	345	523	309	2,044 (54.5%)
Administration	0	520	203	237	156	1,116 (29.8%)
Affiliated groups	0	149	59	32	13	253 (6.8%)

Note
The percentages indicate the intensity of threat to face of a given target relative to the total number of questions ($n = 3,748$).

Reactions of Interviewers to the Interviewees' Replies and Interviewees' Feedback

The second aspect of control over content is how interviewers and interviewees reacted to each other's utterances. Did interviewers accept the replies provided by the interviewees or did they further pursue the answers they wanted to obtain? Conversely, how did the interviewees react to the questions posed?

Interviewers' response to replies: To observe the way interviewers reacted to the interviewees' replies, the cohesive ties that existed between questions and the answers preceding them were evaluated. That is, the tendency of interviewers to either request more information on prior remarks ("topic extension") or to raise a question related to the general theme under discussion ("topical shift") was noted if they evaluated the reply as an adequate answer. Conversely, the interviewers' inclination to ask for an explanation or expansion ("reformulation") or to challenge aspects of the interviewees' intentions or attitudes ("challenge") was noted if they regarded the response as a non-answer. Table 3.6 details the interviewers' responses, combining *topic extension* and *topical shift* under the category of *accept replies*; *reformulation* and *challenge* were placed in the category *challenge replies*.

An overwhelming majority of the replies were generally accepted by the interviewers; in other words, interviewers found more than 81% of the interviewees' replies to be satisfactory (with slight variations between local and national level politicians, as well as between the coalition and opposition camps' members). Only about 19% of the questions challenged the interviewees' replies. These were classified as either asking for clarification (*reformulation*, 13.5%), which is attributed mainly to the interviewers' desire to simplify the jargon and technical terms politicians used in their replies so that they would be better understood by the audience, or confronting interviewees regarding their answer to a previous question and inviting them to defend or justify their actions or attitudes (*challenge*, 5%).

From a comparative context, data for interviewers and interviewees in the three countries reveal very different patterns (Table 3.7). In the Netherlands, interviewers did not make significant attempts to challenge the replies of interviewees: Only 4.9% of the journalists' responses expressed dissatisfaction with the politicians' replies. This is in complete contrast with the UK, where a large proportion of the interviewers' questions (41%) aimed to further probe the interviewee by repeating or re-defining previous questions. Interviewers in Japan fall somewhere between these two countries as they accepted most politicians' replies, challenging them in only 19% of their questions.

Interviewees' reactions to questions posed: The interviewees' responses also differed by country. Whereas about 33% and 17% of the politicians in the UK and the Netherlands challenged questions that were put to them, respectively, almost 60% of them did so in Japan. Politicians in the Netherlands and the UK frequently challenged the interviewer's inquiry by changing or redefining the

TABLE 3.6 Interviewers' reactions to replies of interviewees from different groups ($n = 3{,}748$)

		Politicians			Local level	Total
		Diet members				
		Coalition members	Opposition members	Total		
Accept replies	Count	1,598	1,118	2,716	338	3,054
	Percentage	80.8%	81.9%	81.3%	83.3%	81.5%
Challenge replies	Count	379	247	626	68	694
	Percentage	19.2%	18.1%	18.7%	16.7%	18.5%
Total	Count	1,977	1,365	3,342	406	3,748
	Percentage	100%	100%	100%	100%	100%

TABLE 3.7 Cross-national comparison on the reaction to questions and replies (in percentages)

	Japan	UK	Netherlands
	(n = 3,748)	(n = 127)	(n = 154)
Interviewers			
Accept reply	81.5	58.7	95.1
Challenge reply	18.5	41.3	4.9
Interviewed politicians			
• Accept question	41.8	66.7	83.1
• Challenge question, of which	58.2	33.3	16.9
• Incomplete answer	45.3	0	0
• Make political point	43.6	0	0
• Acknowledge the question without answering on it/dismissal of question	5.1	42.9	15.4
• Change/redefine topic	4.0	35.7	49.9
• Attack the question	0.9	0	0
• Decline/refuse to answer a question	0.5	0	7.7
• State or imply that the question has already been answered	0.3	0	0
• Question the question (reflecting a question back to the interviewer)	0.2	0	0
• Repeat answer to previous question	0.1	21.4	26.9

Notes
n indicates the number of exchanges (question–reply pairs). The samples of the UK and the Netherlands are based on Voltmer and Brants (2011).

problem (49.9% of the challenges in the Netherlands and 35.7% in the UK) or by dismissing the question (15.4% and 42.9%, respectively). In Japan, the majority of politicians provided incomplete answers (45%) or tried to make a political point in their reply without directly replying to the question (44%).

To further detail interviewees' reactions to questions, the study attempted to identify the specific level (position) of politicians that most often tended to challenge questions in Japan, as well as the subject matter they did not provide direct replies to. For this purpose, the sample was divided into five groups as follows: prime ministers ($n = 48$, n = number of responses to questions asked), ministers and vice ministers ($n = 989$), ruling coalition party members ($n = 940$), opposition party members ($n = 1,336$), and local politicians ($n = 406$).[5]

Figure 3.1 shows the tendency of members of the different groups to provide direct replies to interviewers' questions. Prime ministers and ministers and vice ministers most often tended to equivocate in their replies. They gave full replies to less than 40% of the questions, and opted over and over again to make political points, provide incomplete answers, and acknowledge the questions without answering them (Feldman, Kinoshita, & Bull, 2017).

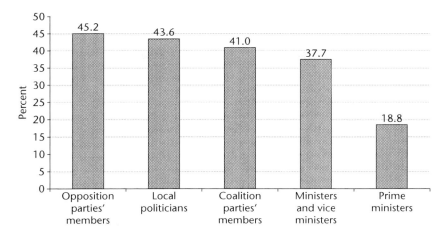

FIGURE 3.1 Proportions of direct replies to questions by politicians from different groups

Note
Means of the "direct reply" dimension for the different groups (ranging from [1] "This is a direct answer to the question asked," through [6] "Totally unrelated to the question"): opposition parties' members, 2.33; local politicians, 2.44; ruling parties' members, 2.45; ministers and vice ministers, 2.57; prime ministers, 3.31.

An in-depth analysis revealed a pattern that consisted of two opposing clusters of politicians (see Feldman et al., 2017). On one side are members of the ruling parties, in particular members of the Cabinet and prime ministers, who often tended to provide less complete and vague replies. On the other side are members of the opposition parties and local politicians, who replied to questions by providing clearer messages. These results demonstrate that "elite" politicians, that is, the high-echelon members of the administration, who are most up-to-date about the latest details concerning political dynamics and decision-making processes in the government and who serve most often as information sources to the media, tended to equivocate a great deal more than other politicians in replying to interview questions.

The analysis further identified the subject matters at the center of the "elite" politicians' equivocation. When asked questions regarding non-issues (subdivided into five categories, as noted in Table 3.3), they tended to equivocate less than when they were asked about issues. That is, politicians tended not to fully reply when asked about politics, society, and the economy. This suggests that *communicative conflicts*, resulting in indirect, ambiguous, and tangential responses, are more likely to occur when interviewees are asked about issues rather than when they are asked about non-issues (Feldman et al., 2017).

"Elite" politicians tended to equivocate on a range of issues, most notably in regard to two topics: the economy, and energy and nuclear power. Specifically, questions concerning the effect of so-called *Abenomics* (the economic policies of Prime Minister Abe Shinzō) and regarding the Great East Japan Earthquake of 2011 and the use of nuclear power as a major element of electricity production were often met with equivocation. Similarly, there were equivocal replies to questions on nuclear safety, nuclear waste disposal, and reviving nuclear power plants in Japan. Questions related to these two issues are arguably the most difficult to handle by leading politicians during political interviews. In contrast, these same high-echelon politicians had no trouble responding to questions about non-issues; for example, they directly replied to questions when asked to detail their knowledge of political events or to share their stances on human affairs and the political process (Feldman et al., 2017).

Discussion

Two main findings are suggested in this study in regard to televised political interviews in Japan and the participants' (interviewers and interviewees) dominance over the content of these shows. The first is related to the type and mood of the questions asked and the corresponding type of the replies provided. The second concerns control over content, that is, the reactions of interviewers to the replies provided by the interviewees and the interviewees' feedback to the questions posed. Both findings reflect cultural and political cultural features, which in turn affect the political and the rhetorical cultures in Japan.

The Type and Mood of the Questions Asked and the Corresponding Type of the Replies Provided

Three primary features were identified for questions:

1. Televised interviews in Japan consist mostly of *open questions* (almost 58%) that give the interviewees a large degree of freedom to form their responses and choose the perspective and rationale to support their answers. The ratio of open questions in Japan is much higher than those in the UK and the Netherlands, revealing the large amount of flexibility that Japanese interviewers allow interviewees to enjoy when describing and explaining events and issues in the public sphere.
2. The majority of the questions posed to Japanese politicians on both the national and the local levels sought information on views prevalent in their political groups rather than on the politicians' own personal or private ideas. The majority of the questions centered on political and social issues, presumably because interviewers were interested in learning about subject matter that affects the public at large more than in discussing non-issue matters. In particular, coalition party members were presented with questions related to political, economic, and social issues more often than their

counterparts from opposition parties. Conversely, members of opposition parties were asked about non-issues more often than their colleagues from the coalition.
3. Interviewers used slightly more *grammatically incomplete* questions, which are considered less formal and friendlier, thereby indicating their intention to carry on a relaxed, easy-going, and cordial communication with the interviewees. The majority of questions did not involve a great deal of threat to the interviewees. Tough questions, including ones that objected to, attacked, or criticized opinions or activities, most often posed a threat to the face of either political parties, the government, or other groups, rather than to the face of the individual interviewees.

As for the corresponding type of responses, Japanese politicians demonstrated a higher level of equivocation as compared with their Dutch and British counterparts (Table 3.2). Leading national and local politicians often exploited the use of vague impressions, bland statements, and incomplete replies, and they tended to channel attention to topics other than ones they were asked about. Moreover, only a small proportion of politicians in the UK and the Netherlands challenged questions in some way, whereas almost 60% of Japanese politicians did so (Table 3.7). These results also suggest the relatively high degree of interviewers' success in controlling the content of the interviews in the UK and the Netherlands, in contrast to Japan, where politicians were able to successfully control the content and interactions during political interviews through their equivocation. Even as they speak unclearly, conceal their own thoughts and views, and appeal to the general public and voters with their vague replies, they also make every effort to justify their policy decisions and activities and improve their political standing (Feldman et al., 2015, 2016).

This verbal behavior on the part of Japanese politicians might have a crucial consequence on the open, democratic process in this society that needs informed citizens who are aware of developments in public policy and political issues, and are able to understand the course of political events. As long as trustworthy, unbiased, and comprehensible information is available, people are able to sufficiently evaluate the various alternatives from which they are asked to choose, and a democratic society can function. In contrast, intentionally vague and incomplete information negatively affects people's attitudes toward politics: It decreases their level of interest and efficacy, and it weakens their motivation to take an active part in public affairs.

Political information, including information that is disseminated through televised interviews, is an essential parameter in this regard. The attitude demonstrated by political communicators in Japan who are reluctant to clearly disclose information may be one of the reasons for the public's increased distrust in politics and politicians, their increasing political cynicism, and the decline in voting turnout in recent years in Japan.

Control Over Content, i.e., the Reactions of Interviewers to the Replies Provided by the Interviewees and the Interviewees' Feedback to the Questions Posed

Clearly, interviewers accepted the majority of the replies given by politicians, challenging only a small proportion of them (Table 3.7). The high level of reply acceptance leads to the conclusion that interviewers were not very aggressive, assertive, or persistent in their questioning. By refraining from directly challenging interviewees, Japanese interviewers propelled interviews forward by extending or shifting the topics of discussion rather than by pressuring interviewees to clarify their positions or by challenging their stated standpoints to provoke debate (Table 3.6).

The data for interviewers and interviewees revealed very different patterns in our international comparison, reflecting differences in the political cultures of the countries. In the Netherlands, politicians enjoy a cordial interview environment to the extent they have an adequate amount of flexibility to present their views and arguments, and interviewers rarely expressed dissatisfaction with politicians' replies. In comparison, in the UK, where political interviews can be extremely confrontational encounters with verbal attacks and counter-attacks, in which the ultimate goal seems to be "winning" the interview, interviewers expressed frequent discontent with politicians' responses (Voltmer & Brants, 2011). The attitudes of interviewers in Japan, who accept the majority of the replies given by politicians, fall between those of their counterparts in these two countries but closer to the consensus-oriented Dutch political culture. Japanese interviewers are not inclined to accept whatever interviewees present to them, but unlike the British case, interviews are not dominated by charismatic, forceful journalists who see adversarial journalism as their trademark.

In terms of the interviewees' feedback to the questions posed to them, the high level of equivocation on the part of Japanese politicians has been discussed in many contexts. In fact, this is one of the most notorious characteristics of political interviews in Japan. Equivocation by utilizing vague impressions, making bland statements, and channeling attention to other topics may be seen as part of a strategy of Japanese politicians for turning difficult communicative conflict situations, in which they tackle tougher interview questions, to their own advantage. Rhetorical equivocation appears thus to be an effective and valuable instrument of self-disclosure and self-presentation for leading Japanese politicians to affect their own and their groups' images and to mobilize public support for the issues they promote.

Equivocation and Political Dominance

Equivocation is particularly prevalent among members of the coalition parties who control Japan, especially among those at the helm of political power, including ministers and prime ministers, who equivocated more often than politicians from the opposition camp or from local communities. Members of the administration and of the parties that dominate political power equivocated when they were asked to address issues, especially the ones that have a special weight on the national agenda and on which public opinion is divided, for example, the economy, and energy and nuclear power policy, as well as matters related to national security and foreign policy.

Because this study took place at a time when the government changed, it was possible to follow the stances of politicians from diverse political parties as they switched from ruling coalition to opposition and vice versa. Without regard to their political party, those who rule the country and dominate political power at any given time communicate in the same style. That is, as compared with members of the opposition camp, members of the ruling parties (whether from the Democratic Party of Japan or the Liberal Democratic Party) replied less directly to interview questions.

This finding is of importance and indicates that those who are in control of the country are more vulnerable to communicative conflicts; that is, they face tougher interview questions that will lead them to equivocate when responding to questions. This is in contrast to members of the opposition parties, who face less controversial questions and have less responsibility in the decision-making process. They can thus, relatively speaking, "say what they wish." In this sense, the position of interviewed politicians in government dictates their rhetorical style and content during televised interviews.

Amicable Rhetorical Culture of Japan

Equivocation during interviews is thus one of the most important factors in the rhetorical culture of elite politicians in Japan. A second factor in this rhetorical practice is the minor amount of threat to face of interviewees, implying that political interviews in Japan are not an arena of tough interrogation posing risks for politicians. This feature has cultural connotations that dictate the tone of the interview and the interaction between the participants.

The fact that interviewers approached politicians in a calm manner, posing often easy, open-ended questions, most of which were not "very tough" or face-threatening, is related to Japanese interpersonal attitudes. Interviewers persistently avoid direct public confrontation that may result in embarrassing their counterparts and instigating their "loss of face." The awareness and consideration that interviewers showed during televised interview programs to the interviewees' face (including their status, honor, and standing within their political parties and groups) is the social norm that determines the rarity of a hardline attitude mirrored in "very tough" and intimidating questions. Even when interviewers asked tough questions, most of them posed a greater threat to face of the collective membership – political parties, factions, and the administration – than to the individual interviewees.

Moreover, even though politicians did not reply to their questions, interviewers seldom "challenged" the interviewees by, for example, persistently repeating the question or by pointedly stating, "you haven't answered my question – please do so." An interviewer's explicit comment noting that the interviewee did not answer a question might be regarded as the most face-threatening type of question because it brings attention to the fact that the interviewee has avoided answering the question. Yet, in our sample of more than 3,700 questions, there was not even one such case with this or a similar form.

However, if interviewers do not re-ask the questions that have not been answered, what is the journalistic point of these interview shows? Indeed, by pretending as if the public is receiving genuine answers from their leaders, perhaps there is more harm than benefit from the programs. In Japan, however, the interviewer's desire to refrain from an unmannerly and offensive attitude often outweighs their social obligation to pursue detailed information. This is probably the strongest evidence of cultural norms and values affecting the interaction of interviewers with political (and other) sources.

Rather than posing adversarial questions that place pressure on interviewees and stirring debate, interviewers approached politicians in a relatively friendly and gentle communication style. The amiable interview milieu was further exemplified by the frequent use of *grammatically incomplete* (i.e., lacking the questioning particle *ka*), and therefore gentler and less formal, questions. In the formal, honorific, hierarchy-oriented Japanese language, this communication style reduces status differentials between conversation participants and therefore also the formality of the discussion.

The flow of information through the televised interviews we viewed was generally conducted in a tranquil and peaceful manner, marked by an exchange of opinion in which interviewers shared their own ideas and assessments of events along with their questions, rather than relying on outside sources that may have irritated the interviewers, to back up their arguments (Table 3.4).

The outcome is often unexciting and tedious interview sessions in which the interviewers' sensitivity to the interviewees' face along with their equivocating replies determines the distinct nature of the rhetorical culture of these interview shows in Japan. Whether or not this pattern of behavior also typifies the print media, to the extent it is less intrusive and investigative, is worth examining. These results definitely portray a different perspective when looking at the ongoing debate on the limits the government puts on media and the information it can disseminate to the public in Japan.

Acknowledgments

Financial support during this study and the writing of this chapter came through Grants-in-Aid for Scientific Research awarded to the first author by the Japanese Ministry of Education, Culture, Sports, Science, and Technology 2012–2015, and 2016–2018.

Notes

1. This study is part of a broader project that, for comparison purposes, also included interviews with 49 non-politicians (e.g., subject-matter experts and retired politicians) along the same period of time. See Feldman et al. (2015).
2. In Japanese, vowels can either be short or long; a diacritical mark, e.g., ō, ū, ē, or ā, over the vowel indicates that it is a long vowel.
3. *Puraimu Nyūsu* is broadcast through BS (Broadcasting Satellite) every day from Monday through Friday (20:00 to 21:55), *Shin Hōdō 2001* every Sunday (7:30 to 8:55), and *Gekiron Kurosufaya* broadcasts through BS every Saturday (10:00 to 10:55).
4. The sample consisted of the Liberal Democratic Party, 61 members; the Democratic Party of Japan, 38; Japan Restoration Party, 7; the Kōmei Party, 6; Your Party, 6; People's Life Party, 3; Japanese Communist Party, 3; the Social Democratic Party, 2; the People's New Party, 1; the New Renaissance Party, 1; the Sunrise Party of Japan, 1; Tax Cuts Japan, Anti-TPP, Nuclear Phaseout Realization Party, 1; New Party Daichi – True Democrats, 1; Green Wind, 1; and one unaffiliated politician. On the selection of these interviews, see Feldman et al. (2015).
5. The sample consisted of two prime ministers, 31 ministers and vice ministers, 43 ruling coalition parties' members, 57 opposition parties' members, and 12 local level politicians.

References

Bavelas, J. B., Black, A., Chovil, N., & Mullett, J. (1990). *Equivocal communication*. Newbury Park, CA: Sage.

Bull, P. (1994). On identifying questions, replies and non-replies in political interviews. *Journal of Language and Social Psychology*, 13, 115–131.

Bull, P., & Mayer, K. (1993). How not to answer questions in political interviews. *Political Psychology*, 4, 651–666.

Cohen, J. (1960). A coefficient of agreement for nominal scales. *Educational and Psychological Measurement*, 20, 37–46.

Feldman, O., & Kinoshita, K. (2017a). Do important questions demand respectful replies? Analyzing televised political interviews in Japan. *Journal of Asian Pacific Communication*, 27, 121–157.

Feldman, O., & Kinoshita, K. (2017b). Expanding factors in threat to face: Assessing the toughness/equivocation connection in Japanese televised political interviews. *Language & Dialogue*, 7, 336–359.

Feldman, O., Kinoshita, K., & Bull, P. (2015). Culture or communicative conflict? The analysis of equivocation in broadcast Japanese political interviews. *Journal of Language & Social Psychology*, 34, 65–89.

Feldman, O., Kinoshita, K., & Bull, P. (2016). "Ducking and diving": How political issues affect equivocation in Japanese political interviews. *Japanese Journal of Political Science*, 17, 141–167.

Feldman, O., Kinoshita, K., & Bull, P. (2017). Failures in leadership: How and why wishy-washy politicians equivocate on Japanese political interviews. *Journal of Language & Politics*, 16, 285–312.

Voltmer, K., & Brants, K. (2011). A question of control: Journalists and politicians in political broadcast interviews. In K. Brants, & K. Voltmer (Eds.), *Political communication in postmodern democracy: Challenging the primacy of politics* (pp. 126–145). New York: Palgrave Macmillan.

4

COMPARING JAPANESE AND US LEADERS' COMMUNICATION

The Construction of Meaning in Addresses to the United Nations General Assembly

Sarah Tanke

Introduction

This chapter presents differences and similarities between Japanese and United States (US) political communication as observable in a diplomatic context. Diplomacy can be seen not only as an "essentially political activity," but also as an important tool of power (Berridge, 2005, p. 1). In fact, it is closely linked to communication, which is often part of its definition. Melissen (1999, p. xvii), for instance, defines diplomacy as "the mechanism of representation, communication and negotiation through which states and other international actors conduct their business." Some authors claim that communication plays a central role in order for international society to function (Melissen, 1999, p. xviii), while others put diplomacy on the same level as communication: "Diplomacy is basically communication between rulers or governments, be they individual or collective" (Jönsson & Hall, 2005, p. 88).

Successful diplomatic communication needs communicators to share certain codes, to share the same interpretation of linguistic signs to understand a message. While a certain "diplomatic code" is widely shared in the international political sphere, there remain local or regional codes based, for instance, on different cultures. Thus, the same sign may be interpreted differently by persons basing their understanding on different cultural codes (Jönsson & Hall, 2005, pp. 72, 77). Moreover, the tension between incentives to communicate clearly but also ambiguously makes diplomatic language an interesting object of study (Jönsson & Hall, 2005, p. 77).

Within global diplomacy, multilateralism and multilateral institutions such as the United Nations (UN) play an important role, especially since 1945 (Badie & Devin, 2007). The multilateral environment chosen for this chapter is, in particular, the United Nations General Assembly (UNGA), which can be considered the main international scene for national presentations during its annual general debate in September.[1] Also, since these speeches address an international audience, they are part of public diplomacy, trying to gain understanding and support from foreign peoples (Jönsson & Hall, 2005, p. 90).

Multilateral diplomacy in general and the United Nations in particular play different roles for Japan and the US. As pointed out by Shinyō (2016, p. 10),[2] the US as a superpower does not depend on the UN to conduct its foreign policy. Japan, on the other hand, can benefit from the UN in order to participate in international rule-making and decision-making and in order to be recognized as a somewhat big power (Shinyō, 2016, pp. 11–12). In general, Japan is a particularly present player in multilateral diplomacy. There seems to be a Japanese "preference" for multilateral institutions (Berger, 2007, pp. 288–289), and a valorization of international coordination in multilateral settings (Lebow, 2008, p. 491).

The United Nations, in particular, have played a considerable role in Japan's foreign policy, as well as in domestic politics and as a way to achieve international status (Pan, 2005); its financial contributions to the regular UN budget as well as voluntary contributions are significant (Hook, Gilson, Hughes, & Dobson, 2012, p. 331; Rana, 2009, p. 95). The 1957 Diplomatic Bluebook, an annual publication by the Japanese Ministry of Foreign Affairs summarizing Japan's diplomacy and vision of world affairs, declares three pillars of Japanese diplomacy: the United Nations, the US, and Asia (Ōshiba, 2013, p. 298). Moreover, given that the security alliance makes the US Japan's most important bilateral partner, a comparison between these two countries' diplomatic communication and interpretations becomes particularly interesting (Iokibe, 2011).

Addresses by Japanese and US leaders at the UNGA build the linguistic basis for discourse analyses in this chapter. Language shows how communicators create meaning and make sense of the world. These UNGA discourses can be seen as a process to create a certain meaning of messages (Jönsson & Hall, 2005, p. 72). Following a constructionist approach, this chapter focuses on the creation of political messages. Examining the process of how "political 'realities' are shaped and transformed" allows one to show "how people make sense of a world of political events, personalities, and images" (Crigler, 1996, p. 7). To understand how meaning is created and how leaders interpret issues and make sense of the political world, the following discussion focuses on the discourse of political leaders.

Specifically, this chapter focuses on the language used by Japanese and US political figures when addressing the public in front of the UNGA. How do these political leaders communicate? Are there differences and similarities regarding their framing of political issues? How do they construct meaning and what can their political discourse tell us about their way of interpreting key terms of international politics? How do they make use of their addresses to the

UNGA? This chapter aims at contributing to the scholarly debate on political communication by examining how these political leaders construct and shape political discourse.

Theoretical Background: The Construction of Meaning in Political Discourse

The study of political communication analyzes "the processes of persuasion, message construction, and interpretation of meaning" (Crigler, 1996, p. 1). From the perspective of this constructionist approach, all those who play a role in a communication process, such as political leaders, media, and the public, can be seen as engaging in constructing messages and meanings (Crigler, 1996, p. 1). Meaning is constructed, in the sense that certain elements are integrated into political messages and others are not. This means simply that "what will be picked out for description will vary" according to the communicator (Potter & Wetherell, 1987, pp. 33–34). It is in the constructionist sense of generating meaning that I speak of discourses as "systems of meaning-production that fix meaning, however temporarily, and enable actors to make sense of the world and to act within it" (Dunn & Neumann, 2016, p. 4). Foucault famously recommended to "treat discourses [...] as practices that systematically form the objects of which they speak" (Foucault, 1971, pp. 66–67), acknowledging that discourses play a role in reinforcing and creating non-discursive objects. Thus, discourse not only shows previously created meaning, but also contributes to its construction.

At the same time, discourse transports certain social, political, and cultural phenomena (Dunn & Neumann, 2016, p. 3). Thus, even if pronounced by an individual, political discourse will also reveal to a certain extent a broader social and cultural impact on the construction of meaning. What makes the study of discourse further interesting is that by constructing meaning, discourse influences what is being seen as "normal," natural, or true, and thus limits action that will be considered appropriate and possible (Dunn & Neumann, 2016, p. 4). However, discourses are not only formed by socio-cultural factors, but also by individuals' interpretations, framings, and categorizations of new information, which themselves are based on one's "unique set of prior experiences" (Crigler, 1996, p. 9). Thus, having experienced similar and different situations throughout their life, there will be similarities and differences in the way different individuals categorize and frame the same issues, leading to possible misunderstandings and tensions between them.

Framing has been linked to the study of media effects and agenda-setting in the field of political communication (Crigler, 1996, p. 3); this chapter follows Wittgenstein to base the notion of "frames" on his general idea that, in order to find meaning, one needs to examine how language is used: "the meaning of a word is its use in the language" (Wittgenstein, 1968, para. 43). Thus, the context in which a concept is used is crucial for understanding its meaning. Frames are then useful to analyze the way a speaker organizes their thoughts and interprets knowledge; they are "collective, intersubjective understandings" used for construction and interpretation, for instance, of the causes of violence (Autesserre, 2009, pp. 250–251). Furthermore, this shared understanding then "makes certain actions possible while precluding others" (Autesserre, 2009, p. 252).

Since Japan considers the US its most important bilateral ally, the main question this chapter asks is: How do Japanese and US leaders differ in their beliefs and worldviews as presented during the general debate of the UNGA? What do these political discourses reveal about different perceptions and conceptualizations of ideas that are central to the speeches? I argue that it is helpful to compare the Japanese and US frames in their political discourse in order to better understand their foreign policies and international actions and to uncover possible misunderstandings.

Based on the above, two hypotheses can be formulated. First, one can expect different frames used in the political discourse, caused by differing cultural, social, and political factors and codes, but also by different individual experiences and beliefs (Crigler, 1996; Dunn & Neumann, 2016; George, 1967). Second, Japanese and US speakers may make different use of their UNGA addresses, based on their different positions in world politics. While the US is widely perceived as a superpower without a certain need to prove this position, Japanese speakers may use the stage at the UNGA to construct a certain worldview where Japan's international role is valorized and recognized, aiming for international recognition (Lindemann & Ringmar, 2012; Pan, 2005; Shinyō, 2016).

Methodology and Data: Word Context and UNGA Addresses

As outlined above, this chapter examines frames, understood as the context of words in use, as seen in collocations, n-grams, and concordances (defined in the following paragraphs), rather than focusing, for instance, exclusively on transitive verbs such as in the "Verbs in Context System" (VICS) (Schafer & Walker, 2006). Collocations, in general, are words that appear near each other. In linguistics, the term has been famously linked to a word's "company" by the British linguist Firth (1957, as cited in Partington, 1998, p. 15). One of Firth's students defines a collocation as "the occurrence of two or more words within a short space of each other in a text" (Sinclair, 1991, p. 170, as cited in Partington, 1998, p. 15). The idea behind this concept is that a word's collocates will contribute to and explain this word's meaning "in use." Words that frequently co-occur will become habitually associated with each other and will even be expected to appear in close proximity. According to Partington, this "could be referred to as the 'psychological' or 'associative' definition" (Partington, 1998, p. 16). While a word's collocates are all those that appear "near" to it, n-grams (or clusters) are more narrowly defined as words that appear immediately next to each other (Anthony, 2016, p. 5).

A word thus acquires a certain connotation which may "establish an aura" around this word. When a word or phrase connotes "threat or reassurance for a group," it can indirectly evoke certain emotions for a political cause. At the same time, commonly used, abstract terms such as "public interest" or "national security" do not have only one, fixed meaning, but they mean "different specific things to different groups" (Edelman, 1985, p. 116).

A useful way to examine the framing and context of the central notions within a discourse is via concordance lines, i.e., "a list of all of the occurrences of a particular search term in a corpus, presented within the context that they occur in; usually a few words to the left and right of the search term" (Baker, 2006, p. 71). This is particularly helpful in order to see directly and in detail how and in which context a certain term is actually used in the discourse, leaving the quantitative level and adding a qualitative element to the analysis.

Apart from collocates, n-grams, and concordance lines, this chapter also looks into occurrences and keywords. As for occurrences, the main focus is on the most frequently used words in a given text, i.e., concerning the absolute number of certain words. Keywords, on the other hand, are words that are unusually frequent as compared to a certain reference corpus, i.e., this is a measure interested in relative numbers. Using the software AntConc (Anthony, 2014), their "keyness" is calculated based on the log-likelihood measure, meaning that for significance values a keyness of at least 3.84 refers to a p-value smaller than 0.05 (Anthony, 2016, p. 7).

This chapter compares Japanese and US addresses to the UNGA on the national level (i.e., between Japan and the US) and on the individual level (i.e., between different speakers of the same country), conducting both quantitative and qualitative analyses. The first analysis, on the national level, looks into the most frequent words used by Japanese and US speakers, as well as their collocates. The second analysis on the national level compares keywords in the Japanese and US addresses, i.e., unusually frequent words in each corpus as compared to both the Japanese and US corpora together as a reference corpus. On the individual level, the first analysis will again deal with keywords; however, this time comparing individual Japanese and US speakers. The reference corpus in this case is the total of all chosen UNGA addresses given by the leader's fellow countrymen, i.e., all the Japanese UNGA addresses for the case of a Japanese leader, and all the US addresses to the UNGA for the case of a US leader. The second analysis on the individual level aims at n-grams used by individual leaders. The third and final analysis on the individual level deals with concordances of three key areas (freedom, North Korea, and the Middle East, as well as women).

With regard to the data, this chapter presents a case study based on a comparative discourse analysis of the official addresses by the Japanese and US representatives delivered at the UNGA during ten years, that is, from 2006 to 2015. More specifically, these are the addresses made during the general debate at the UNGA usually taking place in September in New York and lasting for about

TABLE 4.1 List of examined addresses to the UNGA, 2006–2015

Year	Japanese speaker	US speaker
2006	Ōshima Kenzō (Permanent Representative)	George W. Bush (President)
2007	Kōmura Masahiko (Foreign Minister)	George W. Bush (President)
2008	Asō Tarō (Prime Minister)	George W. Bush (President)
2009	Hatoyama Yukio (Prime Minister)	Barack Obama (President)
2010	Kan Naoto (Prime Minister)	Barack Obama (President)
2011	Noda Yoshihiko (Prime Minister)	Barack Obama (President)
2012	Noda Yoshihiko (Prime Minister)	Barack Obama (President)
2013	Abe Shinzō (Prime Minister)	Barack Obama (President)
2014	Abe Shinzō (Prime Minister)	Barack Obama (President)
2015	Abe Shinzō (Prime Minister)	Barack Obama (President)

seven to nine days, and for which each speaker has a "voluntary 15-minute time limit" (United Nations General Assembly, 2017).

During the chosen period, the US speaker has always been the US president, i.e., George W. Bush (three addresses) or Barack Obama (seven addresses) (Table 4.1). In the Japanese case, the speaker has been the Japanese prime minister since 2008 (including Asō Tarō, Hatoyama Yukio, Kan Naoto, Noda Yoshihiko [two addresses], and Abe Shinzō [three addresses]). The Japanese speaker in 2006 was the Japanese permanent representative to the United Nations in New York, Ōshima Kenzō, and the Japanese foreign minister, Kōmura Masahiko, in 2007. In this way, altogether a corpus of 20 speeches has been constructed (Table 4.1).[3]

Analyses and Empirical Evidence

This chapter presents five analyses, quantitative and qualitative ones, regarding first the national and then the individual level, based on the computer software AntConc (Anthony, 2014).[4]

Analyses on the National Level
Occurrences: Comparing Japan and the US

A first analysis with AntConc compares the occurring words in both corpora and shows as a first difference the number of words that are used. In theory, there is a "voluntary 15-minute time limit […] to be observed" by the UN member states during the general debate (United Nations General Assembly, 2017), but as noted, this time limit is only voluntary. While the US speakers pronounced almost 41,000 words in their ten addresses to the UNGA (word tokens), Japan's ten addresses comprised only approximately 25,000 words in total, i.e., approximately 61% of the US word tokens. Another difference concerns the number of different words (word types) used by the representatives of the two countries: The US speakers reached 4,242 different words while the Japanese speakers managed to do with only 3,409 word types – a number amounting to about 80% of the US word types. This difference of absolute word types can first be linked to the longer US addresses (word tokens) but also to the fact that these are composed in the speakers' mother tongue. When comparing the relative numbers, the difference is less obvious: Around 14% of the Japanese word tokens are used only once as compared to approximately 10% of the US word tokens, which again can be explained by the longer US speeches.

As for the most frequent words occurring in both corpora, Table 4.2[5] lists the semantically most interesting words among the 50 most frequent ones for the Japanese and the US case. This means that in both lists the following words – judged as semantically less interesting and occurring in both corpora among the 50 most frequent words – have been omitted: *the, of, to, and, in, a, is, that, for, as, will, on, this, I, with, we, has, it, be, s ['s], its, by, have, are, from, our, an, all.*[6]

For the Japanese case, the table then shows that the most frequent noun is

TABLE 4.2 Frequent words in the Japanese and US corpora (AntConc)

Japan			*US*		
Rank	*Frequency*	*Word*	*Rank*	*Frequency*	*Word*
6	465	japan	14	311	people
18	147	international	18	262	world
23	120	at	22	235	nations
26	106	united	26	225	their
29	98	world	27	216	not
30	97	nations	29	209	must
32	91	also	30	199	who
33	91	efforts	31	197	can
34	91	security	32	188	united
35	91	which	33	178	but
36	87	president	35	163	they
38	82	mr [Mr.]	39	148	peace
39	81	peace	40	136	or
41	76	human	41	133	more
42	75	nuclear	42	131	those
43	73	community	43	130	america
44	70	year	44	127	us
46	66	people	45	124	states
47	64	countries	46	123	so
48	63	such	47	107	these
49	61	council	48	106	no
50	60	my	50	103	you

Japan (rank 6, 465 occurrences) and the most frequent adjective is *international* (rank 18, 147 occurrences). They are followed by *united* (rank 26, 106 occurrences), *world* (rank 29, 98 occurrences), and *nations* (rank 30, 97 occurrences). When looking at the analysis of collocations in AntConc, it is interesting to note that the main collocates of *united* are *nations* (i.e., *United Nations*, 82 occurrences) and *states* (i.e., *United States*, 20 occurrences). Ranks 33 and 34, with 91 occurrences each, are occupied by *efforts* and *security*. After *the*, *to*, *in*, and *of*, the most frequent collocate of *efforts* is *Japan* (22 occurrences). As for *security*, it co-occurs often with *council* (i.e., [UN] *Security Council*, 50 occurrences; 17 times linked to *reform* as well) and *human* (i.e., *human security*, 24 occurrences). Other frequently mentioned words are *peace* (rank 39, 81 occurrences), *human* (rank 41, 76 occurrences), *nuclear* (rank 42, 75 occurrences), *community* (rank 43, 73 occurrences; in 71 cases occurring as *international community*), and *people* (rank 46, 66 occurrences). Important collocates of *human* are *security* (24 occurrences), *rights* (17 occurrences), and *beings* (12 occurrences).

In the case of the US, the most frequent noun (excluding pronouns) is *people* (rank 14, 311 occurrences), followed by *world* (rank 18, 262 occurrences), and *nations* (rank 22, 235 occurrences, out of which only 81 times as *United Nations*), all of which occur frequently in the Japanese corpus as well. Further frequently used words are, similar to the Japanese case, *united* (rank 32, 188 occurrences) and *peace* (rank 39, 148 occurrences). The collocates show that *united* is most often mentioned as *United States* (98 occurrences) and then as *United Nations*. Used as a synonym for *United States*, *America* occupies rank 43 (130 occurrences, out of which 8 times as *the United States of America*). In contrast to Japan, the US corpus frequently speaks of *their* (rank 26, 225 occurrences), *they* (rank 35, 163 occurrences), *us* (rank 44, 127 occurrences), and *you* (rank 50, 103 occurrences) as well, addressing the audience in a more direct and inclusive way. The US speakers also frequently use verbs such as *must* (rank 29, 209 occurrences) and *can* (rank 31, 197 occurrences), as well as negations using *not* (rank 27, 216 occurrences) and *no* (rank 48, 106 occurrences).

In comparison, the Japanese speeches focus more on UN topics and on the UN in general (out of 97 occurrences of *nations*, 82 refer to *United Nations*, while in the US speeches only 81 out of 235 occurrences of *nations* refer to *United Nations*), which indicates a particular Japanese commitment to the UN. The Japanese corpus also dedicates a special place to Japanese contributions to the UN, possibly linked to the less powerful Japanese international status and to a wish for recognition as a somewhat big power; something the US as a recognized superpower may consider less crucial.

The US speeches, on the other hand, indicate a more direct way of communication (*must, can, not, no*), clearly pointing out obligations, possibilities, and limits. Since these words are not among the most frequent in the Japanese case, this points to a less direct way of communication for Japanese speakers and a less "direct" Japanese culture. When distinguishing between "high-context" and "low-context" cultures, Hall (1989) clearly categorizes Japan among the high-context ones, meaning that a relatively large part of communication happens in the context, i.e., messages carry implicit meanings with more information outside of the actual message. This also means then that, compared to low-context cultures, communication in high-context cultures is relatively indirect – a finding which this chapter supports for the Japanese case.

Keyword Analysis Comparing Japan and the US

A second analysis on the national level looks at keywords in both corpora. As mentioned above, keywords are unusually frequent words in a certain corpus as compared to a reference corpus. With a p-value of 0.05 and the log-likelihood measure, the critical value for a keyword here is a keyness of at least 3.84. The reference corpus is the total of all 20 UNGA addresses by both Japanese and US speakers.

Table 4.3 shows the unusually frequent words in each corpus (i.e., the Japanese or the US corpus) as compared to both corpora together (keywords that have been omitted from the table in the interest of space can be found in the notes).[7] This analysis confirms several results seen in the previous analysis of occurrences. The direct comparison of keywords demonstrates that the Japanese speakers are relatively frequently referring to Japan itself (*Japan/Japanese*) and its international efforts (*efforts, contribution*), the international community (*international, community*), North Korea (Democratic People's Republic of Korea, *DPRK*), the United Nations Security Council and its possible reform (*council, reform*), but also to the United Nations in general (*UN, member, resolution*) as well as to the field of development aid (*assistance, development, peacebuilding, TICAD* [Tokyo International Conference for African Development]).

The US speakers, on the other hand, when compared to Japan, talk unusually often about their reference group (*we, our*), addressing directly the audience, but also more often about their own country than the Japanese speakers do (*America*). There is also a relatively high frequency of talking about other reference groups (*they, their*), about "people" in general, about abilities (*can*), necessities (*must*), and values such as *freedom/free*, but also about *extremists* and *terror*.

In comparison, the US speakers speak more about the US than the Japanese speakers do, but at the same time do not focus as much on the US as the Japanese speakers focus on Japan.[8] Also, clearly, the Japanese speak more about Japan than the US speakers do. This linguistic asymmetry reflects a political asymmetry between the two countries: in their bilateral relationship but also concerning their international status where Japan has relatively less power than the US. This is again confirmed by the Japanese tendency to focus on Japanese contributions and the US's use of *they* and *their*, suggesting

TABLE 4.3 Comparison of keywords in the Japanese and US corpora (AntConc)

Japan				US			
Rank	Frequency	Keyness	Keyword	Rank	Frequency	Keyness	Keyword
1	465	208.427	japan	1	780	32.827	we
2	147	25.655	international	3	423	19.782	our
5	45	20.314	japanese	4	130	14.694	america
8	38	17.154	dprk [DPRK]	5	311	13.695	people
9	56	16.444	assistance	7	197	11.195	can
10	91	15.899	efforts	9	163	9.962	they
13	73	14.980	community	10	225	9.848	their
14	61	12.410	council	11	178	9.283	but
15	70	11.921	year	12	216	7.683	not
16	26	11.737	contribution	13	123	6.984	so
17	48	11.158	un [UN]	15	209	6.868	must
18	55	10.923	development	17	89	6.380	do
19	24	10.834	peacebuilding	18	52	5.877	israel
23	38	10.381	member	19	127	5.822	us
24	22	9.931	area	20	61	5.703	freedom
25	47	9.895	general	23	67	4.972	because
27	21	9.480	ticad [TICAD]	29	37	4.182	extremists
28	39	9.350	issues	30	47	4.142	free
29	39	9.350	reform	31	38	3.887	institution
31	37	9.000	resolution	32	34	3.843	terror
32	23	8.981	important	33	262	3.843	world

Note
Only statistically significant keywords with a keyness of at least 3.84 have been included in the table.

that the Japanese speakers focus more on Japan's role and less on other groups. The use of *can* and *must* indicates again a more direct communication on the US side.

Thus, both occurrences and keywords show that, on the national level, Japanese and US speakers communicate differently and indicate that they use their UNGA addresses in different ways – according to their different international roles and different cultures.

Analyses on the Individual Level

For the analyses on the individual level, I have chosen Abe Shinzō, Barack Obama, and George W. Bush in order to be able to use a minimum of three texts per person for the analysis. This subsection will first compare keywords used by the three leaders, then n-grams, and finally have a closer look at the frames of certain key concepts using concordance lines.

Keyword Analysis Between Individual Speakers

For the keyword analysis of individual speakers, Abe's speeches are compared to the whole Japanese corpus of ten speeches, while the speeches of Bush and Obama are compared to each other in their addresses to the General Assembly, i.e., by using all the ten US speeches as a reference corpus. This comparison clarifies how these three individual leaders emphasize different ideas in their respective discourses as compared to other leaders of their own country.

In Abe's remarks, one notices his frequent references to women (*women, Ms., her, she, woman, shine*), as well as to certain development and aid-related issues (*police, medical, health, refugees*) (Table 4.4; keywords that have been omitted from the table in the interest of space can be found in the notes[9]). As for Bush, one sees the direct address to the audience (*you, your*), while the focus of his speeches turns around the "pair" between freedom (*free, freedom*) and terrorism/extremism (*terror, terrorism, terrorists, extremists*). Moreover, he also speaks unusually often of help (*help, helping, aid*), indicating his worldview where the US helps the rest of the world (to achieve freedom and democracy) and justifying his criticized foreign policy in the Middle East (Lindsay, 2011, pp. 769–770).

TABLE 4.4 Comparison of keywords between individual leaders (AntConc)

Abe			Bush			Obama		
Freq.	Keyness	Keyword	Freq.	Keyness	Keyword	Freq.	Keyness	Keyword
57	35.147	women	51	30.808	your	859	19.175	that
17	9.398	ms [Ms.]	50	15.395	you	171	9.219	but
16	8.759	her	86	14.272	nations	123	7.237	us
14	7.484	she	23	11.255	terror	199	6.356	not
15	6.779	police	26	9.845	free	375	6.289	our
11	5.580	child	22	9.203	extremists	129	6.015	or
16	5.186	ladies	25	7.316	help	299	5.707	will
8	5.161	medical	14	7.113	declaration	670	5.310	we
8	5.161	refugees	10	6.023	multilateral	86	4.939	do
18	4.932	health	68	5.860	their	100	4.369	no
26	4.852	un [UN]	15	5.715	good	219	3.983	it
15	4.627	gentlemen	58	5.444	united	73	3.929	war
7	4.519	woman	9	5.333	aid			
6	3.874	anniversary	8	5.091	hopeful			
6	3.874	cultivating	9	4.912	helping			
6	3.874	handbook	9	4.518	terrorism			
6	3.874	participation	8	4.232	democracies			
6	3.87	shine	13	4.209	terrorists			
			23	4.137	freedom			

Note
Only statistically significant keywords with a keyness of at least 3.84 have been included in the table.

Specific to Obama's addresses as compared to those of Bush are mainly "grammatical" words, such as conjunctions (*but, that, or*), but also those referring to oneself as a group (*we, us, our*) – indicating a more inclusive worldview, – referring to *war* and to the future (*will*), possibly showing his more optimistic view on foreign policy (Lindsay, 2011, p. 777). This first comparison of keywords demonstrates differences in political communication due to domestic policies (on women), international status and recognition, and individual differences in worldviews and one's approach to a more or less cooperative foreign policy.

N-Grams of Individual Leaders

As described above, one way of approaching fixed schemes in a leader's speaking, close to frames or collocates, are n-grams, which show frequently occurring clusters of words. In the case of Abe, for instance, among n-grams that return in each of his three speeches are the following ones, ordered by decreasing size/length (number of occurrences in brackets): *a society in which women shine* (5 times), *a permanent member of the* (4), *Japan will continue* (4), *Japan has been* (6), *the international community* (11). For Bush, among others one can find in all three speeches: *the United Nations must* (7), *the United Nations is* (5), *the people of* (13), *will continue to* (7). As for Obama, at least five of his seven addresses contain the following n-grams: *the United States and* (13), *the people of* (19), *all of us* (17), *around the world* (17), *and we will* (15), *I believe that* (15), *men and women* (14), *together we must* (10).

For Abe, the n-grams show his focus on women, i.e., domestic politics, and on Japan's international role. Bush's focus on the UN's obligations can be seen as a confirmation of his unilateralist approach to foreign policy, believing that the US should lead world politics and the UN should follow (Hirsh, 2002, p. 20). In his view, multilateral organizations might help and follow the US, but were not necessary and clearly not telling the US what to do (Lindsay, 2011, p. 767). Obama, on the contrary, shows a more cooperative view in his n-grams, talking about *the United States and* or *all of us*, indicating his worldview that accepts globalization as given and his pragmatic stance that the US needs to cooperate with partners in international politics (Lindsay, 2011, p. 765).

Concordances

In this qualitative part of the analysis, several key ideas in the three political leaders' UNGA addresses are compared. By looking at concordance lines, the aim is to put together the different elements that constitute the frame of these key ideas for each political leader. The first out of three larger topics chosen in this subsection is linked to the recurring notion of freedom, as seen in the keyword analyses. The second topic deals with two of the most present geographical entities, namely North Korea and the Middle East. Since, as is again shown by the keyword analysis, this is the most specific topic distinguishing Abe from the other two speakers, the third one focuses on "women."

Freedom as a Key Concept

When George W. Bush talks about freedom (i.e., *free, freedom, freedoms, freely, freer*) at the UNGA, these utterances can be grouped into several categories. Out of 53 concordance lines, the following eight elements can be identified. First, Bush emphasizes free elections, free institutions, a free society, nation, justice, and peace in general (18 times). Second, he refers to concrete freedoms such as *free speech, religious freedom, free to pursue [one's] dreams, free assembly*, etc. (12). In a third element of his frame of freedom, Bush mentions concrete regions such as *Afghanistan, Europe, Middle East, Cuba, Burma, Zimbabwe*, and *Asia* (8). Fourth, he opposes freedom to *extremists, terrorists, repression, tyranny and violence, hunger and disease, cruel dictator*, and a situation where *women are oppressed, and all dissent is crushed* (6). A fifth constitutive element of freedom for Bush is the fact that it is and *must be chosen: choice for freedom, desire for freedom, they choose freedom* (6). Sixth and seventh, he also refers to *economic freedom* (3) and that *freedom can change things* (3). Finally, Bush evaluates freedom as something *noble*.

The texts clearly show a particular frame of *freedom* for Bush. The elements he uses in front of the UNGA together with *extremism/terrorism*[10] can be divided into three main groups: In the first group, extremism/terrorism is linked to *tyranny, weapons, attacks, threat, death, fear, violent, evil*, etc. In the second group, the self and those opposed to extremists/terrorists are described with positive expressions such as *together, cooperate, democracy, help, protect, moderate, innocent, peace, victim, free, hope*, etc. The third group confirms a struggle between *us* and *them, a battle of ideas, a great ideological struggle*, which one *must continually confront*.

Freedom, of course, has been a central theme during Bush's presidency. Not only can freedom be considered "the most central of [the US'] founding principles," according to certain authors the maximization of freedom is its "very reason for existence" (Hirsh, 2002, pp. 32, 43). After the terror attacks of September 11, 2001 occurring during Bush's presidency, the black-and-white "Bush Doctrine," in which "Either you're with us, or you are with the terrorists," allowed Bush to preemptively strike against Afghanistan and Iraq (Datta, 2009, p. 270; Hirsh, 2002, p. 19). While the United Nations did authorize "all necessary steps" in order to respond to 9/11, it did not support Bush's intention to go to war against Iraq on the assumption to find weapons of mass destruction (WMD) there (Lindsay, 2011, pp. 768–769). Especially when these WMD could not be found, Bush increasingly used goals of freedom and democracy in Iraq and the region in order to justify his war (Lindsay, 2011, pp. 769–770).

As for Obama, one can distinguish some elements of the *free(dom)* frame that are similar to Bush's. Obama emphasizes concrete freedoms, mainly free speech, freedom of religion, and dignity (30). He also links freedom to a free society, free elections, justice, peace, and democracy (12), and insists that people *long* to be free, *love freedom*, and *refuse to give [it] back* (5). Obama similarly mentions *economic freedom* (4), certain *free regions* (3), and considers freedom as *preferable* to suppression. He contrasts freedom with *poverty, a closed society, war, suppression*, and *want* (6). There is no reference as to terrorism or extremism being the opposite of freedom.

So while freedom is still a major value of US foreign policy under Obama, it is less central than under George W. Bush, showing Obama's more pragmatic approach to diplomacy (Lindsay, 2011, p. 773). Under Obama, "ideological objectives" such as a democratic Afghanistan are abandoned and the "global war on terror" is not anymore the defining factor of the US's international role (Brzezinski, 2010, pp. 16–24). These changing foreign policies are reflected in the way Obama frames freedom differently than Bush (Nau, 2010).

Concerning Abe, the compared texts show a clear difference: *freedom/free* is not mentioned a single time.

Key Regions: North Korea and the Middle East

As seen in the keyword analysis, North Korea is very present in the Japanese addresses. Abe mentions it six times, putting it four times in relation to nuclear weapons or missiles and four times to the issue of the abduction of Japanese citizens, an important domestic topic under Abe. On the US side, Bush mentions it twice, once with regard to nuclear issues and once with regard to human rights. As for Obama, he talks about North Korea four times: three times for nuclear concerns and once for concerns over human rights. There is a slight difference in framing North Korea linked to domestic circumstances: While for Abe the abduction issue is very present and human rights issues absent, the opposite is true for Bush and Obama.

Concerning another much-discussed region in the UNGA addresses, the Middle East, Bush combines four elements in his frame. The first one is stability (in seven out of 11 occurrences), the second one is violence and extremists (3), the third element is the opposition to moderate, democratic, civilized citizens (3), and finally he declares his desire for peace (1). Obama refers to extremism or conflicts in six out of 17 cases mentioning the Middle East, three times to peace, and twice to stability. However, in nine cases he talks not only about the Middle East, but about "the Middle East and North Africa," showing a different frame. This may reflect the changing international environment with the "Arab Spring" starting around 2011. Abe mentions the Middle East four times, three times referring to peace and once to stability. More interesting is, however, that he mentions Japan and Japan's contributions in three cases of referring to the Middle East as well, putting Japan at the center of the text. Again, a concern about Japan's international status influences Abe's frames.

Women as One of Abe's Key Policies

One of Abe's main policies is his commitment to "women issues." In fact, he mentions *women* 64 times in his three addresses to the UNGA. There are several elements in his *women frame*: In 14 cases, he depicts them as victims (*crimes against women, protection, violence, exposed to danger, whose hearts have suffered grievous harm, vulnerable*, etc.). Second and third, he emphasizes the *participation* of and other *opportunities* for women (10), as well as the *power* of women and their *empowerment* (10). In nine cases, Abe refers to "female" characteristics such as *mother, pregnant, shine* (as the stereotypical beautiful women). Another element is Japan's contributions to international women issues (8) and Abe shows particular concerns about their health (5), but less about their (human) rights (3). Most interesting, however, especially in comparison to the US texts, is the complete absence of "man"/"men." Abe's frame of *women* as presented in these three texts is completely cut off from the one of men.

In this context, it is interesting to note that Japan's performance in gender equality is relatively poor: It occupies the 111th rank out of 144 countries in the World Economic Forum's (2016) Global Gender Gap Index and has a very low number of women in positions of power (e.g., 12% of Diet members, 1.8% of mayors, 7.2% of heads of companies, 14% of university professors) (Dalton, 2017, pp. 95–96). While "womenomics" – certain policies to help women to become and stay part of Japan's workforce and leadership – are a part of Abe's economic plan, "Abenomics," the term "womenomics" itself originated in the 1990s based on the idea that Japan's economy should take advantage of women as a labor force (Dalton, 2017, p. 96). Thus, Japan's policies focusing on women's empowerment need to be considered in a domestic and economic context.

The opposite is true in Bush's speeches, which mention women far less often, but where in five out of eight cases he talks about *men and women*. Obama as well talks in 20 out of 34 cases about men and women (and children). When excluding men, Bush refers once to women as *oppressed* and once as *allowed to vote and run for office*. As for Obama, when only talking about women, he sees them five times as victims (*abused, bully, enslaves, political barriers*) and refers to positive achievements in eight cases (*opportunity, potential, participation, rights*, etc.).

The different frames of women as either separated from or linked to men can show, but also lead to, a different understanding of how women's empowerment should be addressed and what kind of policies should be implemented. Since Japan's policies on women's empowerment are closely linked to Japan's economic situation, the reason for Abe's women frame clearly separated from men may be based on "gendered social roles in Japan" where women are still often seen as in charge of family and home, while working practices have a "male style" in Japanese culture (Dalton, 2017, p. 99).

Discussion

In summary, the analyses of occurrences, keywords, collocates, n-grams, and concordances on the national and individual level provide several elements for the two hypotheses. The first hypothesis, namely that different frames in political discourse can be explained by cultural, social, and domestic political factors and codes, but also by different individual experiences and beliefs, is confirmed by the following aspects. First, culture can be seen as having an impact on a relatively more direct communication in the case of the US as compared to Japan, shown in the use of words such as *can, must, not, no,* but also on the central place of *freedom* in the US discourse, as well as on socio-culturally different frames of *women* (to which degree women are categorized as victims or in a more positive light; and whether it appears "normal" to categorize women together with men or separately as a unique group). Second, domestic political factors influence frames, for instance, when Abe focuses on women (keywords, n-grams), but also in different frames of North Korea. Third, individually different beliefs and worldviews have an influence on political discourse as shown in the keywords, n-grams, and concordances. While Bush sees the US as "helping" others and the UN as having mainly obligations, showing a more unilateral approach to world politics, Obama demonstrates a more optimistic, inclusive, and cooperative view of international politics, emphasizing the importance of a community and of cooperation, based on a more multilateral perspective. Furthermore, the two US presidents frame freedom differently; Bush opposing it to violence and Obama to poverty.

The second hypothesis, i.e., that different international roles and positions will lead to differences in political discourse, is supported as well. All analyses conducted in this chapter, i.e., occurrences, keywords, n-grams, and concordances, show how the Japanese speaker dedicates a considerable part of the discourse to Japan's international role and to its contributions. This is possibly linked to the fact that Japan's international status is relatively less powerful than the US (being more self-confident about their role as a superpower) and more dependent on international recognition as a somewhat big power, using the attention at the UNGA to present their country in a positive way.

Outlook

Since diplomacy is intrinsically linked to communication, this chapter compares Japanese and US addresses to the UNGA based on the assumption that discourse not only shows how people make sense of the world but at the same time constructs meaning and defines what is being seen as "normal" and possible. Shared codes are needed for successful communication to interpret linguistic signs in similar ways, and differing frames of political concepts (such as *freedom* or *women*) can cause diplomatic misunderstandings and possibly lead to different ways of seeking means to act on these issues, creating tensions in international cooperation. This chapter presents two hypotheses, claiming that individual, socio-cultural, and domestic political differences will lead to differences in frames; and that different roles and positions in world politics can explain different ways to use UNGA addresses. Analyzing political discourse can help approach political leaders' interpretations and frames which then help understand that country's foreign policy measures.

Political discourse at the United Nations is particularly interesting since the audience can be considered the "voice of global public opinion," judged as valuable in democracies. Even if voted resolutions at the UNGA are not binding, the votes matter in the political domain, which is, for instance, shown by the fact that the US Congress ordered the Department of State to present an annual report on UN voting behavior (Datta, 2009, p. 271). When a state accumulates too many votes against them at the UNGA, this public disapproval can have a serious impact, for instance, by deteriorating its international image and recognition in Japan's case, or by making it difficult for the US to believe in its "moral authority" (Datta, 2009, p. 281). In the end, despite all criticism, the UN serves as a platform of political legitimacy. While individual, domestic, and cultural factors may cause differing codes to make sense of political events and to frame central concepts and construct meaning, the United Nations can serve as a forum contributing to forming common and shared codes of interpretation to improve diplomatic communication.

Acknowledgments

I am very grateful to Sciences Po, Center for International Studies (CERI), CNRS, Paris, the German Institute for Japanese Studies (DIJ) in Tokyo, and the Columbia University Alliance Doctoral Mobility Grant for their financial and institutional support.

Notes

1. In particular, diplomats having worked in a multilateral setting confirmed the importance attached to the annual addresses during the UNGA general debate within the diplomatic community in interviews conducted with the author.
2. Japanese names in this chapter follow the Japanese order, i.e., family name followed by given name. Long vowels in Japanese are indicated by a diacritical mark, e.g., ō.
3. Since the addresses of the US representatives are being held in English, for the Japanese case the English version has been chosen for the comparative analysis as well. This is the official translation of the Japanese Ministry of Foreign Affairs, i.e., the official version of the speech created and diffused by Japan with the clear intention to address an international audience/the world.
4. AntConc is a free software tool developed by Laurence Anthony (www.laurenceanthony.net) for corpus linguistics research. The user can open their corpora via the software, which will generate concordance lines, n-grams, collocates, word lists, keyword lists, etc. More details on AntConc can be found on www.laurenceanthony.net/software/antconc/.
5. Since Tables 4.2, 4.3, and 4.4 are based on AntConc, which works with lowercase letters, capital letters and apostrophes have been added in brackets in some cases for better understanding.
6. This order refers to the Japanese corpus. The order of the same omitted words in the US corpus is as follows: *the, and, to, of, that, a, in, we, is, our, for, this, will, be, are, have, with, it, s ['s], on, as, I, by, from, an, has, all, its.*

7. Omitted keywords from Table 4.3 (rank, frequency, keyness): (1) for Japan: *mr [Mr.]* (3, 82, 24.886), *the* (4, 1,839, 23.148), *such* (6, 63, 17.843), *which* (7, 91, 17.423), *as* (11, 247, 15.666), *president* (12, 87, 15.548), *at* (20, 120, 10.710), *in* (21, 627, 10.667), *session* (22, 23, 10.383), *excellency* (26, 21, 9.480), *also* (30, 91, 9.324), *ms [Ms.]* (33, 19, 8.577); (2) for the US: *that* (2, 954, 23.714), *who* (6, 199, 11.398), *and* (8, 1,627, 10.042), *those* (14, 131, 6.978), *or* (16, 136, 6.692), *ve ['ve]* (21, 48, 5.425), *are* (22, 289, 5.205), *re ['re]* (24, 43, 4.860), *applause* (25, 41, 4.634), *have* (26, 286, 4.587), *when* (27, 75, 4.313), *where* (28, 80, 4.273).
8. Even if the occurrences of *United States* (98) and *America* (130) are added (without counting the *United States of America* [8] twice), a frequency of 220 would only mean rank 27 in the US corpus, far behind *Japan* on rank 1 in the Japanese corpus. Also, the word *us* in the list only refers to the pronoun, not to the US (United States).
9. Omitted keywords from Table 4.4 (frequency, keyness): (1) for Abe: *that* (122, 7.146), *who* (21, 6.570), *years* (26, 5.529), *th ['th]* (13, 4.982), *working* (13, 4.459), *been* (27, 4.373), *has* (60, 4.105), *become* (17, 4.011), *Nilufa [individual's name]* (6, 3.874), *Sato [individual's name]* (6, 3.874); (2) for Bush: *chamber* (12, 8.363), *working* (16, 6.996), *education* (13, 6.076), *requires* (11, 5.869), *Aids* (10, 5.594), *Malaria* (9, 5.333), *m ['m]* (9, 4.912), *re ['re]* (19, 4.911), *Georgia* (7, 4.878), *the* (538, 4.846), *Afghanistan* (13, 4.773), *Lebanon* (8, 4.644), *in* (190, 4.221), *Doha* (6, 4.182), *developing* (9, 4.152).
10. Refers to *extremism/extremist/extremists/terror/terrorism/terrorist/terrorists*.

References

Anthony, L. (2014). AntConc (Version 3.4.4) [Windows]. Tokyo: Waseda University. Retrieved July 13, 2017 from www.laurenceanthony.net.

Anthony, L. (2016). AntConc help file version 002: October 20, 2016. Retrieved July 13, 2017 from www.laurenceanthony.net/software/antconc/releases/AntConc344/help.pdf.

Autesserre, S. (2009). Hobbes and the Congo: Frames, local violence, and international intervention. *International Organization*, 63(2), 249–280.

Badie, B., & Devin, G. (2007). Avant-propos [Foreword]. In B. Badie, & G. Devin (Eds.), *Le multilatéralisme: Nouvelles formes de l'action internationale* [*Multilateralism: New forms of international action*] (pp. 7–9). Paris: Découverte. [in French].

Baker, P. (2006). *Using corpora in discourse analysis*. London, New York: Continuum.

Berger, T. U. (2007). The pragmatic liberalism of an adaptive state. In T. U. Berger, M. Mochizuki, & J. Tsuchiyama (Eds.), *Japan in international politics: The foreign policies of an adaptive state* (pp. 259–299). Boulder, CO: Lynne Rienner Publishers.

Berridge, G. R. (2005). *Diplomacy: Theory and practice* (3rd ed.). New York: Palgrave.

Brzezinski, Z. (2010). From hope to audacity: Appraising Obama's foreign policy. *Foreign Affairs*, 89(1), 16–30.

Crigler, A. N. (1996). Introduction: Making sense of politics; constructing political messages and meanings. In A. N. Crigler (Ed.), *The psychology of political communication* (pp. 1–10). Ann Arbor, MI: University of Michigan Press.

Dalton, E. (2017). Womenomics, "equality" and Abe's neo-liberal strategy to make Japanese women shine. *Social Science Japan Journal*, 20(1), 95–105.

Datta, M. N. (2009). The decline of America's soft power in the United Nations. *International Studies Perspectives*, 10(3), 265–284.

Dunn, K. C., & Neumann, I. B. (2016). *Undertaking discourse analysis for social research*. Ann Arbor, MI: University of Michigan Press.

Edelman, M. J. (1985). *The symbolic uses of politics*. Urbana, IL: University of Illinois Press.

Foucault, M. (1971). *L'archéologie du savoir* [*The archaeology of knowledge*]. Paris: Gallimard. [in French].
George, A. (1967). *The "operational code": A neglected approach to the study of political leaders and decision-making*. Santa Monica, CA: The RAND Corporation.
Hall, E. T. (1989). *Beyond culture*. New York: Anchor Books.
Hirsh, M. (2002). Bush and the world. *Foreign Affairs*, 81(5), 18–43.
Hook, G. D., Gilson, J., Hughes, C. W., & Dobson, H. (2012). *Japan's international relations: Politics, economics and security* (3rd ed.). New York: Routledge.
Iokibe, M. (Ed.). (2011). *The diplomatic history of postwar Japan*. (R. D. Eldridge, Trans.). London, New York: Routledge.
Jönsson, C., & Hall, M. (2005). *Essence of diplomacy*. London: Palgrave Macmillan.
Lebow, R. N. (2008). *A cultural theory of international relations*. Cambridge, New York: Cambridge University Press.
Lindemann, T., & Ringmar, E. (Eds.). (2012). *The international politics of recognition*. Boulder, CO: Paradigm Publishers.
Lindsay, J. M. (2011). George W. Bush, Barack Obama and the future of US global leadership. *International Affairs*, 87(4), 765–779.
Melissen, J. (1999). Introduction. In J. Melissen (Ed.), *Innovation in diplomatic practice* (pp. xiv–xxiii). Basingstoke: Macmillan Press.
Nau, H. R. (2010). Obama's foreign policy. *Policy Review*, (160), 27–47.
Ōshiba, R. (2013). Takokukan gaikō to takokukan shugi: kokuren, G8/G20, bureton uzzu kikan. [Multilateral diplomacy and multilateralism: UN, G8/G20, Bretton Woods institutions.] In T. Inoue, S. Hatano, T. Sakai, R. Kokubun, & R. Ōshiba (Eds.), *Nihon no gaikō. Taigai seisaku: kadaihen.* [*Japan's diplomacy. Foreign policy: The subjects.*] (pp. 291–319). Tōkyō: Iwanami Shoten. [in Japanese].
Pan, L. (2005). *The United Nations in Japan's foreign and security policymaking, 1945–1992: National security, party politics, and international status*. Cambridge, MA: Harvard University Press.
Partington, A. (1998). *Patterns and meanings: Using corpora for English language research and teaching*. Amsterdam, Philadelphia, PA: John Benjamins.
Potter, J., & Wetherell, M. (1987). *Discourse and social psychology: Beyond attitudes and behaviour*. London: Sage Publications.
Rana, K. S. (2009). *Asian diplomacy: The foreign ministries of China, India, Japan, Singapore, and Thailand*. Washington, DC, Baltimore, MD: Woodrow Wilson Center Press, Johns Hopkins University Press.
Schafer, M., & Walker, S. G. (2006). Operational code analysis at a distance: The verbs in context system of content analysis. In M. Schafer, & S. G. Walker (Eds.), *Beliefs and leadership in world politics: Methods and applications of operational code analysis* (pp. 25–51). New York: Palgrave Macmillan.
Shinyō, T. (Ed.). (2016). *Nihon to kokuren: Kyōto kara sekai heiwa o negatte.* [*Japan and the UN: Wishing for world peace from Kyōto.*] Nishinomiya: Kwansei Gakuin University Press. [in Japanese].
United Nations General Assembly (2017). *General debate: Frequently asked questions (faq)*. Retrieved July 29, 2017 from https://gadebate.un.org/en/faq.
Wittgenstein, L. (1968). *Philosophical investigations*. Oxford: Basil Blackwell.
World Economic Forum (2016). *The global gender gap report 2016: Rankings*. Retrieved December 15, 2017 from http://reports.weforum.org/global-gender-gap-report-2016/rankings/.

Japanese Addresses During the General Debate at the UNGA

Abe, S. (2013). http://japan.kantei.go.jp/96_abe/statement/201309/26generaldebate_e.html.
Abe, S. (2014). http://japan.kantei.go.jp/96_abe/statement/201409/unga2014.html.
Abe, S. (2015). http://japan.kantei.go.jp/97_abe/statement/201509/1213007_9928.html.
Asō, T. (2008). http://japan.kantei.go.jp/asospeech/2008/09/25speech_e.html.
Hatoyama, Y. (2009). http://japan.kantei.go.jp/hatoyama/statement/200909/ehat_0924c_e.html.
Kan, N. (2010). http://japan.kantei.go.jp/kan/statement/201009/24speech_e.html.
Kōmura, M. (2007). www.mofa.go.jp/policy/un/state0709.html.
Noda, Y. (2011). http://japan.kantei.go.jp/noda/statement/201109/23enzetu_e.html.
Noda, Y. (2012). http://japan.kantei.go.jp/noda/statement/201209/26un_e.html.
Ōshima, K. (2006). www.mofa.go.jp/announce/speech/un2006/un0609.html.

US Addresses During the General Debate at the UNGA

Bush, G. W. (2006). http://georgewbush-whitehouse.archives.gov/news/releases/2006/09/20060919-4.html.
Bush, G. W. (2007). http://georgewbush-whitehouse.archives.gov/news/releases/2007/09/20070925-4.html.
Bush, G. W. (2008). http://georgewbush-whitehouse.archives.gov/news/releases/2008/09/20080923-5.html.
Obama, B. (2009). https://obamawhitehouse.archives.gov/the-press-office/remarks-president-united-nations-general-assembly.
Obama, B. (2010). www.whitehouse.gov/the-press-office/2010/09/23/remarks-president-united-nations-general-assembly.
Obama, B. (2011). www.whitehouse.gov/the-press-office/2011/09/21/remarks-president-obama-address-united-nations-general-assembly.
Obama, B. (2012). www.whitehouse.gov/the-press-office/2012/09/25/remarks-president-un-general-assembly.
Obama, B. (2013). www.whitehouse.gov/the-press-office/2013/09/24/remarks-president-obama-address-united-nations-general-assembly.
Obama, B. (2014). www.whitehouse.gov/the-press-office/2014/09/24/remarks-president-obama-address-united-nations-general-assembly.
Obama, B. (2015). www.whitehouse.gov/the-press-office/2015/09/28/remarks-president-obama-united-nations-general-assembly.

PART II
Populist Communication and Negative Campaigning

5
THEY CAUSED OUR CRISIS! THE CONTENTS AND EFFECTS OF POPULIST COMMUNICATION

Evidence from the Netherlands

Michael Hameleers

Introduction

Although a growing body of literature has pointed to the pervasiveness and persuasiveness of populism all around the globe (e.g., Mudde, 2004), systematic research on the content and effects of populist communication is still extremely scarce (for exceptions, see Bos, van der Brug, & de Vreese, 2013; Hameleers, Bos, & de Vreese, 2017a). Especially in the Dutch context of highly salient and electorally successful populism, it is relevant to assess how populist messages affect voters' opinions. Indeed, those studies that *did* investigate populist communication ascribed a central role to the media in disseminating populist messages to the people (e.g., Hameleers et al., 2017a). Against this backdrop, it is crucial to understand *which* elements of populist communication affect the perceptions of *which* citizens.

The Dutch political landscape has been characterized by electorally successful populist movements. In 2017, the right-wing populist Freedom Party became the second largest party in the general elections. Situated in this context, this chapter aims to dissect the core message of populism, both communicated by populist actors and disseminated by the media. In the next step, this chapter presents an overview of systematic research on the effects of populist communication in the Netherlands. Taken together, this chapter aims to present in-depth insights into the discursive strategies of populism expressed by the media and politicians, and the effects of such populist discourse on citizens' political perceptions. To do so, this chapter draws on an extensive review of literature on populist communication, enriched by evidence from empirical case studies on populist communication in the Netherlands originally conducted by the author of this chapter.

To set the stage, this chapter will first of all present a definition of populism's ideational core, enriched with examples from the Dutch context. In brief, the central idea of populist communication can be defined as the attribution of blame for the ordinary people's problems to the elites and societal out-groups (Hameleers et al., 2017a). This definition is in line with conceptualizations that have defined populism as a relational concept, marking the central causal and moral boundary between the "good" people and the "corrupt" elites, potentially supplemented by the exclusion of societal out-groups (e.g., Jagers & Walgrave, 2007; Mudde, 2004). This definition forms the starting point for explaining how populist discourse is expressed by politicians and the media in the Dutch context.

Next, this chapter will present empirical work indicating the central content features of populist communication. In line with a recent, yet growing body of research, the role of social network sites in providing a platform for populist discourse will also be discussed here (Bartlett, Birdwell, & Littler, 2011). Expanding the concept of populism *by* the media or media populism (e.g., Mazzoleni, 2008), this chapter will also present research on populist framing by traditional Dutch media. Moving beyond the central content features of populist communication, the next part of this chapter will delve deeper into the effects of populist communication, and the mechanisms underlying these effects. Drawing on experimental research conducted in the Netherlands, this chapter hereby aims to demonstrate *how* populist communication can affect populist perceptions and populist voting behavior.

The Core Ideas of Populist Communication

Epistemological Underpinnings

Despite its growing popularity among scholars, populism continues to be a contested concept. The most salient disagreement on populism's definition concerns its epistemological and ontological underpinnings. More specifically, authors have disagreed on defining populism as a style, strategy, discourse, frame, rhetoric, or ideology. Next to this, some authors have defined populism as a binary label that is either on/off (e.g., Heijne, 2011), whereas another line of research actually studies populist discourse as a matter of degree (e.g., Akkerman, Mudde, & Zaslove, 2014; Bos et al., 2013; Jagers & Walgrave, 2007). To circumvent these inconsistencies, and to aim for more conceptual clarity, this chapter will define populism by its ideational core – marking the Manichean opposition between the ordinary people as a "good" in-group opposed to the "corrupt" elites or "evil" others as out-groups. These core ideas are typically expressed, experienced, and communicated by various actors, such as politicians, citizens, and journalists. Although the conceptualization of populism has been surrounded by a fierce scientific debate, most definitions have started to agree on its core components. The "thin cored" ideology rationale has been the starting point for many definitions (e.g., Mudde, 2004). This agreement implies that populism revolves around the construction of a societal divide between the "good" ordinary people and the "evil" elites that pose a severe threat to the well-being of the people (Mudde, 2004). This anti-elitist core can be supplemented by the exclusion of various out-groups, which is a core element of right-wing populist rhetoric (e.g., Jagers & Walgrave, 2007). Taking these defining characteristics as the point of departure, the ideational core of populism consists of three central components: people centrality, anti-elitism, and the potential exclusion of societal out-groups.

People Centrality

The most basic component of populist ideas is the centrality of the ordinary people's will (Jagers & Walgrave, 2007). In populism, the people are constructed as a morally superior in-group belonging to the heartland (Taggart, 2000). This heartland is typically understood as a mental representation of the ordinary people's community. However, "the people" can mean different things in populist discourse. Situated in the context of right-wing populism, "the people" in the Netherlands refers to a nativist perception of a morally superior people who are deprived from what they deserve (van Kessel, 2011). This, for example, means that populist ideas stress how the in-group of "own" people should have more rights than other groups because of their belonging to the nativist heartland. In the Netherlands, this argument is frequently emphasized in chauvinist constructions of the welfare state: Resources as health and unemployment benefits should only be distributed among members of the ordinary people's in-group; others do not deserve to receive these profits.

On a socio-political level, the people's in-group is perceived as a relatively powerless group of Dutch citizens, who are not represented by the elites in government. Geert Wilders, the right-wing populist party leader of the Freedom Party (PVV), frequently communicates how the ordinary people of the Netherlands are neglected by the elites, despite the fact that the people's will *should* be central in political decision-making. By speaking on behalf of the people, and as part of the people, populist actors claim to give the power back to the ordinary men on the street.

Anti-Elitism

It has been argued that populism is a *relational* construct, which implies that the people as the "good" and morally superior in-group is constructed in opposition to a threatening "evil" enemy (e.g., Taggart, 2000). One way in which the central divide can be emphasized is by articulating the divide between the "hardworking ordinary people" and the "corrupt self-interested elites."

Just like "the people" can mean different things in different contexts, the people's opposition to the elites can be constructed in different ways. This "flexibility" in populist discourse ties in with a large body of literature that has conceptualized populism as a chameleonic concept: Populist ideas can adapt themselves to different situations in different ways (Mazzoleni, Stewart, & Horsfield, 2003). More specifically, the opposition between the "good" people and the "evil" elites attaches itself to different sentiments of crisis and emergency (Mazzoleni et al., 2003; Taggart, 2000). Such contexts provide the fertile breeding ground in which populist sentiments are rooted. In the Netherlands, the perceived crises of the influx of migrants, negative developments in the labor market situation, and the allegedly failed representation of Europe are all interpreted in line with the opposition between the people and the elites: The elites are failing to solve these crises and fail to solve the problems facing the nativist heartland.

There are various elites that can be constructed as a threat to the people's in-group. Most saliently, politicians in government are attributed the negative qualities of being corrupt, self-interested, dishonest, and insensitive to the people's needs and desires (e.g., Canovan, 1999; Mudde, 2004). Next to this, on an economic level, banks and global financial institutions are held accountable for the people's crisis. In the European context, the European Union is also a salient target of out-group hostility. Traditional media are also constructed as culprits: They are presenting the people with a distorted, inconsistent and "fake" reality. Instead of spreading false information, they *should* provide a central stage to the ordinary people who can vocalize what is really going on in society.

Exclusionism

In right-wing populism, which is highly salient in the Dutch landscape in particular and in Europe more generally, the anti-elitist message is frequently supplemented by the exclusion of horizontally defined others. The horizontal opposition between the people and out-groups presumes that the culpable out-group lives amongst the ordinary people, without being part of its superior community. The threat to the populist heartland thus resides from *within* the nation. In the context of Dutch politics, this means that immigrants and other minority groups in Dutch society are constructed as a threatening out-group. Wilders, for example, frequently stresses how Dutch norms and values, as well as economic benefits, are taken away by immigrants and people with different religious backgrounds. Next to this, these others pose a threat to the safety of the native people. Therefore, as argued in Dutch right-wing populist discourse, these culpable societal out-groups should be excluded from the people's in-group.

The boundary between the "good" in-group and the "evil" out-group can be consolidated in various ways, such as economically or cultural-symbolically. Out-groups are excluded economically as they profit from the in-group's resources without giving anything in return. Dutch populist actors, for example, argue that refugees are taking "free" health-care and unemployment benefits that *should* be reserved for people with an original Dutch background. On a cultural-symbolic level, they pose a threat as their beliefs and value systems, most saliently Islam, are a threat to "real" Dutch norms and values.

Populist Blame Attribution

These central components of populist discourse can be synthesized in one core interpretation that lies at the heart of populist communication: the causal and moral opposition between the "good" people and the "culprit" others. Populism thus revolves around shifting blame from the innocent people's in-group to the causally responsible others. This blame frame is highly salient in the Dutch political landscape, where Wilders frequently blames the elites for not representing the will of the "silenced majority" of the ordinary citizens. The elites are, for example, accused of filling their pockets at the cost of the people's well-being. In a similar vein, horizontally opposed out-groups, such as immigrants, are blamed for depriving the nativist heartland from material and cultural resources. In the Dutch case of populism, it is argued that the immigrants are responsible for an erosion of traditional Dutch norms and values. *Because* of the influx of migrants, Dutch traditions will be attacked by foreign elements that pollute the in-group's purity.

In the next section, the foregrounded integration of the three salient populist elements in populist blame attribution will be used to explain *why* populist ideas may be so persuasive. These theoretical explanations will allow us to answer the central questions of this chapter: What are the mechanisms behind the persuasiveness of populist ideas? And who is most likely to be persuaded by them? Before delving deeper into these specificities, it is important to discuss *who* can actually communicate populist ideas.

Who Is Communicating Populist Ideas?

Populist Communication by Politicians

Populism has mainly been studied on the supply-side of populist political parties and their communication (e.g., Jagers & Walgrave, 2007). In the Dutch context, the most visible and electorally successful populist politician is Geert Wilders, party leader of the right-wing populist party PVV (Freedom Party). Moving further back in time, the Center Democrats (e.g., Mudde, 1996) and The Farmers' Party (e.g., van Kessel, 2011) have also been considered as right-wing populist political parties. Only the Socialist Party has been considered as a left-wing populist party, although authors disagree whether it can actually be classified as a populist party after the 2000s (e.g., Rooduijn, de Lange, & van der Brug, 2014).

Zooming in on the type of populist rhetoric communicated in Dutch politics, extant research considers the Freedom Party as an example of "complete right-wing populism" (Jagers & Walgrave, 2007). This means that all three elements of populism's ideational core discussed above are present in the populist ideas communicated by right-wing populist politicians in the Netherlands. Specifically, Wilders' party refers to the ordinary, native Dutch people as an "innocent" in-group. Next to this, his Freedom Party stresses the central causal and moral opposition between the ordinary people and the elites, most saliently on the level of the national government and the European Union. An exclusionist interpretation is salient as the Islam, refugees, and immigrants are excluded from the people, as they are perceived as a severe threat to the Dutch nation (e.g., Rooduijn et al., 2014). In the Dutch context, the exclusion of out-groups has a political, cultural, and economic component. The other populist political parties that have been successful in the Netherlands, Pim Fortuyn's LPF List and Rita Verdonk's Proud of the Netherlands, can also be described as complete right-wing populist parties.

Populist Communication in and by the Media

A growing body of literature has ascribed a central role to the media to explain the success of populism (e.g., Krämer, 2014; Mazzoleni, 2008). The media's role has been described in both a *passive* and an *active* way. The passive role of the media can be understood as the media's dissemination of the ideas of populist actors, sparked by a resonance between journalistic values and populist ideas. In the European context, it has in particular been argued that the media logic prioritizes negativity, simplification, a sense of conflict, and people-centered news coverage (e.g., Mazzoleni et al., 2003). The core ideas of populism can easily be aligned with such journalistic routines: They simplify issues into black-and-white terms; they highlight a sense of urgency and conflict by arguing that the nation and the people's in-group are in a severe state of crisis; they emphasize a central conflict between the people and the elites; and their negative problem interpretations and blame-shifting rationale highlights the negative aspects of societal issues. Against this backdrop, media outlets are presumed to provide a favorable stage to populist actors and viewpoints, which ties in with a passive role of spreading populist ideas among society.

A second line of literature on the relationship between populism and the media has argued that the media can play a more active role in framing issues in populist ways. This active role presumes that the media act separately from the ideas communicated by populist politicians (e.g., Krämer, 2014; Mazzoleni, 2008). More specifically, this implies that journalists draw on their agency to frame issues along the populist divide between the "good" us versus the culpable "them." This active role of the media in disseminating populist messages has been labeled as media populism (Krämer, 2014; Mazzoleni, 2008) or populism *by* the media (Bos & Brants, 2014). In the Dutch case, media populism postulates that tabloid and entertainment media, in particular, frame societal issues, such as the immigration debate, in terms of the populist divide between the innocent native Dutch people and the culpable elites and immigrants. In line with the literature on the alignment between media logic and populist ideas, such populist biases should be most salient in tabloid and entertainment outlets (e.g., Mazzoleni, 2008).

Empirical Evidence for Media Populism

But are the media actually populist themselves, or are they just giving a voice to allegedly newsworthy populist actors? The evidence regarding the media's role is still mixed. Some have found no consistent empirical evidence that media content actually contains populist framing (Bos & Brants, 2014), whereas others continue to argue that populism can be found in various media outlets (Mazzoleni, 2008). To shed more light on the presence of populist ideas in the media, an extensive content analysis of various Dutch media outlets[1] ($N=867$) has been conducted (Hameleers, Bos, & de Vreese, 2017b). In this content analysis, we coded for the type of media outlet, the presence of populist attributions of blame, indicators of journalistic styles (interpretative versus more objective), and the source of the message.

As a first result, we found that different actors are disseminating populist messages through the media (see Figure 5.1). As can be seen in Figure 5.1,

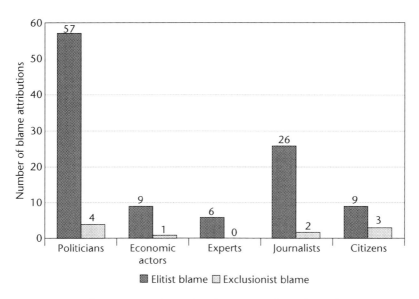

FIGURE 5.1 The presence of populist ideas in Dutch media outlets

Note
The presence of blame attribution is graphically depicted as the exact number of populist messages communicated by each sender (see Hameleers et al., 2017a).

politicians are the most likely source of populist blame attributions in the media. It must be noted that the populist exclusion of societal out-groups is extremely scarce. The second most salient actor is the journalist him- or herself, which does indicate that journalists are also spreading populist ideas via the media.

Journalists are most likely to communicate populist ideas when an interpretative journalist style is used. As can be seen in Figure 5.2, the likelihood of the presence of populist ideas by the media is only significantly different from zero and *positive* when an interpretative journalistic style is used. This means that populism is more likely to be present when an interpretative versus a neutral journalistic stance is used. When conflict framing is used – focusing on the reproach of one actor to another – populist blame attribution is not more likely to be present compared to neutral coverage (see the lower graphs in Figure 5.2).

Compared to all other outlets, tabloid media are most likely to engage in interpretative populist blame attributions. Broadsheet outlets are in comparison less likely to actively interpret issues in terms of populist blame attributions. Based on this empirical evidence, it can be concluded that the media can both act as a passive disseminator of populist messages *and* as an actor actively involved in the construction of populist ideas. The media's role in the spread of

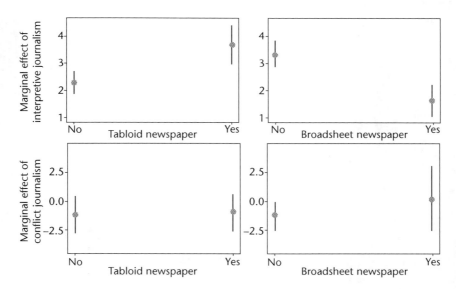

FIGURE 5.2 Comparing the presence of populist ideas in the media across outlets and journalistic routines

Note
The reference category for interpretative and conflict journalism is neutral coverage. "Yes" on the horizontal axes indicates the presence of the outlet type (tabloid on the left, broadsheet on the right) and "No" indicates all other outlets (see Hameleers et al., 2017a).

populist ideas in society is thus twofold: They cover newsworthy populist actors and directly respond to the media logic by framing issues into black-and-white terms of the "good" us versus the evil "them."

Populist Communication by Citizens

Just like politicians and journalists, citizens can also interpret societal issues along the lines of a divide between their in-group of ordinary people and out-groups of elites and "evil" others. This premise corroborates a growing body of empirical research that has measured citizens' populist interpretations as individual-level attitudes (e.g., Akkerman et al., 2014). These conceptualizations are, however, based on only the two most central components of populism: the centrality of the people's will in political decision-making and the people's opposition to political elites. In European countries, such as Austria, Denmark, France, and the Netherlands, right-wing populist movements have been successful. The most salient component of right-wing populist ideas is, next to the centrality of the people and scapegoating the elites, the *exclusionist* perspective taken on various societal issues: Immigrants, refugees, and other marginalized groups are excluded from the nativist in-group of the people because they are perceived as an economic, cultural or political threat (e.g., Albertazzi & McDonnell, 2008). In the Netherlands, for example, refugees entering the country from Syria, economic migrants from Eastern Europe, and immigrants who receive unemployment benefits are the center stage of populist blame attribution: They have caused the people's crisis because they are profiting without giving anything in return.

Empirical Evidence for the People's Populism

Based on the salience of right-wing populist ideas among society, we have proposed an expansion of populist attitudes measured on two core dimensions: anti-elitism and exclusionism. Survey research among a representative sample of Dutch citizens ($N=809$) provided support for such a distinction between populist interpretations among citizens: They perceived the opposition of their in-group of "the people" on both an elitist and societal level (Hameleers, Bos, & de Vreese, 2018). This means that, in the context of right-wing populism, citizens themselves attribute blame for the nation's problems on both a vertical and a horizontal level. Vertically, various elites, such as the government, experts, and economic elites, are perceived as a threat coming from *above*: The self-interested elites are safe in their ivory tower, at a large distance from the experiences of the ordinary people. Horizontally, people living among the in-group of the nativist citizens are also perceived as a threat coming from *within*: They occupy the same streets as the nativist people, but their perceived moral inferiority excludes them from the in-group.

Although we touched upon the key components of the people's populist interpretations, the question remains *where* people communicate such populist interpretations. Circumventing elitist and journalistic gatekeepers, ordinary citizens are empowered as many-to-many self-communicators in online contexts. Reasoned from a technological affordances perspective, communication on social network sites may create a perception of anonymity, asynchronicity, and a pervasive awareness and maintenance of community membership (Ellison & Boyd, 2013; Hampton, 2016). Against the backdrop of the social identification processes central to populism, this means that individuals are empowered to constantly negotiate and compare the boundary between their in-group and out-groups (Tajfel & Turner, 1986). The perception of anonymity and the potential of asynchronous communication may consolidate disinhibition: People experience less inhibition with regards to social norms and values in the online context, which fosters uncivil behavior targeted at the elites and societal out-groups.

Based on the assumptions on the compatibility of the online context for the expression of populist ideas (also see Bartlett et al., 2011 and Engesser, Ernst, Esser, & Büchel, 2017), an extensive qualitative content analysis of citizens' populist discourse on Facebook was conducted in the Netherlands ($N=417$). This content analysis aimed at an in-depth understanding of *how* citizens construct populist worldviews beyond scoring lower or higher on a subset of pre-defined attitude items (Hameleers, 2016). Specifically, publically accessible community pages revolving around criticism of the government, or the establishment and elites more generally, and nationalist communities were analyzed according to the steps explicated in grounded theory approach. Interpreting the results from a social identity perspective, it can be concluded that people constructed the boundary between their superior in-group and the corrupt and unresponsive elites in very hostile ways, frequently accompanied by death wishes targeted at specific politicians.

The following quote in a Facebook group revolving around governmental distrust, posted in July 2015, can be used to illustrate the people's hostile opposition to elites: "It would be a fantastic day if someone would hit this nation's traitor with a bullet through his head." On an exclusionist level, people constructed the boundary between morally and culturally superior native people and "polluting" other elements, who pose a threat to an economic, cultural, and social level. This exclusionist construction of identity can be illustrated by the following quote in a Dutch nationalist Facebook community, posted in May 2015: "Everything needs to go back. This will give us more air to breathe. Their houses will need to be disinfected, but we will do this with pleasure."

In line with the theoretical premises of social identity theory, and the depersonalizing potential of social network sites, ordinary citizens were empowered to become the senders of potentially dangerous, uncivil populist sentiments.

Contextual Factors Surrounding the Presence of Populist Ideas

It has been argued that populist ideas thrive in crisis times (e.g., Mazzoleni, 2008; Taggart, 2000). In such crisis situations, populist ideas are argued to adapt in consistency, depending on the social context in which they are articulated (e.g., Mazzoleni et al., 2003). Still, populist political movements have been successful and persuasive for electorates that have been relatively well-off, such as in Nordic countries (e.g., Danish People Party) and in Western Europe (e.g., the Freedom Parties in Austria and the Netherlands). Against this backdrop, the presence of a crisis in objective and absolute terms, such as a continuing influx of migrants or rising levels of unemployment, may not be the core criterion on which the persuasiveness of populist sentiments is built. It is rather the *perception* and *construction* of a severe crisis to the well-being of the ordinary people's in-group that provide the root for the pervasiveness and persuasiveness of populist sentiments (e.g., Elchardus & Spruyt, 2016).

To explain the success of populism from demand-side factors, previous research has predominately argued that the populist voter can be characterized by a specific socio-demographic profile: Lower educated, younger males who are high in political distrust are most likely to be affected by populist ideas (e.g., Bos et al., 2013). Based on this profile, populist voters have been characterized as the "losers of modernization" (e.g., Kriesi et al. 2006). This means that those people that may have experienced losses in the economic or cultural sphere are attracted to populist ideas. But what drives the appeal of populist ideas: demographic characteristics or feelings of losing out in a crisis that remains unsolved?

Empirical Evidence for Populist Profiles

To provide empirical evidence for this question, we tested the attractiveness of anti-elites and exclusionist populist sentiments discussed earlier (see Table 5.1; Hameleers et al., 2018). As can be seen in this table, the "standard" variables used to explain populist sentiments only play a minor role. The strongest factor is *perceived* relative deprivation: the perception that the people's in-group is relatively worse off than other groups in society, such as those who receive social benefits. This key finding is in line with other research that has argued that the perception of a crisis is a key contextual factor for populism's success (Elchardus & Spruyt, 2016). This notion can be illustrated with evidence from the earlier reported qualitative content analysis, in which the perception of in-group superiority was consolidated by emphasizing how other groups in society are victimized *less* by the problems or crisis situation threatening the people: "The Dutch man can get lost while the poor asylum seeker gets everything he demands from the government."

TABLE 5.1 Exploring the appeal of populist ideas

Variable	Anti-establishment		Exclusionist	
	B	SE	B	SE
Intercept	2.21***	0.29	1.33***	0.26
Gender (female)	0.01	0.07	−0.15*	0.06
Age	0.01	0.01	0.01	0.01
Education (higher)	−0.03	0.10	−0.14	0.09
Working class	0.01	0.10	−0.12	0.08
Relative deprivation	0.31***	0.03	0.40***	0.03
Voting establishment 2012	0.03	0.10	0.09	0.09
Voting populist party 2012	0.52***	0.15	0.24	0.14
Non-voting in 2012	0.26*	0.11	0.11	0.10
Political knowledge	−0.04	0.04	−0.08*	0.03
Left self-placement	0.06	0.11	−0.22*	0.01
Right self-placement	−0.11	0.09	0.13	0.08
Left-inclusionist	−0.01	0.03	−0.08***	0.02
Right-nativist	0.01	0.03	0.20***	0.03
Anti EU-integration	0.06*	0.02	0.07**	0.02
PVV preference	0.03*	0.01	0.11***	0.01
SP preference	0.03*	0.01	−0.01	0.01
Adjusted R^2	0.35		0.66	
F	21.34***		72.84***	
N	809		809	

Source: Hameleers et al. (2017b).

Notes
***$p < 0.001$, **$p < 0.01$, *$p < 0.05$.
See online Appendix for item wordings and scales. The populist attitudes scales were constructed using confirmatory factor analysis (CFA). Model fit for the two-dimension model was satisfactory ($\chi^2(23) = 34.09$, $\chi^2/df = 1.48$, p = 0.06; RMSEA = 0.024, 90% CI [0.00, 0.04]; CFI = 0.99). All measures reported in this table were measured on seven-point scales.

Understanding the Effects of Populist Communication

Populist messages that emphasize the central divide between the people and the culpable elites or societal out-groups have been regarded as persuasive (e.g., Mudde, 2004; Rooduijn et al., 2014). The argument behind this persuasive appeal can be explained from a social identity perspective. Social identity theory holds that individuals have a desire to maintain a positive perception of the self, which may even outweigh people's accuracy motivations (Tajfel & Turner, 1986). To engage in such strategies of positive distinctiveness, favorable situations, outcomes, or characteristics are ascribed to the in-group. Blame attributions may not only consolidate a positive self-concept, they may also activate *negative* stereotypes about the elites and immigrants (Dixon, 2008). To reassure a blameless self-perception in the context of a threat, negative attributes can be assigned to out-groups perceived as the cause for the people's threat (Gordon & Arian, 2001).

This process is strongly related to populism's central ideas. Populist ideas identify external causes for the in-group's deprivation by scapegoating the elites and immigrants: *They* did it. In the Netherlands, for example, the government is frequently accused of only listening to immigrants instead of the in-group of their "own" national citizens. Populist ideas thus enable citizens to maintain their positive self-perception: They can absolve themselves from any responsibility in causing their experienced problems. Having someone to blame hereby fulfils the desire for positive distinctiveness.

The process by which populist messages affect citizens' perceptions can be seen as "media based othering" (Krämer, 2014) or trait activation (Richey, 2012). This means that populist discourse blaming "evil" others for the people's problems activate or prime congruent schemata among those who receive such messages. If a populist message communicated by a populist politician, for example, holds the national government accountable for causing a crisis on the labor market that victimizes helpless, "good," hardworking people, citizens may interpret this issue in terms of similar binary divides: We are innocent and they are to blame! Against this backdrop, it can especially be expected that related attitudes are primed by populist communication, such as populist attitudes, voting, or blame perceptions.

Empirical Evidence for the Effects of Populist Communication

Recent empirical evidence illustrates that this is indeed the case (Hameleers et al., 2017a). Messages that frame issues, such as the labor market situation, as a matter of a societal divide between the "good" people and the "evil" politicians, prime similar interpretations among receiving citizens (see Figure 5.3). First of all, as can be seen in Figure 5.3, blame attributions to the political elites prime similar blame perceptions among receivers. This is mostly the case for blame attributed to the European Union. Next to this, populist attitudes are activated by exposure to populist messages: Those who were exposed to messages that shift blame in a populist way are more likely to interpret reality from a populist mindset.

These effects are, however, not demonstrated for all citizens. As can be expected, some citizens with non-populist priors disagree with populist messages. Empirical evidence demonstrates that those who do not feel attached to the actors who are attributed blame are more likely to accept populist messages than those who feel attached to the out-group attributed blame. In a similar vein, a recent comparative experiment on the effects of populist communication in Austria and the Netherlands demonstrated that source support plays a crucial role: Only those people who perceive the source of the populist message as part of their in-group are positively affected by the populist message (see Figure 5.4; Hameleers & Schmuck, 2017).

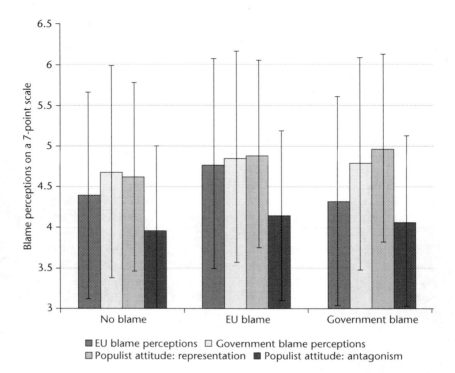

FIGURE 5.3 The direct effects of populist blame exposure on blame perceptions

Note
The direct effects of populist blame exposure on three levels (no blame vs. EU blame vs. governmental blame; see Hameleers, Bos, & de Vreese, 2017d).

This figure shows that, among those people who oppose the source, populist communication can result in a backlash. They already oppose populist actors, and this opposition becomes even stronger as a result of exposure to populist communication. Compared to those who are not exposed to populist messages, their populist attitudes are thus lower. Against this backdrop, exposure to populist messages can lead to polarized audiences: Those citizens who already oppose populist viewpoints are further bolstered in their negative priors vis-à-vis populist communication. Those who are already aligned with populist ideas become even more populist in their interpretations.

Empirical Evidence for Attitudinal Congruent Persuasion

It has been argued that populist ideas are only persuasive for a specific part of the electorate: Lower educated citizens higher in political distrust and cynicism and the so-called "losers of modernization" are identified as the most susceptible

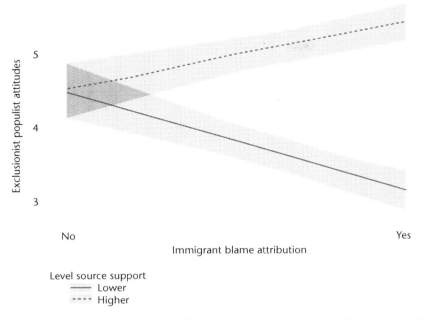

FIGURE 5.4 The crucial role of source support in the effects of populist communication

Source: Hameleers and Schmuck (2017).

audience (Kriesi et al., 2006). In that case, it may be expected that some citizens are also more likely to select populist messages than others. This presumption ties in with the literature on selective exposure and motivated reasoning (e.g., Stroud, 2010). In line with the premises of selective exposure, citizens are most likely to self-select messages that are congruent with their prior attitudes whilst they circumvent incongruent exposure (Taber & Lodge, 2006).

Taking selective exposure and attitudinal congruence into account in an experimental study (see Hameleers et al., 2017c), it was first of all found that people who self-select populist compared to non-populist content are part of a specific audience. More specifically, they have higher perceptions of relative deprivation than citizens who select non-populist content. Other antecedents and demographics play a less prominent role. Against this backdrop, it seems that the populist audience consists of citizens who perceive their in-group as relatively worse off than other groups living among them in society.

Concerning the effects of populist communication in a fragmented media environment, attitudinal congruence plays a key role: Only people who perceive the message as congruent with their prior attitudes of deprivation are affected by populist messages (see Figure 5.5). As can be seen in Figure 5.5, the effects are similar for forced and selective exposure. On both the left and right

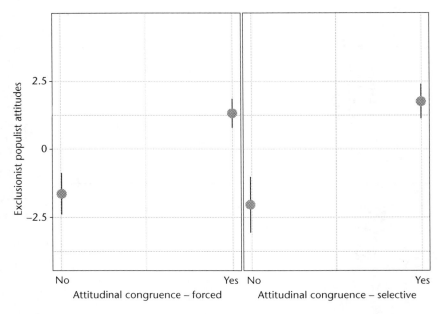

FIGURE 5.5 Marginal effect plots for interaction attitudinal congruence and populist blame attribution in forced (left) and selective (right) exposure conditions

Note
Dots represent regression weights and lines represent 95% confidence intervals. "Yes" on the horizontal axes means that the message was congruent with receivers' prior attitudes, and "No" means exposure to an incongruent populist message (see Hameleers et al., 2017c).

side of Figure 5.5, we see that populist messages only have a positive effect when the message is congruent with people's prior perceptions of relative deprivation. This can be interpreted as evidence that populism's persuasiveness depends heavily on the composition of the audience and their attachment to the people as a deprived in-group.

Discussion

Situated in the context of electorally successful and societally visible right-wing populism in the Netherlands, this chapter has aimed to dissect the core message of populism, its pervasiveness in various media types, and its persuasiveness among the electorate. This chapter started by conceptualizing populist communication by its central ideas: articulating a moral and causal distinction between the "good" people's in-group and the "culprit" elites or "evil" others as vertically and horizontally opposed out-groups. Next, it investigated the presence of populist ideas in the media, and its effect among citizens in public opinion.

With regards to the salience of populist ideas in the Dutch press, it may be concluded that populism is not a dominant frame, which underlines research by Bos and Brants (2014). Still, in tabloid newspapers that draw on an interpretative journalist style, populist frames are used to wrap up different societal issues. This underlines the theoretical expectations of Mazzoleni (2008) and Krämer (2014), who argued that media populism is a practice of active interpretation by journalists writing for tabloid newspapers.

This chapter has also demonstrated that such populist messages are only persuasive for a specific audience. Extending the premises of social identity theory (e.g., Tajfel & Turner, 1986), the empirical evidence presented in this chapter demonstrates that populist messages are most persuasive for citizens who experience a strong connection to the in-group of the "innocent" ordinary citizens and a weak tie to the culpable out-group: either the elites or immigrants. Such biases of in-group favoritism and out-group hostility also drive the selection of populist content: Those citizens who feel connected to an in-group of victimized, relatively deprived Dutch citizens are most likely to select populist communication.

Extending research that has argued that populism attaches itself to crisis sentiments and urgency (e.g., Mazzoleni et al., 2003; Taggart, 2000), this chapter has demonstrated that the people's perception of a threat to their in-group drives populism's persuasiveness. Perceived relative deprivation forms the psychological mechanism for this crisis perception. Extending the traditional demographic analysis of the losers of modernization (e.g., Kriesi et al., 2006), the empirical work highlighted in this chapter shows that it is not necessarily factual deprivation of material resources, but rather the threat of losing out more than undeserving out-groups that creates the context for the success and stickiness of populism (also see Elchardus & Spruyt, 2016).

What do these Dutch case studies tell us about the persuasiveness of populist ideas throughout the globe? As the empirical findings presented here are mostly based on randomized survey experiments, the psychological mechanisms that drive persuasion by populist communication should be applicable to populist uprisings all around the globe, where similar binary identity constructions of "us versus them" are expressed. However, the contextual factors and media content may differ. In the Netherlands, right-wing populist ideas are communicated within a relatively wealthy democracy with a long history of a strong welfare state. Various countries around the world – for example, in Southern Europe and Latin America – have witnessed the rise of left-wing populist movements that are mostly inclusionary opposed to exclusionary (e.g., Mudde & Rovira Kaltwasser, 2012). In these political systems, populist ideas may be expressed differently, revolving around the centrality of the ordinary people's will opposed to the wealthy and self-enriching elites. Yet, the *same mechanism* of in-group favoritism and out-group hostility underlines these populist ideas, making the results presented here relevant for other contexts as well.

In terms of the implications of these findings, it can first of all be noted that populist communication may lead to a polarized electorate, as already hinted at by Pappas (2014). This means that people who already oppose populist viewpoints may become even less aligned with populism as a result of exposure to populist ideas. Indeed, their prior resistance against populist views is bolstered by exposure to populist discourse, as they defend their prior attitudes after the populist challenge. For those aligned with populist viewpoints, in contrast, the message activates their prior convictions of a central divide between their in-group and populist enemies. To reassure their self-concept of belonging to the blameless people, they shift blame to the elites and societal out-groups after exposure to populist communication. Taken together, this means that populist communication can result in a divide between citizens who are aligned with populist views and those who oppose it.

Regarding such biases in the selection of populist media, echo chambers and filter bubbles may be consolidated. Certain media types, such as certain right-wing online media, are strongly associated with populist ideas. This means that citizens with populist viewpoints may read these outlets, whereas those with opposing views circumvent them. But what if selection is merely unconscious and automatic, such as selection driven by algorithms on social network sites? One could argue that the polarizing potential of populism would have even more far-reaching consequences, as people are no longer able to self-select incongruent viewpoints. They may perceive their media diet as balanced and driven by their own choices, but in fact they are exposed to congruent views only.

What may be the antidote for such societal polarizations? As populist self-selection is driven by perceptions of relative deprivation, it is important that these prior sentiments are acknowledged by the media and mainstream political actors. As such perceptions are salient in public opinion, these should be targeted and relativized. Fear and anger toward deprivation are real sentiments, so they should not be ignored. To engage the populist audience, communicators should therefore voice people's concerns related to being worse off than others in society, and relativize this threat by presenting facts on the actual deprivation of native citizens, and the opportunities they have to avert this threat in non-populist ways, also involving the out-groups as part of the solution, instead of the cause.

To conclude, and to end this chapter on a positive note, populist ideas are not as omnipresent as assumed in the "populist zeitgeist" rationale. Rather, they are present in the interpretations of a specific group of citizens, politicians, and journalists. To counterargue populist messages, it is important to acknowledge the anger and fear of citizens, and to relativize these with facts on the actual threat posed by the elites and immigrants. In doing so, their alleged involvement in the causes of the people's problems may be shifted to their contribution of solutions to the people's crisis.

Note

1. This content analysis was conducted on the following national Dutch newspapers: *De Telegraaf* (tabloid); *NRC Handelsblad* (broadsheet); *Volkskrant* (broadsheet); *Metro* (free newspaper); *Elsevier* (magazine); *Vrij Nederland* (magazine). The content analysis was conducted during two different election periods (the general elections of 2002 and 2012) and a routine period, in which the analysis focused on media coverage on the migration and labor market debates (2014–2015). Coding was done on the statement level within articles. The codebook included variables for the presence of populist blame attribution and the indicators of various journalist styles, such as interpretative journalistic stances, conflict strategy and game framing, objectivity, and journalistic interventionism. All variables had a satisfactory inter-coder reliability (Krippendorff's alpha > 0.70).

References

Akkerman, A., Mudde, C., & Zaslove, A. (2014). How populist are the people? Measuring populist attitudes in voters. *Comparative Political Studies*, 47(9), 1324–1353.

Albertazzi, D., & McDonnell, D. (2008). Introduction: The scepter and the spectre, In D. Albertazzi, & D. McDonnell (Eds.), *Twenty-first century populism. The spectre of Western European democracy* (pp. 1–11). Basingstoke: Palgrave Macmillan.

Bartlett, J., Birdwell, J., & Littler, M. (2011). *The new face of digital populism*. London: Demos.

Bos, L., & Brants, K. (2014). Populist rhetoric in politics and media: A longitudinal study of the Netherlands. *European Journal of Communication*, 29(6), 703–719.

Bos, L., van der Brug, W., & de Vreese, C. H. (2013). An experimental test of the impact of style and rhetoric on the perception of right-wing populist and mainstream party leaders. *Acta Politica*, 48(2), 192–208.

Canovan, M. (1999). Trust the people! Populism and the two faces of democracy. *Political Studies*, 47, 2–16.

Dixon, T. L. (2008). Crime news and racialized beliefs: Understanding the relationship between local news viewing and perceptions of African Americans and Crime. *Journal of Communication*, 58, 106–125.

Elchardus, M., & Spruyt, B. (2016). Populism, persistent republicanism and declinism: An empirical analysis of populism as a thin ideology. *Government & Opposition*, 51(1), 111–133.

Ellison, N. B., & Boyd, D. (2013). Sociality through social network sites. In W. H. Dutton (Ed.), *The Oxford handbook of internet studies* (pp. 151–172). Oxford: Oxford University Press.

Engesser, S., Ernst, N., Esser, F., & Büchel, F. (2017). Populism and social media: How politicians spread a fragmented ideology. *Information, Communication & Society*, 20(8), 1109–1126.

Gordon, C., & Arian, A. (2001). Threat and decision making. *Journal of Conflict Resolution*, 45(2), 197–215.

Hameleers, M. (2016). *The populism of online communities: Constructing the boundary between the heartland and polluting others*. Paper presented at the annual Etmaal conference, Amsterdam.

Hameleers, M., & Schmuck, D. (2017). It's us against them: A comparative experiment on the effects of populist messages communicated via social media. *Information, Communication & Society*, 20(9), 1425–1444.

Hameleers, M., Bos, L., & de Vreese, C. H. (2017a). Shoot the messenger? The media's role in framing populist attributions of blame. *Journalism*. doi: 10.1177/1464884917698170.

Hameleers, M., Bos, L., & de Vreese, C. H. (2017b). The appeal of media populism: The media preferences of citizens with populist attitudes. *Mass Communication & Society*, 20(4), 481–504.

Hameleers, M., Bos, L., & de Vreese, C. H. (2017d). "They did it": The effects of emotionalized blame attribution in populist communication. *Communication Research*, 44(6), 870–900.

Hameleers, M., Bos, L., & de Vreese, C. H. (2018). Selective exposure to populist communication: How attitudinal congruence drives the effects of populist attributions of blame. *Journal of Communication*, 68(1), 51–74.

Hampton, K. N. (2016). Persistent and pervasive community: New communication technologies and the future of community. *American Behavioral Scientist*, 60(1), 101–124.

Heijne, B. (2011). The Netherlands: Prosperity and populism. *World Policy Journal*, 28(2), 30–33.

Jagers, J., & Walgrave, S. (2007). Populism as political communication style: An empirical study of political parties' discourse in Belgium. *European Journal of Political Research*, 46(3), 319–345.

Krämer, B. (2014). Media populism: A conceptual clarification and some theses on its effects. *Communication Theory*, 24, 42–60.

Kriesi, H. P., Grande, E., Lachat, R., Dolezal, M., Bornschier, S., & Frey, T. (2006). Globalization and the transformation of the national political space: Six European countries compared. *European Journal of Political Research*, 45(6), 921–956.

Mazzoleni, G. (2008). Populism and the media. In D. Albertazzi, & D. McDonnell (Eds.), *Twenty-first century populism: The spectre of Western European democracy* (pp. 49–64). Basingstoke: Palgrave Macmillan.

Mazzoleni, G., Stewart, J., & Horsfield, B. (2003). *The media and neo-populism: A contemporary comparative analysis*. Westport, CT: Praeger.

Mudde, C. (1996). The paradox of the anti-party: Insights from the extreme right. *Party Politics*, 2(2), 265–276.

Mudde, C. (2004). The populist zeitgeist. *Government and Opposition*, 39, 542–564.

Mudde, C., & Rovira Kaltwasser, C. (2012). *Populism in Europe and the Americas: Threat or corrective for democracy?* Cambridge: Cambridge University Press.

Pappas, T. S. (2014). Populist democracies: Post-authoritarian Greece and post-communist Hungary. *Government and Opposition*, 49(1), 1–23.

Richey, S. (2012). Campaign advertising and the stimulation and activation of the authoritarian personality. *Political Communication*, 29(1), 24–43.

Rooduijn, M., de Lange, S. L., & van der Brug, W. (2014). A populist zeitgeist? Programmatic contagion by populist parties in Western Europe. *Party Politics*, 20(4), 563–575.

Stroud, N. (2010). Polarization and partisan selective exposure. *Journal of Communication*, 60(3), 556–577.

Taber, C. S., & Lodge, M. (2006). Motivated skepticism in the evaluation of political beliefs. *American Journal of Political Science*, 50(3), 755–769.

Taggart, P. (2000). *Populism*. Buckingham; Philadelphia, PA: Open University Press.

Tajfel, H., & Turner, J. C. (1986). The social identity theory of inter-group behavior. In S. Worchel, & L. W. Austin (Eds.), *Psychology of intergroup relations* (pp. 7–24). Chicago, IL: Nelson-Hall.

Van Kessel, S. (2011). Explaining the electoral performance of populist parties: The Netherlands as a case study. *Perspectives on European Politics and Society*, 12(1), 68–88.

6

POPULISM IN SELF-DIRECTED AND MEDIATED COMMUNICATION

The Case of the Five Star Movement in the 2013 Italian Electoral Campaign

Cristina Cremonesi

Introduction

In recent years, a number of populist movements and parties have experienced renewed political success in countries with different economic and political characteristics. In order to understand the reasons behind this widespread success, the electoral communication of these parties and their media coverage are crucial factors to be considered. In fact, due to the ideology crisis of the last decades (Lyotard, 1984) the role of political communication is increasing in importance in determining voters' electoral choices (Manin, 2014). Moreover, the relationship between populist parties and the media needs to be reassessed in light of the new hybrid media environment, characterized by social media and new logics of political information production (Castells, 2007; Chadwick, 2013).

This research addresses this topic by focusing on the case of the Five Star Movement (FSM), an Italian populist party led by the former comedian Beppe Grillo, which was in its "insurgent phase" during the 2013 Italian electoral campaign.[1] The full image of the FSM conveyed to Italian voters is reconstructed by analyzing both direct communication by the party and newspaper coverage. In this way, similarities and differences between self-directed and mediated communication of FSM are shown, and it verifies whether the self-directed communication of this populist formation has been monolithic or has changed according to the communication channel used to deliver its message. In the same way, the differences in the coverage of FSM by newspapers characterized by dissimilar political positions and pro/anti-system attitudes are highlighted.

The chapter is structured as follows. First, a brief revision of the existing literature on populism and on the relation between media and populism is provided. Second, the case study is presented and the methods applied to conduct the analysis are explained. Finally, three sections discuss the results of the self-directed communication of FSM and its leader, Beppe Grillo, its coverage by the Italian newspapers, and the relationship between these two factors.

Theoretical Considerations

Populism: Conceptions and Fundamental Elements

In social science literature, the term populism has been applied to a wide range of objects (parties, ideologies, leaders, etc.) across a variety of contexts, so that multiple definitions of this phenomenon have been developed. They can be grouped into three main conceptual approaches (e.g., Gidron & Bonikowski, 2013) that, however, are not mutually exclusive. As already presented by Hameleers in this volume, populism has been conceived, respectively, as a political strategy (e.g., Germani, 1974; Kornhauser, 1959; Weyland, 2001), as a discursive style (e.g., Laclau, 2005; Taguieff, 2002), and as a set of ideas or thin-centered ideology (e.g., Mény & Surel, 2002; Mudde, 2004; Taggart, 2002).

The ideological approach to populism is nowadays the most common in the empirical works, according to which populism is a set of ideas about how politics should function in order to truly represent the interests of the people. In this regard, populism can be considered a "thin-centered ideology," i.e., an ideology that does not provide answers to all the major socio-political questions (as the thick ideologies, such as liberalism, do), and could therefore be compatible with other ideologies (Gidron & Bonikowski, 2013). This is demonstrated by the existence of both right-wing and left-wing populism.

Many scholars following the ideological approach have defined populism by identifying the core elements of populist manifestations (e.g., Mény & Surel, 2002; Stanley, 2008; Taggart, 2002). The most inclusive among these definitions, i.e., the one that accounts for the majority of the movements conventionally labelled as populist (Mudde & Kaltwasser, 2013), is elaborated by Mudde (2004). According to this definition, populism is:

> an ideology that considers society to be ultimately separated into two homogeneous and antagonistic groups, "the pure people" versus "the corrupt elite," and which argues that politics should be an expression of the *volonté générale* (general will) of the people.
> (Mudde, 2004, p. 543, parentheses in original)

From Mudde's definition, it emerges that almost all manifestations of populism refer to a conflict between the people and the elites, and that the key features of populism are the reference to "the people," the elite, and the aim to restore the "general will."

Typical of all kinds of populism is the valorization of "the people" conceived as a homogeneous and virtuous entity. Multiple meanings are associated with the populist formations and this entity depending on the aspects (e.g., political or economic position, origin) they consider.[2] What "the people" indicates is always defined in opposition to a series of enemies, since according to the populist logic "the people" hold the victim role, and populist formations offer them redemption and revenge against their antagonists (Tarchi, 2003, p. 24). Consequently, those who are not part of the homogenous group of "the people," such as national (political, economic, media, etc.) elites and external agents, i.e., immigrants coming from different cultural or religious contexts and supranational elites (e.g., the European Union, the IMF), are conceived as a menace and an obstacle to be removed.

Concerning the political elites, they are accused of hindering the exercise of the legitimate sovereignty of the people, an element strictly connected to the populist valorization of "the general will." Populist formations hold a simplifying vision of politics that consists of a direct realization of the will of the people. It explains both populists' strong and personalistic leadership style (as it emerges from the direct relationship between the leader and his supporters, and from the marginal role of populist parties' apparatus) and their criticism of the mechanisms of representative democracy (Chiapponi, 2008; Tarchi, 2003). In fact, populists demand that the political decision-making process completely reproduces the people's will. It is at odds with the so-called distortions they impute to the mechanisms of representative democracy, but the populist disapproval of democratic institutions does not automatically evolve into a rejection of democracy per se; quite the contrary, it usually realizes itself in a demand for more democratization in the relationship between citizens and institutions (Canovan, 1999).

Following the ideological approach to populism means focusing on the sole content of populist communication. However, how populist ideas are communicated is also relevant, since populism is often associated with a certain style of communication (Engesser, Fawzi, & Larsson, 2017). According to the literature (Albertazzi, 2007; Bos & Brants, 2014; Mols & Jetten, 2014), a series of elements characterizes the communication of populist political actors: reference to the *nation* facing a critical juncture (i.e., a situation that has to be addressed urgently to ensure historical continuity, since the *nation* is under extreme conditions and its future is at risk), the presence of emotional language (when the events reported are dramatized by presenting them as exceptional, exciting, or thrilling; and affective wording and speech is proposed through the use of multiple strong adjectives, present tense in the description of past events, pronounced accentuation, etc.), explicit reference to negative emotions (such as anger, disappointment, disgust, fear, and sadness), and the use of peculiar language devices (such as irony, metaphors, and offensive language). A series of scholars have underlined the connection between populism as a thin ideology and as a style developing a twofold approach to populism (Bos & Brants, 2014; Bos, van der Brug, & de Vreese, 2010). Following these previous studies, this research considers both the ideological and the stylistic elements of populist communication.

While many studies have already analyzed the elements of populism as both ideology and style in political actors' self-directed communication on a specific communication channel, few studies have considered how the political actors' reference to populist elements changes in different communication sets (Cranmer, 2011), and no study has analyzed the differences between online and offline populist communication. The first aim of this chapter is to fill this gap.

Populism Through and by the Media

The current theoretical conceptualization of the relationship between populism and the media is mainly based on the comparative studies of Mazzoleni (2003, 2008, 2014), which explained how the media may favor populism success through the coverage of populist parties, and on the research of Krämer (2014), which demonstrated that the media may also be proper populist actors and spread populism by themselves. While these lines of research are valid starting points, the evidence provided by other empirical studies (e.g., Bos & Brants, 2014) suggests that they need to be refined in order to be adapted to the current media environment.

According to Mazzoleni (2003, 2014), the attention that the media pay to populist formations and the way they speak about them varies according to a series of variables: populist parties' lifecycle phase, the characteristics of the media outlets (upmarket quality vs. mass-market media), and the degree of integration of the media system with the political elites. In particular, mass-market media are more prone to cover new populist formations, since populist parties and popular media share the same objective of gaining support via sensationalism. In fact, populist formations are "newsworthy" for mass-market media since they fit the news values of these outlets. So, mass-market media tend to cover a populist party from its insurgent phase (Mazzoleni, 2003). By contrast, upmarket quality media are reluctant to cover new populist parties because these media reflect the values and the views of the elites and they tend to defend the status quo (Mazzoleni, 2008; Mudde, 2007). Consequently, upmarket media ignore new populist parties as far as they can, and only when these parties become popular do they start to cover them (Mazzoleni, 2003). In addition, upmarket quality newspapers may favor the success of insurgent populist parties when their deferential attitude toward the political elites breaks because of a political crisis (Mazzoleni, 2014). In this case, quality media offer negative coverage of the political class and of its actions, and so spread disaffection toward mainstream parties that indirectly may increase voters' support for new populist formations (Mazzoleni, 2003).

It is important to underline that, while Mazzoleni's arguments had for a long time been the main theoretical reference for understanding the differences in populist parties' media coverage, a number of recent empirical contributions (e.g., Akkerman, 2011; Bos & Brants, 2014) have questioned its validity in the current media environment characterized by the diffusion of commercial media logic in both mass-market and upmarket media outlets (Strömbäck & Esser, 2014).

Beyond populism through the media, populism by the media also needs to be taken into account, according to Krämer (2014), in order to understand the relation between media and populism. In fact, by investigating media logics and behaviors, Krämer individuated a series of properties of media populism concerning ideological elements (Krämer, 2014, p. 49): (1) "the unmediated appeal to 'The People'," since media outlets gain their strength from a close connection to the audience, (2) "the representation of society as divided into homogenous groups," since the media usually select and report issues and events by mirroring the divisions in society and adopting an ethnocentric frame, and (3) "the anti-institutional attitude," as news media conceive themselves as a "fourth estate" and assume a watchdog function with respect to the establishment (especially if media have given up their deferential attitude toward politicians). This suggests that the presence of populism in the media does not need to be connected to the coverage of a populist party, but that the media may be populist themselves. It is a relevant assumption, but, as also highlighted by Krämer (2014), further research is needed on the relationship between populist media and populist parties in order to understand whether and how the former contributes to the containment or success of the latter.

With regard to the Italian case, no studies have focused on the coverage of populist parties by the Italian media or considered the degree of populism of the Italian media. These deficiencies are significant, since Italian populist parties have been very successful even though Italy has the peculiarity of lacking mass-market tabloid newspapers. This condition makes Italy the perfect case study in order to understand if there are differences in how the media cover populism beyond the classical distinction between upmarket quality and mass-market tabloid newspapers, which has been losing its explanatory power in the current media environment where the commercial media logic has permeated all kinds of newspapers (Strömbäck & Esser, 2014). Consequently, the second aim of this research is to understand whether among the same kind of media, in this case upmarket newspapers, differences exist in the support of populism and which media characteristics they depend upon. This aim is pursued by focusing on the case of the 2013 Italian electoral campaign. The next section discusses the relevance of this object of analysis and describes the data analyzed.

Case Study and Data

In order to investigate populism and its propagation in the new media environment, focusing on the Italian case is a valid choice since Italy may be defined as a "laboratory of populism," given the many and multifaceted populist political formations that have characterized the country's political history (Bobba & McDonnell, 2015). Moreover, to consider the 2013 Italian general election for investigating the role played by self-directed and mediated communication in determining the success of a populist party is particularly relevant. Not only was the 2013 campaign the first one in which the internet (and therefore politicians' self-directed communication) played a significant role in Italy, but also the Five Star Movement was in its "insurgent phase" (Mazzoleni, 2014); thus, that is the moment in which both self-directed communication and media coverage are crucial for determining the success of a political formation. Finally, Italy is the only Western European country where populist parties were successful even though they could not count on the coverage of mass-market tabloid newspapers.

Many studies have addressed the topic of Grillo and his party's communication in the 2013 campaign (e.g., Cosenza, 2013; Mazzoleni, 2014). According to these sources, it was characterized by: the extensive use of online communication (Bartlett, Froio, Littler, & McDonnell, 2013, pp. 13–14); an ambivalent relationship with traditional offline media (Corbetta & Gualmini, 2013, p. 25); and noteworthy personal communication, as shown during the electoral tour (Cosenza, 2013, p. 217). Moreover, a number of recent research studies have considered the elements of populism deployed by Grillo and his party's online self-directed communication (e.g., Bracciale & Martella, 2017). However, to what extent Grillo's communication differs via diverse communication channels and how it was covered by newspapers have not yet been investigated.

In order to fill this gap in the literature and to reconstruct the full image conveyed to the Italian voters about Grillo's insurgent populist formation, this analysis considers both Grillo and FSM's self-directed communication on different media channels and its coverage by the Italian press by focusing on the last week of the 2013 Italian electoral campaign (i.e., February 16–23, 2013).

The choice to consider only the last week of the campaign is due to the fact that almost no media attention had been paid to the FSM before this point in time (Bobba, Legnante, Roncarolo, & Seddone, 2013). In fact, all the Italian media nearly ignored the FSM, considering it politically marginal, until it became clear from electoral surveys and the citizens' participation in Grillo's electoral rallies that the FSM was going to receive a considerable share of votes.

Regarding self-directed communication, five channels were included in the analysis, because the current media environment offers political actors many ways to reach voters, and this may entail a differentiation in their message. For the offline communication, both FSM's 2013 party manifesto and three speeches given by Beppe Grillo at the main electoral rallies of the closing week of the campaign were analyzed. The Web 1.0[3] communication was considered through 22 blog posts on the official website of the FSM.[4] In terms of social media sites, both Facebook and Twitter were taken into account, and all the Facebook posts ($N=381$) and tweets ($N=221$) published on the official pages and accounts of Grillo and his party during the considered week were analyzed.

With regard to the mediated communication, the analysis of FSM and Grillo's coverage focused only on printed newspapers, since they play a central role in the Italian media system. Printed newspapers have more political journalists and publish more political articles than any other media outlet in Italy. Moreover, in general, newspaper coverage may be considered a trustworthy proxy of political parties' media representation, even in contexts where newspapers do not determine the media's political agenda-setting (Walgrave & Van Aelst, 2006). In order to reconstruct the full spectrum of the Italian newspapers, and given that the distinction between upmarket quality and mass-market tabloid newspapers is not relevant in the Italian case, five newspapers were selected according to their diffusion, partisanship, and pro- or anti-system orientation (Ceron & Splendore, 2016): *Corriere della Sera*, *La Stampa*, *La Repubblica*, *Il Fatto Quotidiano*, and *Il Giornale* (Table 6.1).

The articles published by the five newspapers were gathered from the *Eco della Stampa* database, and automatically and manually selected in order to individuate the articles that mentioned Grillo and the Five Star Movement.

Table 6.2 shows the main characteristics of the data about the self-directed and mediated communication of Grillo and the FSM described so far.

Hypotheses and Method

With regard to the self-directed communication of FSM and Grillo, since parties nowadays usually use tailored strategies on different media (Strandberg,

TABLE 6.1 Main characteristics of the press outlets analyzed

Newspaper	Daily readership in February 2013	Partisanship	Pro-/anti-system
Corriere della Sera	430,283	Neutral	Pro
La Repubblica	372,654	Left-wing	Middle position
La Stampa	240,008	Neutral	Pro
Il Giornale	123,901	Right-wing	Anti
Il Fatto Quotidiano	53,153	Left-wing	Anti

Source: The data on newspapers' daily readership were collected from the website Accertamento Diffusione Stampa (www.adsnotizie.it) in February 2013; the data on newspapers' partisanship are based on the research of Lizzi and Pritoni (2014) and Mancini (2008); the data on newspapers' pro- or anti-system orientation are based on the study of Ceron and Splendore (2016).

TABLE 6.2 Information on the analyzed data (time frame: February 16–23, 2013)

Type of communication	Communication channel/outlet	Unit of analysis	N
Offline self-directed communication	Leader's speeches at the electoral rallies of Turin, Milan, and Rome	Thematic unit	70
	Party manifesto for the 2013 general elections	Thematic unit	7
Online self-directed communication	Official Facebook page of Beppe Grillo	Post	216
	Official Facebook page of FSM	Post	165
	Official Twitter account of Beppe Grillo	Tweet	81
	Official Twitter account of FSM	Tweet	140
	Official party website	Blog post	22
Mediated communication (newspapers)	*Corriere della Sera*	Article	18
	La Repubblica	Article	23
	La Stampa	Article	34
	Il Giornale	Article	27
	Il Fatto Quotidiano	Article	27

Source: Cremonesi (2017, p. 62).

2013), I expected that (H1) *The self-directed communication of FSM and its leader differs on different communication channels.* More specifically, since the content of parties' messages reveals their ideology (Battegazzorre, 2013), I supposed that (H1a) *Grillo and FSM place different emphasis on the elements of populism "as a set of ideas" according to the media used to communicate.* Moreover, since different communication channels influence the type of communication delivered by posing restrictions regarding its register and possibility to use emotionality devices (Engesser, Ernst, Esser, & Büchel, 2017), I also expected that (H1b) *Grillo and FSM's use of populist stylistic devices differs on different media.*

In terms of the coverage of FSM, according to Mazzoleni (2003, p. 225), different kinds of media react in different ways to the populist parties in their early growth phase. In order to verify this in the Italian context, the following hypothesis was put forward: (H2a) *Italian newspapers cover the populist elements of Grillo and FSM discourse in different ways and give a different connotation to these elements.* Moreover, in order to increase the comprehension of the differences in newspapers' coverage and support for populist elements in the current media environment, particular attention was paid to the newspapers' attitudes toward the political system. In fact, anti-elites' rhetoric and criticism of the representative democracy institutions are distinctive traits of both populist parties and the newspapers most critical of the political system. Consequently, another more specific hypothesis was stated as (H2b) *Newspapers' attitudes toward the political system influence their coverage of FSM and Grillo, as well as their support for populist elements mentioned by these political actors.*

Finally, the relationship between FSM self-directed and mediated communication was also investigated with the objective of understanding whether the Italian press owns proper populist ideology traits. Since, according to Krämer (2014), the presence of populism in the media does not have to be connected to the coverage of a populist party, I expected that (H3) *The Italian press deployed independent elements of populist ideology during the 2013 electoral campaign.*

In order to address the hypotheses mentioned above, a quantitative manual content analysis was initially conducted of both self-directed and mediated communication data. For this purpose, an original and detailed codebook that considers both the fundamental dimensions of populism as a set of ideas and the elements of populism as a discursive style was constructed referring to the aforementioned theoretical knowledge. Tables 6.3 and 6.4 show the dimensions and indicators employed in the analysis. Successively, the self-directed and mediated communication of FSM was investigated by calculating and comparing the frequencies of the populism indicators;[5] the newspapers' support for the mentioned populist traits was examined; and these steps were followed by a comparison of the frequencies of mentioning the elements of populism as an ideology in the self-directed communication of Grillo and his party and in the coverage of the Italian newspapers.

TABLE 6.3 Operationalization of populism "as a thin-centered ideology"

Dimension	Codebook variable	Answer
Valorization of "the people"	Does the text mention the people?	Yes
	Does the text mention the people in general?	Yes
	Are the people conceived as a homogeneous group?	Yes
	How are the people evaluated? (−2 = strongly negative to +2 = strongly positive)	≥1
Negative evaluation of the elites	Does the text mention the elite (the parties/professional politicians; the European Union elite and politicians; the bureaucrats/technocrats; the economic powers; the media; the intellectuals) or a member of the elites?	Yes
	Does the text mention this elite in general?	Yes
	Is the elite conceived as a homogeneous group?	Yes
	How is the elite evaluated? (−2 = strongly negative to +2 = strongly positive)	≤−1
Opposition between the people and the elites (this element is coded only if both the elites and the people in general and as an homogeneous group are mentioned)	One of these questions:	Yes
	Are the people depicted as being oppressed by the elite?	
	Are the elite's actions depicted as being a threat to the well-being of the people?	
	Is the political elite depicted as not listening to the people's requests?	
	Is the political elite depicted as neglecting the people's interests/necessities?	
Negative evaluation of the out-groups	Does the text mention a social out-group?	Yes
	How is the out-group evaluated? (−2 = strongly negative to +2 = strongly positive)	≤−1
Criticism toward representative institutions and valorization of the instruments of direct democracy	One of these two questions:	Yes (or)
	Does the text contain a general critique toward the functioning, the characteristics, and/or the rules of representative democracy and its institutions?	Yes
	Does the text mention the instrument of direct and participatory democracy? How are they evaluated? (from −1 = negatively to +1 = positively)	1
Focus on the leader only	Does the text/speech mention or refer to the leader's actions/programs/intentions?	Yes
	Does the text/speech mention the party's support for the leader?	No

Source: Cremonesi (2017, pp. 65–70).

TABLE 6.4 Operationalization of populism as a communication style

Dimension	Indicators	Answer
Reference to the nation facing a "critical juncture"	One of these questions: Does the text/speech refer to the fact that the nation is facing a "critical juncture"? Does the text/speech refer to the fact that the nation has faced a "critical juncture" and that, thanks to the intervention of the author's party/leader, it has been overcome?	Yes
Presence of emotional language	One of these questions: Does the speaker dramatize events? Does the speaker use affective wording and speech? Does the speaker use explicit expressions of emotions?	Yes
Explicit reference to negative emotions (this element is coded only if an explicit use of emotion is identified)	Which emotions are expressed in the text/speech?	One of the negative emotions listed[a]
Use of peculiar language devices	Does the text/speech contain a "distinctive use of the language" such as: • irony (the use of words to convey a meaning that is the opposite of their literal or actual meaning) • metaphor (figure of speech used for describing an object or a situation by suggesting a comparison of it with a different object or situation) • offensive language (i.e., bad language and swear words, personal offense and offensive nicknames; evocation of vulgar images)	Yes

Source: Cremonesi (2017, pp. 65–70).

Note

a The negative emotions listed in the codebook are: anger, contempt, disappointment, disgust, fear, guilt, hate, regret, sadness, and shame. This list was created by referring to the work of the *GERG – Geneva Emotion Research Group*, and to the *Geneva Emotion Wheel* – a research tool that organizes emotions around two dimensions (valence: positive-negative, and control: high-low) and that has been built on the base of empirical data and theoretical considerations (see, for example, Sacharin, Schlegel, & Scherer, 2012; Scherer, 2005).

110 Cristina Cremonesi

Results

Grillo and FSM's Self-Directed Communication

The study of FSM and Grillo's communication on different channels reflects a variegated picture of "populism as a thin-centered ideology" (Table 6.5). Criticism of the elites is the only element that is strong in all of them. In fact, while elements of populism are marginal on social media in general, this theme was evident in 34.6% of Facebook posts and 33.1% of the analyzed tweets. As regards the neutral or positive valorization of "the people," it is particularly strong in the website posts (47.6%) — where there is also the greatest focus on the explicit opposition between "the people" and elites, 23.8% — and in the party manifesto (28.6%). This result is particularly remarkable, since it indicates that the programmatic document of FSM's political action makes explicit reference to the positive connotation of "the people" as a homogeneous group; in addition, 42.9% of the thematic units of this document report criticism of the elites and 14.3% explicit opposition between these two groups. It is a sign that the fundamental dimensions of "populism as a set of ideas" drive FSM's political action.

Lastly, particular attention must be paid to the elements of populism individuated in Grillo's speeches at the rallies. This type of communication stresses many populist traits almost absent on the other channels. First, only in Grillo's speeches is the role of the leader especially highlighted (22.9%). Second, the out-groups are almost exclusively pointed out in this kind of communication. Third, the criticism of representative democracy and the related positive evaluation of instruments of direct democracy are particularly strengthened in Grillo's

TABLE 6.5 Reference to the elements of populism as a "thin-centered ideology" by communication channel (in percentages)

	FB post	Tweet	Website post	Oral speech	Party manifesto	Total
Positive or neutral mention of "the people" as a homogeneous group	14.1	11.0	47.6	20.0	28.6	15.6
Negative evaluation of the elites as a homogeneous group	34.6	33.1	52.4	48.6	42.9	36.9
Explicit opposition people vs. elites	4.2	2.8	23.8	7.1	14.3	5.1
Explicit focus on the leader only	1.8	0.7	4.8	22.9	0.0	4.4
Against representative democracy/ pro direct democracy	3.5	3.4	14.3	25.7	14.3	7.0
Negative evaluation of out-groups	0.0	0.7	0.0	4.3	0.0	0.8
Total (N)	283	145	21	70	7	526

Source: Cremonesi (2017, p. 88).

oral communication (25.7%), but they also emerge as characteristic traits on FSM's website posts (14.3%) and are mentioned in the party manifesto.

With regard to the elements of populism as a communication style, the differences among communication channels are also pronounced (Table 6.6). As before, the populist characteristics are more common in oral speeches and website posts than in social media communication, where the use of emotional language is the only extensive feature (it characterized 26.9% of Facebook posts and 23.4% of tweets). Moreover, the party manifesto does not show elements of populist style in this case: unsurprisingly, it contains only one device of emotionalization.

In contrast to what was individuated with regard to the elements of populism as a "thin-centered ideology," the oral speech does not present a particularly higher level of populist style, but it is quite similar to the one registered on FSM's website. Only the use of offensive language is significantly more marked in Grillo's oral communication; it characterizes 27.1% of oral thematic units analyzed and only 14.3% of website posts. Presumably, this is due to the higher degree of freedom permitted by the oral communication in which Grillo could express his opinions without too much control by his communication experts, than by the written communication where communication experts played a major role. Lastly, the use of emotional language is slightly more common in the oral communication (62.9%) than in the website posts (52.4%), despite being quite high in the latter case.

In light of these data, it appears clear that the type of media channel used to communicate also influences the content and style of populist messages. Given that in Grillo's oral communication several elements of populism as a thin-centered ideology are more marked than in the written communication, and that the mention of all populist elements is rarer on Facebook and Twitter than in other types of online and offline communication, it is possible to state that H1a is confirmed. Regarding the use of populist style, H1b seems to be only

TABLE 6.6 Reference to the elements of populism as a communication style by communication channel (in percentages)

	FB post	Tweet	Website post	Oral speech	Party manifesto	Total
"Critical juncture"	3.9	2.1	19.0	17.1	0.0	5.7
Presence of emotional language	26.9	23.4	52.4	62.9	14.3	31.6
Explicit reference to negative emotion	3.9	1.4	9.5	12.9	0.0	4.6
Use of irony	3.9	4.8	28.6	34.3	0.0	9.1
Use of metaphor	5.7	4.8	19.0	4.3	0.0	5.7
Use of offensive language	1.8	0.0	14.3	27.1	0.0	5.1
Total (N)	283	145	21	70	7	526

Source: Cremonesi (2017, p. 88).

partially confirmed. In effect, while differences between the media channels have been highlighted, they seem to be only partially caused by the media channel characteristics.

For example, there are no significant differences[6] between the communication on Facebook and Twitter, even though the characteristics of these two platforms are different. Moreover, website communication and oral communication appear to be quite similar regarding the presence of populist style elements. This suggests that, in the use of populist stylistic devices, the differences between different media are not related to media outlets' characteristics but to the strategic choice to convey different messages to the different audiences of offline, Web 1.0, and social media communication.

Grillo and FSM's Newspaper Coverage

The analysis of the coverage of FSM's populist message by the Italian newspapers depicts a variegated picture of populism both as a "thin-centered ideology" and as a discursive style. Concerning the mention of the elements of populism as a set of ideas, *Il Fatto Quotidiano* and *Il Giornale*, the two anti-system outlets, display the highest percentage of articles (88.9%) referring to populism (see Table 6.7). By contrast, *La Stampa*, a pro-system newspaper, shows the lowest percentage of references to populism (nonetheless, at least one element of populism is displayed in 70.6% of its articles about Grillo and FSM). Nevertheless, the pro-system newspaper *Corriere della Sera* refers to populism in 83.3% of its articles.

The prominence of populism in *Corriere della Sera*'s coverage is clearly visible when the elements of populism as a thin-centered ideology are considered separately. *Corriere della Sera* shows the highest percentage of articles referring to "the people" and those expressing an explicit opposition between "the people" and the elites. The same holds for the criticism of the elites, a populist element that *Il Fatto Quotidiano* also mentions in a high percentage of its articles (63%). Finally, the criticism of representative democracy is most common in *Il Fatto Quotidiano* (occurring in one-third of its articles), but *Corriere della Sera*, *Il Giornale*, and *La Stampa* also display such criticism in a relatively high percentage share of articles. By contrast, *La Repubblica*, which occupies the middle ground in regards to the Italian political system, deals with this trait of populism only rarely (8.7%). Thus, the differences in Grillo and FSM's coverage mentioned above cannot be explained by the newspapers' attitudes toward the Italian political system. However, the way in which the populist elements are connoted (Table 6.8) suggests a different scenario.

Il Fatto Quotidiano and *Il Giornale* connoted the ideological elements of populism very differently (Table 6.8). *Il Fatto Quotidiano* supported populist elements in 51% of cases, while *Il Giornale* mainly gave them a negative connotation (45%). Similarly, *La Repubblica* did not support the elements of populism as a

TABLE 6.7 Articles containing a reference to elements of populism as a "thin-centered ideology" by newspaper (in percentages)

	Corriere della Sera	La Repubblica	La Stampa	Il Giornale	Il Fatto Quotidiano	Total
Positive or neutral mention of "the people" as a homogeneous group	33.3	17.4	20.6	14.8	11.1	18.6
Negative evaluation of the elites as a homogeneous group	66.7	52.2	47.1	51.9	63.0	55.0
Explicit opposition people vs. elites	16.7	4.3	0.0	7.4	7.4	6.2
Explicit focus on the leader only	50.0	34.8	52.9	59.3	37.0	47.3
Against representative democracy/pro direct democracy	27.8	8.7	23.5	25.9	33.3	24.0
Negative evaluation of out-groups	0.0	8.7	0.0	0.0	3.7	2.3
All populist ideology elements	83.3	78.3	70.6	88.9	88.9	81.4
Total (N)	18	23	34	27	27	129

Source: Cremonesi (2017, p. 131).

TABLE 6.8 Connotations given to the elements of populism as a "thin-centered ideology" by newspaper (in percentages)

Connotation	Corriere della Sera	La Repubblica	La Stampa	Il Giornale	Il Fatto Quotidiano	Total
Negative	12.9	30.8	10.4	45.0	12.1	21.9
Neutral	83.9	61.5	81.3	32.5	36.4	59.6
Positive	3.2	7.7	8.3	22.5	51.5	18.5
Total (N)	31	26	48	40	33	178

Source: Cremonesi (2017, p. 132).

thin-centered ideology that it had quoted. Finally, *Corriere della Sera* (which displayed a very high number of elements of populism as a set of ideas) and *La Stampa* distinguish themselves in terms of their mainly neutral reporting of these elements of populism, an approach in line with their pro-system attitude. It is interesting to note that the newspapers closer to the Italian elites did report populist elements and did not give them a negative connotation. This suggests that in 2013 a fracture between Italian quality media and political elites had opened up because of the series of scandals that had hit the Italian ruling elite since 2012, and that the newspapers had given up their deferential attitude toward the political class (Bobba et al., 2013).

As concerns the elements of populism as a communication style (Table 6.9), they are used more by the pro-system newspapers *Corriere della Sera* and *La Stampa*. They use a language device typical of populism in 55.6% and 47.1% of their articles, respectively. While *Il Fatto Quotidiano* also displayed these elements of populism quite frequently (44.4%), *Il Giornale* and *La Repubblica* contained these populist elements in a very low percentage of articles (22.2% and 17.4%). By looking at single dimensions of populism as a style, the general trend individuated is confirmed, with the sole exception of the very low level of use of negative emotions in *Il Giornale* (3.7%).

With regard to the support of elements of populism as a communication style (Table 6.10), the anti-system newspapers *Il Fatto Quotidiano* and *Il Giornale* employed very few populist language devices, but they are clearly supportive. On the other hand, *Corriere della Sera* and *La Repubblica* never gave them a positive connotation, and *La Stampa* did so only in 15% of cases.

The data presented address the hypotheses formulated in terms of populist message coverage. Regarding H2a, there is no doubt that Italian newspapers displayed different coverage of Beppe Grillo and his party. However, the most significant differences between the newspapers concern the connotations that they gave to the elements of populism. For H2b, the results are contradictory. On the one hand, some results suggest that the outlets' attitudes toward the political system may have influenced the connotation given to the elements of

TABLE 6.9 Articles containing reference to the elements of populism as a communication style by newspaper (in percentages)

	Corriere della Sera	La Repubblica	La Stampa	Il Giornale	Il Fatto Quotidiano	Total
"Critical juncture"	16.7	4.3	20.6	11.1	14.8	14.0
Presence of emotional language	50.0	13.0	38.2	22.2	40.7	32.6
Explicit reference to negative emotion	22.2	13.0	17.6	3.7	22.2	15.5
All populist style elements	55.6	17.4	47.1	22.2	44.4	37.2
Total (N)	18	23	34	27	27	129

Source: Cremonesi (2017, p. 131).

TABLE 6.10 Connotations given to the elements of populism as communication style by newspaper (in percentages)

Connotation	Corriere della Sera	La Repubblica	La Stampa	Il Giornale	Il Fatto Quotidiano	Total
Negative	16.7	25.0	20.0	22.2	20.0	20.0
Neutral	83.3	75.0	65.0	33.3	40.0	58.3
Positive	0.0	0.0	15.0	44.4	40.0	21.7
Total (N)	12	4	20	9	15	60

Source: Cremonesi (2017, p. 133).

populism – in fact, the pro-system newspapers did not support the elements of populism reported, while the anti-elite *Il Fatto Quotidiano* gave them a positive connotation.

On the other hand, the low interest in and negative approach toward the elements of populism of *La Repubblica*, a medium only partially supportive of the political system, as well as the negative connotation given to the ideological elements of populism by the anti-system newspaper *Il Giornale*, suggest that other characteristics might explain the media coverage of populism.

Echoes of a Populist Message or Proper Populist Media?

The comparison between the elements of populism expressed in the self-directed communication and the ones reported in the press coverage highlight some interesting differences (Table 6.11). These discrepancies become even more marked in the case of *Il Fatto Quotidiano*, given that it was the most supportive newspaper of the elements of populism. First, the press placed far more emphasis on the role of the leader than did the self-directed communication: 47.3% of the press articles contain this trait, but only 4.4% of the direct messages mention it. While this discrepancy may be attributed to the general tendency of the media to personalize political news (e.g., Strömbäck & Esser, 2009), the ones regarding the dimensions of "negative evaluation of the elites" and "criticism toward representative democracy and demand for direct democracy" are less justifiable. In both cases, the newspapers as a whole and *Il Fatto Quotidiano* in particular stressed these traits more than the self-directed communication.

First, only 36.9% of the self-directed communication messages criticize the elites, while they are attacked in 55% and 63% of the articles of all newspapers and of *Il Fatto Quotidiano*, respectively. Second, as regards the "criticism toward representative democracy," a third of *Il Fatto Quotidiano* articles contain this element of populism, as do a quarter of all the newspaper articles analyzed. By contrast, only 7% of the direct messages of Beppe Grillo and his party contain this populist trait.

TABLE 6.11 References to the elements of populism as a populist "thin-centered ideology" by type of communication and media outlet (in percentages)

	Self-directed communication	Mediated – all newspapers[a]	Il Fatto Quotidiano
Neutral or positive mention of "the people"	15.6	18.6	11.1
Negative evaluation of the elites as a homogeneous group	36.9	55.0	63.0
Explicit opposition people vs. elites	5.1	6.2	7.4
Explicit focus on the leader only	4.4	47.3	37.0
Against representative institutions/pro direct democracy	7.0	24.0	33.3
Negative evaluation of out-groups	0.8	2.3	3.7
Total (N)	526	129	27

Source: Cremonesi (2017, pp. 137–138).

Note
a Including also *Il Fatto Quotidiano*.

These results confirm that the detachment between the political class and the upmarket media was very strong in the 2013 Italian electoral campaign. In fact, the dimensions of populism most popular in the press were the ones connected to criticism of the political and economic elites and of the functioning of Italian democracy. Moreover, these criticisms were particularly strong in *Il Fatto Quotidiano*, an Italian newspaper that is less connected to the Italian political and economic elites.

Given the results presented so far, it is possible to state that H3 is partially confirmed. The Italian press in general has fostered the populist message of Grillo and the FSM, giving considerable relevance to Grillo's criticism of the Italian ruling elite and political system, an attitude that, according to Mazzoleni (2014), may indirectly support populist claims. Moreover, it has been demonstrated that *Il Fatto Quotidiano* displayed an independent populist communication focused on criticism of the institutions, rules, and practices of Italian democracy. In fact, if this latter dynamic is interpreted in combination with the results of the previous section about the positive connotation given by *Il Fatto Quotidiano* to populist elements, it appears clear that this newspaper has not only fostered this (marginal) aspect of Grillo's communication but has also autonomously promoted it.

Conclusion

This chapter addressed the relationship between populist parties and the media in the new media environment by focusing on the case of the Five Star Movement, an Italian populist party that, during the 2013 Italian electoral campaign, was in its insurgent phase. In order to fulfil this objective, the chapter reconstructed the full image of the FSM conveyed to Italian voters by analyzing both self-directed communication by the party on different media channels and its coverage by print media with diverse characteristics and attitudes toward the political system.

With regard to the self-directed communication, the analysis demonstrated that Grillo and FSM's populist messages change according to the type of media channel used and that these differences are not determined by the media outlet characteristics but by a specific communication strategy. This means that for the elements of populism as a "thin-centered ideology" as well as for the dimensions of populism as a discursive style, their varied use on self-directed communication channels derives from strategic choices to convey different aspects of the populist message to the diverse audiences of offline, Web 1.0, and social media communication.

The study of the media coverage showed that the five newspapers considered displayed a different coverage of Grillo and FSM, particularly regarding the connotations given to the elements of populism. However, these differences cannot be explained by the newspapers' leaning toward the political system. The "pro-system" newspapers *Corriere della Sera* and *La Stampa* mainly used neutral connotations, while *La Repubblica* (which holds an intermediate position regarding the political system) used negative ones. Moreover, the "anti-system" newspaper *Il Giornale* mainly negatively connoted the elements of populism as an ideology, but supported the populist discourse devices. Finally, the articles of *Il Fatto Quotidiano*, the other "anti-system" newspaper, positively connoted most of the elements of populism mentioned and referring to both ideology and discursive style.

Consequently, the distinction between pro- and anti-system newspapers advanced as an explanatory factor in the replacement of the classical opposition between upmarket and mass-market media did not prove completely valid. This suggests that, in order to understand newspapers' populist communication, other characteristics must also be taken into account, such as newspapers' closeness to political parties and the type of relationship between the media and the political class.

For example, *La Repubblica* probably did not support populist stances, since it is a left-wing newspaper and it supported Partito Democratico, the left-wing and not-populist party that was expected to win the 2013 elections. Moreover, *Corriere della Sera* and *La Stampa* probably reported populist elements of critique toward the political elites and democracy in a neutral way because they had abandoned their deferential attitudes toward the political class.

In sum, the comparison between Grillo and FSM's communication and their media coverage has demonstrated that the Italian press fostered the populist message of FSM, and that *Il Fatto Quotidiano* promoted an independent populist message. Consequently, it is possible to affirm that in 2013, despite their late acknowledgment of FSM's importance, the Italian media indirectly promoted the success of this insurgent populist formation. In fact, even if most of the Italian newspapers did not explicitly support populist elements or mention them independently, they reported Grillo and his party's populist message and emphasized its criticism of the ruling elites. Moreover, the "anti-system" newspaper *Il Fatto Quotidiano* also supported Grillo and FSM's populist stances and dedicated considerable space to the criticism of Italian representative democracy.

These results suggest that the relationship between the media and the political class must be taken into primary consideration in future studies that seek to investigate the role of the media in the electoral success of populist formations.

Notes

1. FSM is a political party created in 2009 by Giuseppe Piero Grillo – known as Beppe Grillo – a former Italian popular comedian who funded it after many years of individual political action. Grillo started his political engagement after having been excluded from Italian public television in 1988 because of his strong criticism of the governing party. Grillo subsequently performed in theatres and squares, and during his spectacles he attacked the Italian elites and denounced Italy's problems with a sharp irony. It allowed Grillo to build a solid group of followers, who supported him in the first phases of FSM creation (Corbetta & Gualmini, 2013). Between 2009 and 2012, Grillo's party participated in a series of local elections, obtaining low but increasing support. On the eve of the 2013 Italian general election, FSM was in what Mazzoleni (2014, p. 51) identified as the "insurgent phase": "when populists become outsiders who challenge the existing political balance in elections or parliaments" and the media are more likely to show different responses to their political game (Mazzoleni, 2014, p. 51). It is important to note that even if FSM is named "Movement" and it is not listed in the "Italian Parties' Register," it actually presents all the characteristics of a political party. In fact, beyond these rhetorical appearances (aimed at emphasizing FSM's distance from traditional parties), FSM does not differ from a political party either according to political science theory (see Passarelli, Tronconi, & Tuorto, 2013, p. 134) or from an electoral perspective (Italian law does not distinguish between parties and movements regarding access to electoral competitions).
2. For a classification of the meanings associated with the people, see the research of Canovan (1999), Mény and Surel (2002), and Taguieff (2002).
3. The term "Web 1.0" includes non-interactive informational websites, while "Web 2.0" includes web-based, open, and interactive technologies, such as social networking and media sharing (Wattal, Schuff, Mandviwalla, & Williams, 2010).
4. www.beppegrillo.it.
5. The only difference between the analysis of direct and mediated communication concerns the dimension "Use of peculiar language devices," which was considered only with reference to FSM and Grillo's direct communication.
6. ANOVA test results for all the variables measuring populism as a style in Facebook posts and tweets: $2,854 <= F <= 2,870$, $0,091 <= p <= 0,093$.

References

Akkerman, T. (2011). Friend or foe? Right-wing populism and the popular press in Britain and the Netherlands. *Journalism*, 12(8), 931–945.

Albertazzi, D. (2007). Addressing "the people": A comparative study of the Lega Nord's and Lega dei Ticinesi's political rhetoric and styles of propaganda. *Modern Italy*, 12(3), 327–347.

Bartlett, J., Froio, C., Littler, M., & McDonnell, D. (2013). *New political actors in Europe: Beppe Grillo and the F5M*. Retrieved from www.demos.co.uk/project/new-political-actors-in-europe-beppe-grillo-and-the-m5s.
Battegazzorre, F. (2013). Linguaggio e discorso politico: La prospettiva della scienza politica. In F. Rositi (Ed.), *La ragione politica: I discorsi dei leader, Vol. 1* (pp. 155–183). Napoli: Liguori. [in Italian].
Bobba, G., & McDonnell, D. (2015). Italy a strong and enduring market for populism. In H. Kriesi, & T. S. Pappas (Eds.), *European populism in the shadow of the great recession* (pp. 163–179). Colchester: ECPR Press.
Bobba, G., Legnante, G., Roncarolo, F., & Seddone, A. (2013). Candidates in a negative light. *Rivista italiana di scienza politica*, 43(3), 353–380.
Bos, L., & Brants, K. (2014). Populist rhetoric in politics and media: A longitudinal study of the Netherlands. *European Journal of Communication*, 29(6), 703–719.
Bos, L., van der Brug, W., & de Vreese, C. H. (2010). Media coverage of right-wing populist leaders. *Communications*, 35(2), 141–163.
Bracciale, R., & Martella, A. (2017). Define the populist political communication style: The case of Italian political leaders on Twitter. *Information, Communication & Society*, 20(9), 1310–1329.
Canovan, M. (1999). Trust the people! Populism and the two faces of democracy. *Political Studies*, 47(1), 2–16.
Castells, M. (2007). Communication, power and counter-power in the network society. *International Journal of Communication*, 1(1), 238–266.
Ceron, A., & Splendore, S. (2016). From contents to comments: Social TV and perceived pluralism in political talk shows. *New Media & Society*, 20(2), 659–675.
Chadwick, A. (2013). *The hybrid media system: Politics and power*. Oxford: Oxford University Press.
Chiapponi, F. (2008). *Il populismo come problematica della scienza politica*. Genova: Mauro Cormagi Editore. [in Italian].
Corbetta, P., & Gualmini, E. (Eds.). (2013). *Il partito di grillo*. Bologna: Il Mulino. [in Italian].
Cosenza, G. (2013). Come comunica grillo: Dal turpiloquio al linguaggio del corpo. *Comunicazione Politica*, 13(1), 109–124. [in Italian].
Cranmer, M. (2011). Populist communication and publicity: An empirical study of contextual differences in Switzerland. *Swiss Political Science Review*, 17(3), 286–307.
Cremonesi, C. (2017). Populist parties' campaign communication: Different messages to different voters? The case of the Five Star Movement during 2013 Italian electoral campaign. An analysis of leader and party direct messages and media coverage on various communication channels (Unpublished doctoral thesis). Pavia: University of Pavia.
Engesser, S., Ernst, N., Esser, F., & Büchel, F. (2017). Populism and social media: How politicians spread a fragmented ideology. *Information, Communication & Society*, 20(8), 1109–1126.
Engesser, S., Fawzi, N., & Larsson, O. (2017). Populist online communication: Introduction to the special issue. *Information, Communication & Society*, 20(9), 1279–1292.
Germani, G. (1974). Il peronismo. In L. Garruccio (Ed.), *Momenti dell'esperienza politica latino Americana: Tre saggi su populismo e militari in America Latina* (pp. 85–191). Bologna: Il Mulino. [in Italian].
Gidron, N., & Bonikowski, B. (2013). Varieties of populism: Literature review and research agenda. *Working Paper series, Weatherhead Center for International Affair, Harvard University, No. 13-0004*, pp. 1–38.

Kornhauser, W. (1959). *The politics of mass society*. Glencoe, NY: Free Press.
Krämer, B. (2014). Media populism: A conceptual clarification and some theses on its effects. *Communication Theory*, 24(1), 42–60.
Laclau, E. (2005). *On populist reason*. London: Verso.
Lizzi, R., & Pritoni, A. (2014). Interest group system and media system in Italy: Investigating the national press (1992–2013). *Comunicazione Politica*, 14(2), 287–312.
Lyotard, J. F. (1984). *The postmodern condition: A report on knowledge*. Manchester: Manchester University Press.
Mancini, P. (2008). The Berlusconi case: Mass media and politics in Italy. In I. Bondebjerg, & P. Madsen (Eds.), *Media, democracy and European culture* (pp. 107–119). Bristol; Chicago, IL: Intellect Books.
Manin, B. (2014). La democrazia del pubblico è in pericolo? *Comunicazione Politica*, 14(3), 575–580. [in Italian].
Mazzoleni, G. (2003). The media and the growth of neo-populism in contemporary democracies. In G. Mazzoleni, J. Stewart, & B. Horsfield (Eds.), *The media and neo-populism: A contemporary comparative analysis* (pp. 1–21). Westport, CT: Praeger.
Mazzoleni, G. (2008). Populism and the media. In D. Albertazzi, & D. McDonnell (eds.), *Twenty-first century populism* (pp. 49–64). Basingstoke: Palgrave Macmillan.
Mazzoleni, G. (2014). Mediatization and political populism. In J. Strömbäck, & F. Esser (Eds.), *Mediatization of politics* (pp. 42–56). Basingstoke: Palgrave Macmillan.
Mény, Y., & Surel, Y. (2002). *Democracies and the populist challenge*. Basingstoke: Palgrave.
Mols, F., & Jetten, J. (2014). No guts, no glory: How framing the collective past paves the way for anti-immigrant sentiments. *International Journal of Intercultural Relations*, 43, 74–86.
Mudde, C. (2004). The populist zeitgeist. *Government and Opposition*, 39(4), 542–563.
Mudde, C. (2007). *Populist radical right parties in Europe*. Cambridge: Cambridge University Press.
Mudde C., & Kaltwasser C. R. (2013). Exclusionary vs. inclusionary populism: Comparing contemporary Europe and Latin America. *Government and Opposition*, 48(2), 147–174.
Passarelli, G., Tronconi, F., & Tuorto, D. (2013). Dentro il movimento: Organizzazione, attivisti e programmi. In P. Corbetta, & E. Gualmini (Eds.), *Il partito di grillo* (pp. 123–167). Bologna: Il Mulino. [in Italian].
Sacharin, V., Schlegel, K., & Scherer, K. R. (2012). *Geneva emotion wheel rating study*. Retrieved from https://archive-ouverte.unige.ch/unige:97849.
Scherer, K. R. (2005). What are emotions? And how can they be measured? *Social Science Information*, 44(4), 695–729.
Stanley, B. (2008). The thin ideology of populism. *Journal of Political Ideologies*, 13(1), 95–110.
Strandberg, K. (2013). A social media revolution or just a case of history repeating itself? The use of social media in the 2011 Finnish parliamentary elections. *New Media & Society*, 15(8), 1329–1347.
Strömbäck, J., & Esser, F. (2009). Shaping politics: Mediatization and media interventionism. In K. Lundby (Ed.), *Mediatization: Concept, changes, consequences* (pp. 205–223). New York: Peter Lang.
Strömbäck, J., & Esser, F. (2014). Mediatization of politics: Towards a theoretical framework. In F. Esser, & J. Strömbäck (Eds.), *Mediatization of politics* (pp. 3–28). London: Palgrave Macmillan.
Taggart, P. (2002). *Il populismo*. Enna: Città Aperta Edizioni. [in Italian].

Taguieff, P. A. (2002). *L'illusione populista*. Milano: Bruno Mondadori. [in Italian].
Tarchi, M. (2003). *L'Italia populista: Dal qualunquismo ai girotondi*. Bologna: Il Mulino. [in Italian].
Walgrave, S., & Van Aelst, P. (2006). The contingency of the mass media's political agenda setting power: Toward a preliminary theory. *Journal of Communication*, 56(1), 88–109.
Wattal, S., Schuff, D., Mandviwalla, M., & Williams, C. B. (2010). Web 2.0 and politics: The 2008 US presidential election and an e-politics research agenda. *MIS Quarterly*, 34(4), 669–688.
Weyland K. (2001). Clarifying a contested concept: Populism in the study of Latin American politics. *Comparative Politics*, 34(1), 1–22.

7

FIGHTING WITH FIRE

Negative Campaigning in the 2015
UK General Election Campaign as
Reported by the Print Media

Annemarie Walter

Why Study Negative Campaigning as Reported by Print Media?

"The SNP (Scottish National Party) are lefties on steroids"[1] and "The kingmaker would be Nicola Sturgeon and Ed Miliband would have to dance to her tune"[2] are some examples of attacks that politicians launched on one another in their battle for votes during the 2015 UK general election campaign. As the Conservatives felt the threat of a Labour–SNP coalition government, they attacked the SNP fiercely throughout the campaign. In this context, Conservative London mayor Boris Johnson called the SNP "lefties on steroids," trying to scare voters by emphasizing how "calamitous" a government with the SNP would be.[3] Former Tory MP (Member of Parliament) Kenneth Baker attacked SNP party leader Nicola Sturgeon for enabling such a government and warned voters of who would be really calling the shots when a Labour–SNP government would be realized.

Although negative campaigning is common practice in British elections, not everyone can appreciate it. Labour party leader Ed Miliband called upon Conservatives' leader David Cameron to stop his "gutter" election smears. These were remarks "the prime minister should be ashamed of."[4] Defense secretary Michael Fallon said "Mr. Miliband would stab Britain in the back over the Trident Nuclear deterrent just as he stabbed his brother in the back."[5] Ed Miliband defeated his older brother, David Miliband, in the Labour leadership contest after Gordon Brown resigned in 2010. Trident is Britain's nuclear deterrent system that would come up for renewal in 2016. Cameron backed his defense secretary before admitting that politicians should show opponents respect. Conservative Secretary of State for Health Jeremy Hunt said in defense of Fallon "that the most relentlessly negative campaign has been from Labour for the last five years, where they basically said that you shouldn't re-elect David Cameron because he's too posh."[6]

Negative campaigning is generally believed to be a useful campaign strategy. However, it is not uncontested, as it is strongly disliked by the public and thought to have corrosive effects on democracy (e.g., Lau, Sigelman, & Rovner, 2007). The use of negative campaigning is linked by some scholars to growing public distrust toward politics and decreasing electoral participation (Ansolabehere & Iyengar, 1995; Lemert, Wanta, & Lee, 1999; Thorson, Ognianova, Coyle, & Denton, 2000). Regardless of the omnipresence of negative campaigning, the bulk of research on the use and effects of negative campaigning is conducted in the US. Therefore, much is still to be gained from studying negative campaigning elsewhere, including the UK.

Work on negative campaigning in the UK tends to study negative campaigning in the context of political advertising, such as party election broadcasts (PEBs)[7] and print material (see Scammell & Langer, 2006; Van Heerde-Hudson, 2011; Walter, 2014a). The study of negative campaigning in uncontrolled media (such as newspapers and television coverage) is less common, as the media are expected to paint a distorted picture of the reality, over-representing negative campaigning. However, it is important to move beyond controlled party communication when studying negative campaigning, as it is the uncontrolled communication that is most likely to reach large audiences and they use that information to form perceptions on which they act. The exposure of voters to controlled party communication, such as PEBs, posters, and leaflets, is much smaller, and more likely to consist of the party faithful. We know that how the media report the campaign impacts voters' perceptions of the campaign, including the tone of the campaign (Cheng & Riffe, 2008; Pattie, Denver, Johns, & Mitchell, 2011). Voters' perceptions of parties' campaign tone can, in turn, affect their party preferences, vote choice, participation, and trust in politics.

In this chapter, I examine the extent to which the British print media covered negative campaigning during the 2015 UK general election campaign and which parties were reported as attackers and targets. Second, I will examine whether different newspapers covered negative campaigning in the 2015 general election differently and if there is a selection bias driven by the partisan nature of British newspapers.

The structure of this chapter is as follows. First, it defines negative campaigning and discusses its use in multiparty systems. Second, it reflects on the heterogeneous nature of attacks, and on the relationship between the media and negative campaigning. Third, it explains the research methodology of the findings presented in this chapter. Fourth, it presents the use of attacks and its targets during the 2015 campaign, followed by a discussion on differences in coverage of attack behavior by British newspapers. Finally, conclusions are drawn.

Negative Campaigning in Multiparty Systems

Negative campaigning consists of attacking opponents' abilities, accomplishments, and policies instead of focusing on one's own offering in these respects (Geer, 2006; Lau & Pomper, 2004). The latter is called positive campaigning. The goal of using negative campaigning is to acquire a competitive advantage over the political opponent in the given electoral context. This is realized by diminishing the positive feelings voters have for competitors (Lau et al., 2007). Thereby, the attacking party tries to become voters' most preferred party, to weaken its opponent's support by depressing turnout of its supporters, or to shift voters from supporting the opponent to supporting another party (which may be a third party that is not considered a threat).

The literature generally takes a rational choice perspective: Political parties weigh the costs and benefits when deciding whether to attack or not (Lau & Pomper, 2004). However, negative campaigning as an electoral strategy is not without risks. Parties run the risk that the attack backfires, i.e., instead of decreasing the positive feelings for the political opponent, it may generate negative feelings toward the attacker (Johnson-Cartee & Copeland, 1991). Whether or not parties decide to attack depends on the expected balance between the losses their opponent will suffer from the attack and the risk they face themselves from being perceived negatively.

In a multiparty system, and particularly in the expectation of a coalition government, the cost–benefit analysis is different than in a two-party system. In a multiparty system, parties have to carefully balance their vote-, office-, and policy-seeking objectives. In these systems, the largest party is not guaranteed a parliamentary majority, government office, or influence over policy. As a result, costs of negative campaigning are higher in a multiparty system than in a two-party system, as parties need to worry not only about possible backlash effects, but also about post-election bargaining costs. A campaign which is fought too aggressively and too negatively may lower a party's chances of being included in a subsequent government coalition (Walter & van der Brug, 2013). Additionally, the rewards of negative campaigning are less certain in a multiparty system than in a two-party system. Recent work shows that in multiparty systems voters are most likely to punish the use of negative campaigning and set their sights on a party other than the attacker (Pattie et al., 2011). Although the UK has been traditionally classified as a two-party system, it is safe to say that it cannot be regarded as such any more. Rather, it is a two-party dominated multiparty system (Green & Prosser, 2016). The 2015 UK general election campaign was a campaign fought in the context of a widely shared expectation of another hung parliament. The 2010 elections had led to the first coalition government in the UK since 1931, consisting of the Conservatives and the Liberal Democratic Party.

Heterogeneous Nature of Negative Campaigning

No attack is the same. Although the effectiveness of an attack is linked to its characteristics, research on the variety of attacks is limited (see, for notable exceptions, Fridkin & Kenney, 2011; Mattes & Redlawsk, 2015; Walter, Ridout, & Van der Eijk, 2017). Attacks differ in various aspects, one of which is the message content. The opponent can be attacked on issues or on traits and that can be done prospectively or retrospectively. "Just imagine the chaos with NHS and education spending cuts."[8] This is a prospective issue attack. Liberal Democrats' party leader Nick Clegg warns voters of future policies of the Conservatives. "This exposes Miliband for the hypocrite and champagne socialist he is. He says he's on the side of working people, but in reality his home life's like a scene from *Upstairs Downstairs*."[9,10] This is an example of a trait attack, questioning the integrity of Miliband. According to some scholars (Min, 2004), negative issue attacks are more effective than negative trait attacks; however, others (Brooks & Geer, 2007) argue the opposite. Mattes and Redlawsk (2015) find that attacks that are issue- and qualification-oriented are not seen to be as negative as those focused on the target's family or religion and these types of attacks are most likely to backfire. Positive campaigning on trait and issues looks as follows: "I am a compassionate Conservative"[11] and "We will put a vote to parliament to abolish the 'bedroom tax'."[12]

According to some scholars, the extent to which the public perceives attacks as negative and might retaliate against the attacker is not determined by the topic of the attack but by its (in)civility (Fridkin & Kenney, 2011). Attacks can be civil and uncivil (Brooks & Geer, 2007; Fridkin & Kenney, 2011). The study of incivility, which is a distinct field to negative campaigning, is in its infancy. As a result, no agreed definition exists. I define political incivility in line with Gervais' (2017) focus on norm-defying behavior, as behavior that disregards the dominant norms within the political subsystem, specifically, the norms that make it possible for politicians to interact with each other in the conduct of their business. One long-standing norm is respect for one's political opponents, even when one disagrees. As norms may vary by time and culture, political incivility is a relative concept. In this young field of research, various operationalizations of the concept exist. Brooks and Geer (2007) argue that what makes political talk uncivil, rather than just negative, is that uncivil talk includes superfluous words and actions that actively demonstrate lack of respect and often involves hyperbole. They would classify the following attacks as uncivil. "A match made in hell" is what Cameron said to scare voters of the prospect of a Labour–SNP government.[13] Miliband said that Cameron is "a mortal danger to the NHS."[14] Labour candidate Chuka Umunna said, "A virus of racism runs through UKIP [the UK Independence Party]."[15] However, Mattes and Redlawsk (2015) argue attacks with references to religion and family most aggravate voters and are considered unacceptable. These attacks are rare to absent in British campaign rhetoric. In 2015, the comments referring to Miliband as backstabbing his brother come closest.

Unique to attack behavior in multiparty systems is that the composition of potential coalition governments is the subject of attacks. A substantial part of attacks in this campaign was devoted to the prospect of a hung parliament, which would necessitate a coalition government. The Conservatives continuously pointed out to voters that voting for the SNP would enable a coalition government of SNP and Labour. With these statements, they not only attacked the SNP as well as Labour, but also encouraged voters to vote strategically, i.e., voting for a party other than their preferred party to avoid an unwanted coalition. Examples are "Stop SNP's coalition of chaos."[16] "Vote Tory to stop a Labour/SNP coalition from wrecking the country."[17] The Conservatives not only discouraged voters from voting Labour or SNP, but also UKIP. "A vote for UKIP will make a Labour government more likely."[18] Coalition signals are not only part of negative campaigning, but also of so-called support statements (De Nooy & Kleinnijenhuis, 2015). Support statements are a separate category next to positive campaigning, i.e., all statements praising the opponent(s). Parties speak positively about their political opponent when they wish (to continue) to work with them. "I would work with Cameron again," said Clegg.[19] Some campaign appeals are simultaneously an attack as a support statement. For instance, Nick Clegg said: "The Liberal Democrats will add a heart to a Conservative government and a brain to a Labour one!"[20]

Finally, attacks differ in source and target. We know that the source of an attack matters to voters, as not all sources enjoy the same degree of credibility. The extent to which voters accept persuasive messages is dependent on the credibility of the messenger. This, in turn, is influenced by the source's traits, such as expertise, and the fit between message and attacker's reputation (Iyengar & Valentino, 1999). Partisanship is one of the most important traits impinging on credibility (Lipsitz & Geer, 2017; Pattie et al., 2011). People tend to perceive campaigns run by the party they support more positively than campaigns run by the opponent, regardless of their content. In general, they find attacks by their own party more acceptable than attacks by other parties. Attacks are not necessarily only directed at opposing candidates; they can be aimed at the establishment, the government, a specific party, a specific candidate, and a cluster of parties or politicians. "Everyone is tired of the same old Westminster politics"[21] is an example of an anti-establishment attack. Whom to target is an important strategic question in a multiparty system. Studies not only show that parties tend to attack their ideologically closest neighbors as that is where most potential voters are located, they sometimes attack parties on the other side of the ideological spectrum to signal to their voters what they stand for by attacking their ideological enemy (Walter, 2014b).

The Media and Negative Campaigning

The relationship between the media and negative campaigning is complicated. Although the media have to inform voters about the election campaign, including its use of negative campaigning, the media themselves contribute to the use of negative campaigning. According to Geer (2012), the media have altered the incentives of candidates to produce and air negative ads. They are nothing but press releases designed to cater to the news media. Candidates that want to gain media attention are taught to provide conflict and controversy, which can be realized by waging negative campaigning. Negative campaigning appeals to three important news values, namely the game frame, negativity, and personalization (Ridout & Walter, 2015). First, negative campaigning involves a conflict between competing candidates or parties and therefore fits the "game" news frame. The "game" news frame is broadly defined as the framing of politics as a game characterized by a focus on opinion polls, election outcomes, winners and losers, and the use of sports and war language (Aalberg, Strømback, & de Vreese, 2012). The second news value is negativity; negative campaigning is more newsworthy than positive campaigning. The third value is personalization, where the news tends to report on individuals and presents the news in a personalized way. Since newspapers all deal with declining readership and thus face economic pressure, they increasingly feel the need to tailor the content of their stories to presumed audience preferences, and negative campaigning can sell news. Tabloids can be expected to put more emphasis on news values in their election news coverage than broadsheet newspapers, as they tend to be driven more by commercial incentives.

If media prefer negative campaign appeals in the news, the media might over-represent negative campaigning and thereby amplify its effects. In the US, scholars find that negative ads are more likely to be covered than positive ads (Ridout & Smith, 2008). Only a handful of studies have been conducted in a non-US context examining whether the media over-represent negative campaigning (Haselmeyer, Meyer, & Wagner, 2017; Ridout & Walter, 2015; Walter & Vliegenthart, 2010). Haselmeyer et al. (2017) showed that parties were more successful in making the news with negative press releases in the 2013 Austrian parliamentary elections. Ridout and Walter (2015) found mixed evidence for media amplification of negative ads in the UK. They only found for the UK general election campaign in 2010 evidence that newspapers over-reported negative PEBs, while in 2005 they under-reported them. Walter and Vliegenthart (2010) compared negative campaigning by political parties on the basis of PEBs, televised election debates, and as covered by different kinds of newspapers in the 2006 Dutch parliamentary election campaign. They did not find evidence that newspapers over-reported negative campaign behavior by parties; they did find that newspapers, tabloids, and broadsheets alike, tended to over-report trait attacks relative to issue attacks.

Press–party parallelism is present when ties exist between newspapers and parties. The extent of press–party parallelism varies considerably between countries. It can manifest itself in four ways, namely in media content, in ownership of the news, in the affiliations of journalists, owners, and managers, and in readership patterns (Van Kempen, 2007). Political endorsements – one of the manifestations of the first of these four forms – can translate into differential treatment of political parties throughout the campaign in newspaper coverage. Favorable party treatment by the press can realize itself in three ways, namely the endorsed party can be given more coverage, more unfiltered coverage, or more positive coverage.

Therefore, three possible biases can be distinguished, respectively, a coverage bias, an agenda bias, and a statement bias (Brandenburg, 2006).[22] It is the first bias that is of importance when discussing how negative campaigning is covered. The coverage bias is defined as "the disproportional reporting about different parties, can be measured by simply counting how often different newspapers mention each party over the course of the campaign." This measure serves to investigate whether partisan media support parties by "over-representing them or, whether they spend equal or more time attacking opponents" (Brandenburg, 2006). To my knowledge, no work exists that examines how press–party parallelism translates into differential treatment of parties in the press coverage of negative campaigning. As newspapers in the UK tend to openly back parties during the campaign, one could imagine that the parties supported would receive not only more, but also more favorable coverage and the party that is the main opponent less and less favorable coverage. Thus political bias should be visible not only in how the media interpret campaign events (something that I do not focus on in this chapter), but also in their selection of parties' campaign activities that are reported upon, i.e., the amount and selection of positive and negative campaigning, which is the main focus in this chapter.

Methodology

The data presented in this chapter are part of a unique dataset of campaign appeals that measures the use of negative campaigning on the basis of party behavior as covered by the print media. The study focuses on the main parties competing during the formal campaign of the 2015 UK general elections, namely the five parties that compete nationwide and the two regional parties. The five parties that compete in all three countries of Great Britain (England, Scotland, and Wales) are the Labour Party (LAB), the Conservative Party (CON), the Liberal Democratic Party (LD), the UK Independence Party (UKIP) and the Green Party (Gr). The Scottish National Party (SNP) competes solely in Scotland and Plaid Cymru (PC) competes solely in Wales. The formal campaign is the period from the dissolution of parliament (March 30, 2015) until polling day (May 7, 2015).

I conducted a content analysis of the three main national tabloid newspapers and the three main broadsheet newspapers, respectively *The Sun*, *Daily Mail*, *Daily Mirror*, *Guardian*, *The Daily Telegraph*, and *The Independent*. These newspapers were selected on the basis of their character (tabloid versus broadsheet), partisan color, and the size of their readership (Table 7.1). The British newspapers have no obligation to maintain impartiality. They tend to make no secret of their political sympathies and party preferences, and consequently select and interpret the news in accordance with these. The political bias of newspapers often reflects the established preferences of its readers (Leach, Coxall, & Robins, 2006). For British newspapers, party endorsements are not always the same across elections (Wring & Deacon, 2010). Wring and Deacon (2010) argue that newspaper endorsements are of great importance as the party that won the most votes between 1992 and 2010 received the majority of support in terms of press backing.

All election-related articles in the formal campaign were coded (see Banducci et al., 2017), a total of 5,019 articles. The manual content analysis was conducted by four trained Ph.D. students with a high proficiency in the English language. The coding method to measure campaign tone is similar to the fine-grained method of Geer (2006), except for two adaptations. This coding method was first of all adapted to suit the needs of a multiparty system where coalitions may exist, rather than single-party governments. This led to the option to code a cluster of parties or candidates as the target of attack behavior. Another adaptation is that, for the purpose of measuring party behavior as reported by the media, we only code quotes and paraphrases of parties and their spokespeople, thereby excluding interpretations of these quotes and paraphrases by journalists from the analysis. Lau and Pomper (2004) make a similar selection choice.

The unit of analysis is a natural speaking unit, the appeal, which is any mention of self-praise or criticism of the opponent. We do not code at the level of newspaper articles because single articles often contain both positive and negative appeals (Geer, 2006). The same applies to sentences which often contain

TABLE 7.1 Characteristics of selected newspapers in the 2015 general election campaign

Newspaper	Declaration of support	Circulation in '000s	Type
Daily Mail	Very strong Conservative	1,631	Tabloid
Daily Mirror	Very strong Labour	882	Tabloid
The Sun	Very strong Conservative	1,858	Tabloid
The Daily Telegraph	Very strong Conservative	486	Broadsheet
Guardian	Moderate Labour	176	Broadsheet
The Independent	Weak Liberal Democrat/Conservative coalition	59	Broadsheet

Source: Deacon and Wring (2016, p. 304).

more than one appeal. For example, this attack of Cameron on Miliband: "He still thinks the last Labour government didn't spend too much, didn't tax too much, didn't borrow too much."[23] This sentence contains three attacks. Negative campaigning is measured by coding any appeal as either negative (criticism of an opponent) or positive (self-praise of the party or politician). We only coded explicit and visible instances of criticism of the opponent (negative) or self-praise (positive). A total of 21,346 appeals were coded, respectively, 12,964 positive and 8,382 negative appeals. The inter-coder reliability was measured based on the coding of a random sample of appeals. The most difficult coding category was to determine the unit of analysis, that is, the demarcation of appeals and whether a text segment contains one or multiple appeals. The intercoder reliability (Krippendorff's alpha) for identifying paraphrases and quotes is 0.91 and for demarcating within these paraphrases and quotes is 0.58. Reliability for tone (negative versus positive) Krippendorff's alpha was 0.86.[24]

Use of Negative Campaigning Covered in the Print Media

Negative campaigning featured frequently in the 2015 general campaign in Britain, but not to a degree that was very different from other general elections; 39% of the campaign statements of parties reported by newspapers were attacks. A handful of studies have measured the level of negative campaigning in the UK at other elections on the basis of PEBs (e.g., Dermody & Scullion, 2000; Hodess, Tedesco, & Kaid, 2000; Scammell & Langer, 2006; Van Heerde-Hudson, 2011; Walter, 2014a). Van Heerde-Hudson (2011) reports an average level of 38% between 1964 and 2005. Walter (2014a) measures an average of 43% between 1983 and 2005.

Gauging from newspaper coverage of parties' campaign statements, the Conservatives launched the largest number of attacks: 44% of all attacks reported (Figure 7.1). Previous studies also found the Conservatives to be the largest user of negative campaigning and that their use is not affected by their government or opposition status (Scammell & Langer, 2006; Walter, van der Brug, & van Praag, 2014). This is remarkable because, normally, a government party is less inclined to make use of negative campaigning. First of all, because a government party is quite visible in the media and has a policy record that it can campaign on in contrast to an opposition party. Consequently, it has a strong basis for positive campaigning. It is the opposition party's job to convince voters why it should be in government and is therefore more likely to attack. Second, negative campaigning is not without risks; parties that are in opposition, that are new, or that have a small chance of making it into government are in general more willing to take the risks and go negative (e.g., Walter et al., 2014). Why the Conservatives deviate from this pattern when in government is not clear, but it has been observed repeatedly (e.g., Scammell & Langer, 2006; Walter et al., 2014).

Figure 7.1 is affected by the fact that the two largest parties, Labour and Conservatives, receive more media attention and thus are more likely to have their campaign behavior (including attacks) reported. Figure 7.2 shows for each party the use of negative campaigning compared to positive campaigning (as reported by the print media), thereby correcting for the difference in number of campaign appeals reported. The Conservatives still have the highest level of negative campaigning, namely a level of 45%. With the exception of the Green Party, all parties devoted a substantial part of their campaign rhetoric to negative campaigning. Surprisingly, the use of negative campaigning by UKIP as covered by the print media is actually on the lower end. Anti-establishment parties tend to be frequent users of negative campaigning, as not only is it in their nature to be against all that the established parties represent, but they also have very limited chances of governing and thus can freely take the risks involved with negative campaigning. This divergent finding can partly be explained by the fact that UKIP wanted to avoid being seen as too extreme and as a single-issue party. Consequently, they campaigned heavily on their own policy platform.[25]

When looking at the content of all attacks covered by the print media, we find that the campaign was mostly substantive. Many more issue attacks were launched than trait attacks, respectively 73% versus 27%. The parties differed in their use of trait attacks; the levels varied between 21 to 34%. The outlier was the Greens, with only 8% trait attacks. This supports the image that the Greens waged a

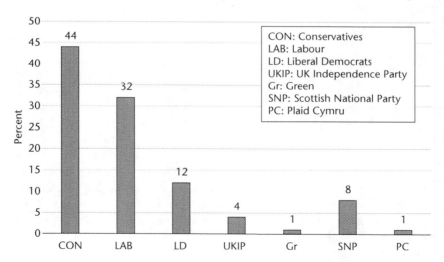

FIGURE 7.1 Use of negative campaigning in the 2015 UK general election campaign in print media (appeals in percentages)

Note

$N = 8{,}382$. In this and subsequent tables and figures, percentages do not always sum to 100% owing to rounding.

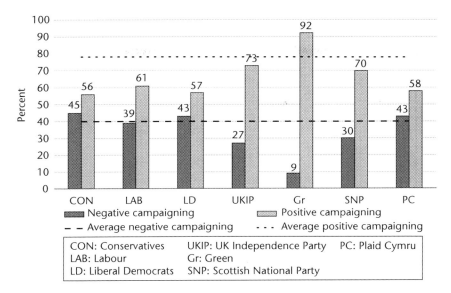

FIGURE 7.2 Use of negative and positive campaigning per party in the 2015 UK general election campaign in the print media (appeals in percentages)

Note
N=21,346.

particularly positive campaign in contrast to the other parties. The Conservatives scored higher than Labour, respectively 27% and 23% issue attacks.

Overall, the 2015 campaign as reported in the media was not out of the ordinary in the use of negative campaigning, with 39% of the campaign appeals reported being negative. In line with "tradition," the Conservatives went negative most often. The Greens ran the most positive campaign. Although attacks feature frequently in news coverage, they are mostly issue attacks, making the campaign still quite substantively oriented.

Targets of Negative Campaigning Covered in the Print Media

To be able to examine who is targeting whom in print media, part of the dataset needed to be transformed. The data were collected in such a way that an attack on the government is counted as a single attack, although it targets (in 2015) both the Conservatives and the Liberal Democrats. In the new dataset, this attack counts as two separate attacks, i.e., one targeting the Conservatives and another targeting the Liberal Democrats. The same was done in the case of attacks targeting clusters of parties or candidates. The total of negative appeals in this dataset is 9,614. The 2015 campaign was different as not only was a hung parliament expected, but also parties other than the traditional three (Conservatives, Labour, and Liberal Democrats) would, in such an outcome, be of importance. The SNP was an important competitor, after achieving a majority in the devolved Scottish Parliament. UKIP had broadened its electoral appeal beyond the anti-EU issue by successfully linking it to the issue of immigration. It has demonstrated its electoral appeal in the 2013 local election and particularly in the 2014 European parliamentary elections, where it emerged as the largest party of the UK (in terms of share of the vote). The traditional parties feared these challengers. In the past, these smaller parties would have been ignored by the traditional three as they would not have been seen as viable spoilers, let alone as contenders for constituency seats.

Figure 7.3 shows who is attacking whom. All attacks of individual candidates are associated to their party. Tracing the edges clockwise shows the direction of the attack. The thickness of the edges reflects the frequency of attacks. Only

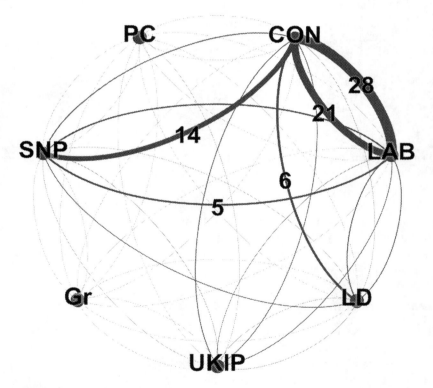

FIGURE 7.3 Overall pattern of attack behavior in the 2015 UK parliamentary election campaign in the print media (percentages of grand total of all attacks across all political parties)

Note
$N = 9,614$. The curvature of the edge shows the direction of the attack. To be read clockwise; see explanation in text.

edges representing more than 5% of the data are labelled. Here we see that a large part of the attacks consisted of the Conservatives attacking Labour and Labour attacking the Conservatives, respectively 28% and 21% of all attacks. The main target of the Conservatives was Labour, but runner up was the SNP – 14% of all the attacks were the Conservatives attacking the SNP.

Figure 7.4 shows us for each targeted party where the attacks came from. Tracing the edges clockwise shows the direction of the attack. Edges are labelled when they represent more than 20% of attacks. We see that the Conservatives were primarily targeted by Labour and their former coalition partner, the Liberal Democrats; respectively, 65 and 20% of all attacks directed to the Conservatives. Labour was primarily targeted by the Conservatives and the SNP; respectively, 79 and 11% of all attacks directed to Labour. It was clear that the SNP was perceived as a threat as it was mainly targeted by the Conservatives and Labour. The same

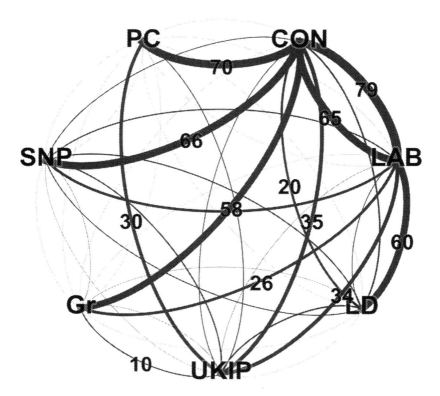

FIGURE 7.4 Party origin of attacks on parties in the 2015 UK parliamentary election campaign in the print media (appeals in percentages)

Note
$N = 9,614$. The curvature of the edge shows the direction of the attack. To be read clockwise; see explanation in the text.

counts for UKIP. This pattern of attack behavior remained quite stable throughout the campaign, so it was not the case that parties shifted target.

Overall, we find that the choice of target was quite stable for the parties throughout the campaign. A substantial part of all attacks reported involved Labour and Conservatives attacking one another. However, unlike other years, parties other than the traditional three were frequently targeted. The Conservatives were responsible for most of the attacks directed at UKIP and the SNP.

Print Media Differences in Reporting Campaign Rhetoric

Do the various newspapers present voters with a similar or different picture of negative campaigning in the 2015 UK general election campaign? And to the extent that there are large differences, do these reflect newspapers' partisan preferences? Do print media bias the image that voters receive of the campaign? Next to type of newspaper (tabloid versus broadsheet), we look at the partisan nature of British newspapers.

Evaluating the coverage of negative and positive campaigning as presented by the print media, we first of all look at the overall percentage of these reported per newspaper (Figure 7.5). The average percentage of attacks reported per newspaper is 41%. The level of negative campaigning as reported by the newspapers seems relatively similar, with two exceptions. Negative campaigning is much more frequently reported by the *Daily Mirror* and less frequently

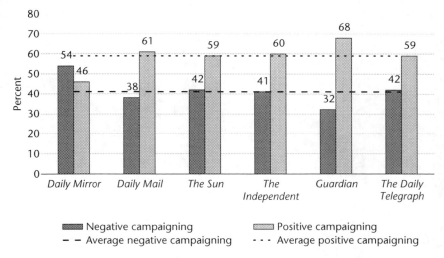

FIGURE 7.5 Reported attack behavior per newspaper (appeals in percentages)

Note
$N = 21,346$.

reported by *Guardian*, respectively 54 and 32%. Tabloids are slightly more likely to report negative campaigning than broadsheets, respectively on average 43% and 37%.

Now, we take a look at which parties received the most coverage as an attacking party, i.e., made most use of negative campaigning as reported by the print media (Table 7.2). The *Daily Mirror* provides again a biased view. More than any other newspaper it gives room to attacks made by Labour, namely 72% of all attacks reported stemmed from Labour. *Guardian*, also supporting Labour through the campaign, almost equally reports attacks from the Conservatives as from Labour, respectively 30 and 36%. All newspapers that declared support for the Conservatives tend to report more attack behavior from the Conservatives than other parties, namely 57% of the attacks in *The Sun*, 58% of the attacks in *The Daily Telegraph*, and 65% of the attacks in the *Daily Mail*. The *Independent* was not part of this pattern. Although weakly supporting a Liberal Democrat and Conservative coalition government, they reported that most negative campaigning was coming from Labour.

We will now examine positive campaigning to see whether these newspapers also give more room for self-praise to the parties that they declared to support (Table 7.3). The *Daily Mirror*'s support for Labour is again reflected in the selection of campaign appeals; 69% of all positive campaigning in the *Daily Mirror* is self-praise by Labour. *Guardian*, which also declared support for Labour, covers more positive campaigning by Labour than the Conservatives, respectively 34 and 28%. The *Daily Mail*, *The Daily Telegraph* and *The Sun*, who supported the Conservatives, again favored the Conservatives when it came to positive campaigning, respectively 46, 42 and 38%. No such pattern was present in *The Independent*; although weakly supporting the Liberal Democrat and Conservative coalition, most positive campaigning reported stemmed from Labour. This all together shows us that the newspapers differed in the quotes and paraphrases

TABLE 7.2 Who attacks the most, as portrayed in the print media (appeals in percentages)

	Daily Mirror	Daily Mail	The Daily Telegraph	The Independent	Guardian	The Sun
CON	9	65	58	28	30	57
LAB	72	20	20	46	36	16
LD	11	7	9	16	18	9
UKIP	5	3	4	4	6	2
Gr	0	0	0	0	1	1
SNP	2	5	8	5	7	16
PC	1	0	1	1	1	0
N	944	1,550	2,479	990	2,061	1,590

Note
$N=9,614$.

TABLE 7.3 Who used positive campaigning the most, as portrayed in the print media (appeals in percentages)

	Daily Mirror	Daily Mail	The Daily Telegraph	The Independent	Guardian	The Sun
CON	20	46	42	28	28	38
LAB	69	31	25	35	34	25
LD	8	7	7	17	14	7
UKIP	3	7	9	7	8	3
Gr	1	1	2	4	6	2
SNP	1	9	15	8.	9	26
PC	0	0	0	1	2	9
N	731	2,104	3,005	1,305	3,821	1,998

Note
$N = 12,964$.

they selected in the coverage of the campaign. Most newspapers were led by their partisan nature when covering campaign rhetoric. We find evidence for a so-called coverage bias. As a result, the readers of these newspapers were presented with different portrayals of the campaign. As a strong pre-campaign relationship exists between partisan leanings of newspapers and those of their readers, most newspaper coverage in this campaign will have strengthened readers' existing preferences.

Conclusion

This chapter examined how the British print media reported negative campaigning in the 2015 UK general election. By doing so, it contributes to the literature on negative campaigning outside the US context and to literature on coverage of election campaigns by newspapers. The print media are often overlooked in the study of negative campaigning as they present a potentially biased representation of the campaign, i.e., being expected to over-report negative campaigning and provide preferential treatment to parties they endorse. However, it is the print and televised media that reach large audiences and they are thus the dominant channels through which voters experience the campaign. It is important to understand on what voters base their perceptions.

The 2015 UK general election campaign was a campaign like most other ones according to the print media. The campaign was not particularly negative and the party attacking the most was, unsurprisingly, the Conservative Party. However, the campaign did differ from previous ones to the extent that the "traditional" parties attacked other parties. The results show that Labour and Conservatives feared the successful challenger parties, consequently frequently attacking UKIP and the SNP. In the past, they would have just ignored these parties. The prospect of a hung parliament also inspired a substantial part of the attack behavior, as, in particular, the Conservatives frequently used fear appeals to scare voters with the prospect of a "disastrous" Labour–SNP coalition government. Although negative campaigning was a substantial part of the campaign, the campaign was still quite informative, as the main bulk of attacks were issue attacks, thereby informing voters about their policy plans and competence on these issues. During the formal campaign, the use and choice of targets was relatively stable for parties throughout.

Besides painting the overall picture of negative campaigning in the 2015 campaign, this study revealed that newspapers significantly vary in how they cover negative campaigning. Different newspapers made different selections of which positive and negative campaign statements to report. This selection reflects in general the partisan nature of the newspaper. The data show a clear selection bias in the coverage of negative campaigning: Newspapers tend to cover both more attacks as well as self-praise from the party they support and attacks targeting the main opponent. We thus find evidence for coverage bias. Readers of different newspapers acquired from their paper different information about the campaign behavior of the various parties and this may have affected their perceptions of the tone of the campaigns of the parties. We know that these perceptions affect, on average, party preferences, vote choice, political participation, and feelings of distrust.

However, newspapers were not the only source of information for voters in the campaign. Further research should assess the influence of the different newspapers on voters' perceptions of the campaign tone. If coverage bias indeed affects voters' perceptions of the tone of parties' campaigns, it is likely that the print media largely reinforces already existing beliefs of their audiences.

On a methodological note, the widespread tendency to group newspapers on the basis of tabloids, broadsheets, and partisanship is, at least for Britain, not good practice, as demonstrated in this chapter. Categorizations like these disguise the variation in news coverage within these categories. Additionally, it shows the potential dangers of measuring negative campaigning on the basis of only a handful of news sources in a context of strong press–party parallelism. This study also had its limitations. Owing to the fact that the data collection did not cover all British print media, no straightforward conclusions can be drawn about population-wide campaign coverage by the entire British newspaper industry.

Acknowledgments

This research is funded by a Marie Curie Intra-European Fellowship (no. 629012: FP7-PEOPLE-2013-IEF), the Centre of British Politics, and the Research Committee of the School of Politics and International Relations of the University of Nottingham. I thank Professor Susan Banducci and Dr. Iulia Cioroianu for providing the newspaper articles.

Notes

1. Boris Johnson (CON), *The Daily Telegraph*, April 20, 2015.
2. Kenneth Baker (CON), *The Daily Telegraph*, April 21, 2015.
3. Boris Johnson (CON), *The Daily Telegraph*, April 20, 2015.
4. Ed Miliband (LAB), *Daily Mirror*, April 10, 2015.
5. Michael Fallon (CON), *Daily Mirror*, April 10, 2015.
6. Jeremy Hunt (CON), *The Daily Telegraph*, April 11, 2015.
7. In the whole of the UK political advertising is prohibited on television. Major parties are allocated rationed blocks of free airtime for party political broadcasts, which are labeled party election broadcasts (PEBs) during official campaign periods. See Scammell and Langer (2006).
8. Nick Clegg (LD), *Daily Mirror*, April 3, 2015.
9. Julian Smith (CON), *The Sun*, April 16, 2015.
10. *Upstairs Downstairs* is a British television drama series about the aristocratic family Bellamy and their servants.
11. David Cameron (CON), *The Independent*, April 8, 2015.
12. Ed Balls (LAB), *The Daily Telegraph*, April 15, 2015.
13. David Cameron (CON), *Guardian*, April 20, 2015.
14. Ed Miliband (LAB), *Guardian*, April 22, 2015.
15. Chuka Umunna (LAB), *The Independent*, April 26, 2015.
16. David Cameron (CON), *The Daily Telegraph*, April 16, 2015.
17. Boris Johnson (CON), *The Daily Telegraph*, April 20, 2015.
18. David Cameron (CON), *The Daily Telegraph*, April 22, 2015.
19. Nick Clegg (LD), *The Daily Telegraph*, April 3, 2015.
20. Nick Clegg (LD), *The Daily Telegraph*, April 16, 2015.
21. Patrick Harvie (Gr), *The Daily Telegraph*, March 31, 2015.
22. Agenda bias measures the extent to which political parties receive coverage that accurately reflects their own issue priorities. A partisan newspaper might be expected to mirror the agenda of its endorsed party [...] Statement bias can be measured by calculating the balance between favourable and unfavourable statements in editorials and commentary, ultimately leading to estimates of the overall attitudes of newspapers towards different political parties.

    (Brandenburg, 2006, pp. 161–162)
23. David Cameron (CON), *The Daily Telegraph*, March 31, 2015.
24. Some aspects of complex coding schemes are coded with higher reliability than others. The detection of quotes and paraphrases was highly reliable, as was the coding of the tone of appeals contained within those. Less reliable was the demarcation of appeals within text segments. Although this is regrettable, it is unlikely to affect our resulting measures of campaign tone systematically, as it affects only the number of appeals coded separately, but not the coding of the tone of each of these.
25. One could wonder whether selection in reporting by print media is responsible for this, but this seems unlikely on account of the high news values inherent in many of the campaign activities of UKIP.

References

Aalberg, T., Strömback, J., & de Vreese, C. (2012). The framing of politics as strategy and game: A review of concept, operationalization and key findings. *Journalism*, 13, 162–178.

Ansolabehere, S., & Iyengar, S. (1995). *Going negative: How attack ads shrink and polarize the electorate*. New York: Free Press.

Banducci, S. A., Cioroianu, I., Coan, T., Katz, G., Kolpinskaya, E., & Stevens, D. (2017). *Content analysis of media coverage of the 2015 British general election.* [data collection]. UK Data Service. SN: 8176, http://doi.org/10.5255/UKDA-SN-8176-1.

Brandenburg, H. (2006). Party strategy and media bias: A quantitative analysis of the 2005 UK election campaign. *Journal of Elections, Public Opinion and Parties,* 16, 157–178.

Brooks, D. J., & Geer, J. G. (2007). Beyond negativity: The effects of incivility on the electorate. *American Journal of Political Science,* 51, 1–16.

Cheng, H., & Riffe, D. (2008). Attention, perception, and perceived effects: Negative political advertising in a battleground state of the 2004 presidential election. *Mass Communication & Society,* 11, 177–196.

De Nooy, W., & Kleinnijenhuis, J. (2015). Attack, support, and coalitions in a multiparty system: Understanding negative campaigning in a country with a coalition government. In A. Nai, & A. S. Walter (Eds.), *New perspectives and negative campaigning* (pp. 75–93). Colchester: ECPR Studies.

Deacon D., & Wring D. (2016). Still life in the old attack dogs: The press. In P. Cowley, & D. Kavanagh (Eds.), *The British general election of 2015* (pp. 302–335). London: Palgrave Macmillan.

Dermody, J., & Scullion, R. (2000). Perceptions of negative political advertising: Meaningful or menacing? An empirical study of the 1997 British general election campaign. *International Journal of Advertising,* 19, 201–223.

Fridkin, K. L., & Kenney, P. (2011). Variability in citizens' reactions to different types of negative campaigns. *American Journal of Political Science,* 55(2), 307–325.

Geer, J. G. (2006). *In defense of negativity: Attack ads in presidential campaigns.* Chicago, IL: University of Chicago Press.

Geer, J. G. (2012). The news media and the rise of negativity in presidential campaigns. *PS: Political Science & Politics,* 45(3), 422–427.

Gervais, B. T. (2017). More than mimicry? The role of anger in uncivil reactions to elite political incivility. *International Journal of Public Opinion Research,* 29(3), 384–405.

Green, J., & Prosser, C. (2016). Party system fragmentation and single-party government: The British general election of 2015. *West European Politics,* 39, 1299–1310.

Haselmeyer, M., Meyer, T. M., & Wagner, M. (2017). Fighting for attention: Media coverage of negative campaign messages. *Party Politics.* doi: 10.1177/1354068817724174.

Hodess, R., Tedesco, J., & Kaid, L. (2000). British party election broadcasts: A comparison of 1992 and 1997. *International Journal of Press/Politics,* 54, 55–70.

Iyengar, S., & Valentino, N. (1999). Who says what: Source credibility as a mediator of campaign advertising. In A. Lupia, M. McCubbins, & S. Popkin (Eds.), *Elements of reason* (pp. 108–129). New York: Cambridge University Press.

Johnson-Cartee, K. S., & Copeland, G. A. (1991). *Negative political advertising: Coming of age.* Hillsdale, NJ: Lawrence Erlbaum.

Lau, R. R., & Pomper, G. M. (2004). *Negative campaigning: An analysis of US Senate elections.* Oxford: Rowman & Littlefield.

Lau, R. R., Sigelman, L., & Rovner, I. B. (2007). The effects of negative political campaigns: A meta-analytic reassessment. *The Journal of Politics,* 69(4), 1176–1209.

Leach, R., Coxall, B., & Robins, L. (2006). *British politics.* London: Palgrave Macmillan.

Lemert, J., Wanta, W., & Lee, T.-T. (1999). Party identification and negative advertising in a US Senate election. *Journal of Communication,* 49, 123–134.

Lipsitz, K., & Geer, J. G. (2017). Rethinking the concept of negativity: An empirical approach. *Political Research Quarterly,* 70(3), 577–589.

Mattes, K., & Redlawsk, D. P. (2015). *The positive case for negative campaigning.* Chicago, IL: University of Chicago Press.

Min, Y. (2004). News coverage of negative political campaigns: An experiment of negative campaign effects on turnout and candidate preferences. *The International Journal of Press/Politics,* 9, 27–38.

Pattie, C., Denver, D., Johns, R., & Mitchell, J. (2011). Raising the tone? The impact of "positive" and "negative" campaigning on voting in the 2007 Scottish Parliament election. *Electoral Studies,* 30, 333–343.

Ridout, T. N., & Smith, G. R. (2008). Free advertising: How the media amplify campaign messages. *Political Research Quarterly,* 61, 598–608.

Ridout, T. N., & Walter, A. S. (2015). How the news media amplify negative messages. In A. Nai, & A. S. Walter (Eds.), *New perspectives and negative campaigning* (pp. 276–285). Colchester: ECPR Studies.

Scammell, M., & Langer, A. (2006). Political advertising in the United Kingdom. In L. Kaid, & C. Holtz-Bacha (Eds.), *Sage handbook of political advertising* (pp. 65–82). London: Sage.

Thorson, E., Ognianova, E., Coyle, J., & Denton, F. (2000). Negative political ads and negative citizen orientations toward politics. *Journal of Current Issues & Research in Advertising,* 22, 13–40.

Van Heerde-Hudson, J. (2011). The Americanization of British party advertising? Negativity in party election broadcasts 1964–2005. *British Politics,* 6, 52–77.

Van Kempen, H. (2007). Media-party parallelism and its effects: A cross-national comparative study. *Political Communication,* 24(3), 303–320.

Walter, A. S. (2014a). Negative campaigning in Western Europe: Similar or different? *Political Studies,* 62(S1), 42–60.

Walter, A. S. (2014b). Choosing the enemy: Attack behaviour in a multiparty system. *Party Politics,* 20, 311–323.

Walter, A. S., & van der Brug, W. (2013). When the gloves come off: Inter-party variation in negative campaigning in Dutch elections 1981–2010. *Acta Politica,* 48, 367–388.

Walter, A. S., & Vliegenthart, R. (2010). Negative campaigning across different communication channels: Different ballgames? *Harvard International Journal Press/Politics,* 15, 441–461.

Walter, A. S., Ridout, T. N., & Van der Eijk, C. (2017). *Explaining voters' campaign tone perceptions.* Unpublished Manuscript.

Walter, A. S., van der Brug, W., & van Praag, P. (2014). When the stakes are high: Party competition and negative campaigning. *Comparative Political Studies,* 47, 550–573.

Wring, D., & Deacon, D. (2010). Patterns of press partisanship in the 2010 General Election. *British Politics,* 5(4), 436–454.

PART III
Media Discourse

8

REPRESENTATIONS OF TELEVISED DEBATES IN THE PRESS AND THEIR INFLUENCE ON POLITICAL CANDIDATES

The Cases of Spain, the UK, and the US

Laura Pérez Rastrilla

Introduction: Debating About Politics on Television

A televised debate is a political activity where candidates have the opportunity to "directly" address a large audience of voters who can listen and judge candidates' proposals and compare them. Although there are ambiguous findings about the immediate effects of televised debates on voters' preferences (Benoit, McHale, Hansen, Pier, & McGuire, 2003; Coleman, 2011; Lanoue, 1991), televised debates also attract voters' and mass media's attention in the days following this event (Gallego Reguera, 2017).

The first televised debate was broadcast in 1956 in the US, when the debate between the Democratic primary candidates of the time was televised. But it was the debate that took place on November 8, 1960, where John F. Kennedy and Richard Nixon faced one another, that became a historical benchmark. Since then, the interpretation of political events mediated by television has had a significant influence on political reality. Television itself became an element of modern democracy, especially affecting campaigning: "The demands of television have dictated the structure and formats of contemporary debates. Television manifests a unique symbol system, which fundamentally shapes what is communicated to receivers, apart from content, and has changed the very nature of presidential debate discourse" (Hellweg, Pfau, & Brydon, 1992, p. xxii).

The appearance of television transformed the whole electoral process. Television made it easier for politicians to establish a closer relationship with their potential voters, as it gave them a platform to talk about personal experiences, open viewers' hearts, and take advantage of their public speaking skills.

The print media, in turn, also tried to make the most of televised debates, and its role is a key element to understanding the interpretation of political debates among audiences (Fridkin, Kenney, Gershon, & Woodall, 2008; Kinder, 2003). Print media coverage of televised electoral debates boosts expectations and defines interpretations. Viewers are encouraged by the press to watch the event, candidates' strategies are forecast, and their performances are analyzed. The audience may also access the newspapers' reports after watching the televised debates. Moreover, many voters may only learn about the TV debates via their coverage in the print media (Benoit & Currie, 2001).

This study is concerned with the importance that the media has in the representation of reality, specifically in the area of politics, and the different meanings it can render of the same political event. This begs the question, first, as to which variables determine which representations. A second objective considered relevant for this study is the influence that the media can exert on behavioral change. Most contemporary studies dealing with media effects pay attention to the impact the media can have on public opinion (Noelle-Neumann, 2010; Wolf, 1987). In this study, however, the focus is on the influence of the media on the represented political candidates themselves.

In this chapter, which centers on print media, press coverage of three rounds of televised debates in Spain, the UK, and the US are analyzed through the lens of qualitative content analysis. In order to tackle the aforementioned aims, this work first addresses the representation of televised debates in the print media by analyzing central elements and comparing the results of this analysis across different newspapers, by country. In regards to the second objective, this work also examines to what extent the print media's representations of the first round of televised debates influenced candidates' behavior during the second round of debates. Thus, this study contributes to our understanding of how the meaning of political events is constructed through their representation in the press and to the empirical research of media influence on politics.

A Theoretical Approach to Media Representations and the Impact of Media Coverage on Televised Debates

Reality Through the Lens of the Media

Media narratives influence our worldviews, and numerous researchers have examined the media's role in shaping perceptions of reality. *Agenda-setting*, formulated by McCombs and Shaw (1972), is still one of the main theories in communication studies about the capacity of the media to establish the public agenda. Based on it, structural theories have been developed where different elements are considered relevant, such as professional routines (McQuail & Windahl, 1981; Tuchman, 1977), media sources (Ericson, Baranek, & Chan, 1989), or the *CNN effect* (Robinson, 1999). All of them accept that news is not an objective reflection of reality, but a process of selection and interpretation of it. Some aspects are thus told, while others are only partially presented or even omitted.

Media interests and bias have also been widely studied. Herman (2000) and Herman and Chomsky (1988) concluded from their research that economic relations impact media practices. Other authors, such as Gerbner (1964) or van Dijk (2009), posit, however, that journalists' political ideology has a heavy impact on news reporting. In these studies, *framing theory* (Goffman, 1974) was decisive in recognizing narrative structures or the framing of discourses, which explain the way representations of political events are constructed.

From the standpoint of critical theory, the ability to represent real discourses, such as by constructing media narratives, is a fundamental factor of power, since discourses are social practices that create worldviews and ideologies. Words are not chosen accidentally, but reflect interpretations of the events that are subject to this discourse. In this vein, we can reveal the production of meaning by studying representations of the real world. When these meanings and representations are articulated, discourses are shaped, offering different versions of reality. Thus, the object of this study should also be conceived of as illustrating forms of socially and politically situated texts. Accordingly, analyses of media representations are studies about power, as they reveal dominant narratives that create the legitimacy of discourses.

Does the Media Shape Candidates' Behavior? The Influence of Media Representations of Televised Debates

To some extent, the impact of media representations of political events can be measured according to their ability to change behavior. Major advances in the study of televised debates, the print media's representations of these, and their impact on voters' behavior have been made in the US. For example, Drew and Weaver (1991) examined the impact of televised debates and media coverage in general during the 1988 presidential election race between Republican candidate George Bush and Democratic candidate Michael Dukakis. They concluded that directly viewing the debates was more influential than one's exposure to all other types of representation of the debates in the news. Their findings, however, were contradicted by more exhaustive studies that came to the conclusion that "news commentary does influence viewers' perceptions about debates" (Hellweg et al., 1992, p. 99). Moreover, Ross's (1992) research demonstrated that both the amount of news coverage concerning a candidate and the tone of this coverage influenced voters.

One of the most famous anecdotes about the impact of media representation concerns the second round of TV debates between Jimmy Carter and Gerald Ford in 1976, in which President Ford committed a major gaffe on foreign policy. Without having noticed this mistake, voters interviewed immediately after the debate thought Carter had lost. However, voters interviewed 48 hours later gave the victory to Carter. In the meantime, the media had proclaimed Carter as the winner of the debate due to Ford's mistake. Researchers concluded that "the passing of time required for the news to reach the public brought with it a virtual reversal of opinion" (Patterson, 1980, p. 123).

Regarding the representation of debates in print media, Kraus (2011) examined samples of newspapers' texts on televised debates within the context of an extensive study on presidential elections in the US. His findings revealed newspapers' tendency to use analogies from sports or entertainment for politics, to emphasize visual elements and to assess winners and losers. By the same token, Benoit (2014) conducted a study about TV debates' media representations, where he compared the content of debates between political leaders in various countries — Australia, Canada, the UK, and the US — with newspaper coverage of them. Results indicated that the press's representations of televised political debates were very selective, with a pronounced tendency to accentuate attacks and focus on the characters of the politicians. Benoit (2014, p. 87) concluded that "those who supplement watching debates with newspaper stories about them, receive a clearly slanted picture."

By contrast, there hardly exist any empirical studies with regard to the effects of media representations on political candidates' behaviors. Graber and Dunaway's (2015) research indicates a transformation of the types of candidates as a result of media trends. Broadcast expansion imposed a new standard on candidates as to who could fit in. This new political standard, characterized by placing a candidate's image at the center of their campaign, has been promoted by the mass media, including the press.

Media interest in TV performance has changed which qualities are valued in a political candidate, so that "a candidate's ability to look impressive and perform well before the cameras has become crucial" (Graber & Dunaway, 2015, p. 392). In the case of the US, these media-driven qualities have made people that are accustomed to acting before the public, such as actors, comedians, or television stars, more likely to run for office than ever before. Graber and Dunaway (2015, p. 393) cite Reagan's presidency as a key moment, since for the first time, "good pictures can counterbalance the effects of unfavorable verbal comments." Currently, media consultants are requisite staff for any candidate's campaign. They give counsel on any subject that may have an impact on the media, from proper attire and appropriate behavior for each occasion to the handling of statements to media (Burton, Miller, & Shea, 2015).

Methodology, Cases, and Data

Qualitative Content Analysis

A common methodology used when studying newspaper coverage is content analysis. Most researchers have traditionally resorted to quantitative content analysis, e.g., Krippendorff (2004), where key elements of a body of news are identified and enumerated, based on manifest content and frequency counts. However, it was considered that a qualitative approach of content analysis, e.g., Schreier (2012), was more appropriate to answer the research questions raised in this study. Using qualitative methods and focusing the scope of analysis on newspaper representations of televised electoral debates allow these texts to be analyzed in context, and for one to explore dominant narratives, specific depictions of these events that are circulated by newspapers, and the character of these outlets. In qualitative content analysis, the meaning of the data and their importance do not depend on its frequency. Data are taken to a higher level of abstraction, which allows one to observe how different parts of the material relate to each other (Schreier, 2014). One disadvantage of qualitative over quantitative analysis, however, is that as the main research task is interpreting the text, there is not a unique procedure to do so (Wiesner, Haapala, & Palonen, 2017). Instead, the researcher is required to focus on select aspects of meaning, those related to the research question.

There are, however, shared steps among researchers that serve as an analytical guide. It is important to keep in mind that these steps are an interactive process, and one may be required to go through them repeatedly as new information is discovered (Schreier, 2014). Hodgetts and Chamberlain (2014) recommend five basic steps. The first one is to identify the topic and scope of the data required. It implies an initial review of the newspaper items and a basic previous knowledge of the reported event. The information to be analyzed will also depend on the research questions. The second step is gridding, an analytical strategy that deconstructs media narratives and identifies key ideas. Gridding is particularly useful in comparative studies like the present one, or when analyzing the evolution of an event, as it allows one to observe trends and patterns, and to compare different parts of the results.

The gridding step can be illustrated by means of a table where information is collected and organized. It is not an attempt to quantify data, but a way to identify the range of news items, elements that are being promoted, and emerging patterns. In this step, key themes are identified, and similarities, differences, and contradictions are analyzed by comparing the results. By selecting key themes, qualitative methodology allows one to consider criteria other than frequency as measures for the relevance of the information gathered. As the current research is about media texts, the criteria applied by the media when emphasizing certain information were taken into consideration. These include, for example, decisions about whether an event is published on the front-page, on even or odd pages, what information headlines will provide, or whether articles are accompanied by graphic items (Pinilla García, 2004).

The third step is coding. This procedure entails categorizing the material which is to be analyzed. An index of terms, linked to key themes identified in the previous step, is created to process the content of the materials. At this point, Hodgetts and Chamberlain (2014) warn that one might be open to the possibility of changing the research aims to better reflect the scope of the data. In the current study, however, the coding procedure was not carried out, as this study focuses on identifying predominant representations and general patterns and, therefore, gridding was the fundamental analytical step. Both themes and codes obtained by gridding and coding may be combined into larger themes or broken down into sub-themes and categories.

In the fourth step, themes are ordered and linked and a new analytical narrative is constructed that responds to the research questions. Comparing these news items from the nine newspapers helped to highlight contrasting representations, shared meanings, and missing information. Giving context to the items identified was key here. It provided a logic for the data interpretation, as the aim of the research is not merely to enumerate the data, but to communicate what the data mean. At this step, it is also important to draw a connection between the theoretical frame and the empirical work. In the fifth and last step, the overall interpretation was ordered in a coherent structure according to the research questions and the obtained results, and the writing was carried out.

Cases and Data

Print media representations of televised electoral debates were chosen from three countries: Spain, the UK, and the US, during three electoral campaigns: 1993, 2010, and 2000, respectively. They were selected because it was considered relevant to compare coverage from countries where debates were being televised for the first time (Spain and the UK) with a country with a long tradition of televised electoral debates (US). Moreover, Spain and the UK were selected because, even though both countries are representative democracies, they have very different political traditions and histories.

In Spain, two rounds of televised debates in 1993 took place between Felipe González, then prime minister, and José María Aznar, the People Party's candidate. These were the first political debates ever televised in the country and they were broadcast on May 25 and June 1.[1]

The 2010 debates between the prime minister, Gordon Brown, from the Labour Party, David Cameron, the Conservative candidate, and Nick Clegg, the candidate from the Liberal Democrats, were the first ones televised in the UK. The debates were organized in three rounds, on April 16, 23, and 30.[2]

Finally, considering that the US has a long tradition of televised debates, one sample from the presidential election in 2000 between the vice-president, Al Gore, and the Republican candidate, George W. Bush, was analyzed. It consisted of three rounds of televised debates, which were broadcast on October 4, 12, and 18.[3]

Televised debates rank among the most-watched political events in all three countries. In Spain, the first round of the previously mentioned debates was watched by 9.6 million people and the second by 10.5 million. In the UK, the first round was watched by 9.6 million viewers, the second by 4.2 million, and the third by 8.6 million. In the US, 46.6 million viewers followed the first round, 37.5 watched the second, and 37.7 tuned into the third round.

Nine newspapers that reviewed these TV debates were analyzed – three from each country – and selected based on circulation numbers and ideological pluralism. The nine observed newspapers rank among the top ten national daily general interest newspapers in their respective countries, according to distribution figures.[4] *El País*, *ABC*, and *El Mundo* were selected to study the Spanish case. Since its foundation in 1976, *El País* has been supportive of socialist and liberal policies, maintaining a close relationship with the Socialist Party. *ABC*, founded at the beginning of the twentieth century, defends the Spanish monarchy and is a supporter of the Popular Party's policies, thereby positioning itself in the right-wing of the political spectrum. *El Mundo* was able to stand out as an alternative to both *El País* and *ABC* during the 1990s. It opposed the Socialist Party's policies and defended the liberal wing within the Popular Party.

The tabloids the *Daily Mail* and the *Daily Express* were analyzed in the UK, as well as the broadsheet *Guardian*. Although the *Daily Mail* is a right-leaning tabloid with traditionally conservative values, it has supported some of the Labour Party's policies. The *Daily Express* altered its political outlook when a change in ownership occurred in 2000. In the wake of it, it backed the Conservative Party and showed a fierce opposition to Prime Minister Gordon Brown during the 2010 election campaign. Finally, *Guardian* is perceived as a fairly or slightly left-wing newspaper, since it frequently supports Labour policies.

From the US, *Washington Post*, *The Wall Street Journal*, and *New York Times* were examined. Since the 1960s and 1970s, *Washington Post* has been known to be a liberal newspaper, with a bias that swings from moderate left to center. *New York Times* has traditionally endorsed Democratic Party nominees, but it also staffs opinionated conservative columnists. Prior to the acquisition of the newspaper by Rupert Murdoch in 2007, *The Wall Street Journal* openly stood for liberal policies and supported Democratic nominees, as those who defended these policies.

Research Questions

The first objective of this research is to analyze the representation of meaning constructed by the newspapers from these three different countries about what occurred in these televised debates. The second objective is to analyze the influence that the newspapers' representations may have had on the candidates over the course of the debates. The following questions aim to guide the research:

1. Were the televised debates subject to the same kind of representations in newspapers from different countries? Were there differences among newspapers from the same country?

    1.1 What aspects did newspapers prioritize in the representation of debates?
    1.2 What differences and common elements could be identified in their representations?

2. Do newspapers' representations influence candidates' behavior? Can we find evidence of this by analyzing newspaper representations?

   2.1 What aspects of a candidate's performance were represented in the newspapers?

   2.2 If there were changes in a candidate's behavior in subsequent debates due to a newspaper's representations of them from previous debates, were these changes reflected by the newspapers later on?

Based on the aforementioned media theories, which highlight the influence different agents and interests have on media representations, it is first of all expected that the specific contexts in which these debates were broadcast influenced their representation. In regards to the second objective, as the media's impact on political candidates is considered a crucial element of influence in political campaigns (Graber & Dunaway, 2015), it is expected that newspapers' assessments of candidates' performances had an effect on them. Since the analyzed televised debates were organized in at least two rounds, the hypothesis is that, if changes in candidates' behavior took place in accordance with newspapers' prior representations, they would be represented in the newspapers' follow-up articles.

Following Hodgetts and Chamberlain's analytical model, the identification of the data required for this project was the first step. The analyzed material was press content directly related to the debates, published two days after each round of the debates. A total of 278 documents were examined. The content analyzed included news articles, op-eds, opinion columns, transcriptions of televised debates, and cartoons. Among the documents analyzed, 43 were published by *ABC*, 30 by *El Mundo*, 20 by *El País*, 23 by the *Daily Express*, 27 by the *Daily Mail*, 31 by *Guardian*, 46 by *New York Times*, 18 by *The Wall Street Journal*, and 39 by *Washington Post*.

Analysis of Newspaper Representations and Their Effects

Three Different Representations of Meaning of Televised Debates

In the Spanish newspapers analyzed, the televised debates were judged positively and generated huge amounts of publicity. In both rounds, the press represented the debates as fine examples of democracy. Their role in Spanish politics was described with distinctly positive adjectives: "It can be considered civilized, a positive test" … "a great event in the history of television" (*El País*, 1993a, May 25),[5] "[Televised debates] have improved politics […] this is an outstanding service to our country" (*ABC*, 1993a, May 25), "Last night, undoubtedly, democracy won" (*El Mundo*, 1993a, May 25). The dictatorial past was frequently recalled, though not explicitly, when expressing the important step toward democracy that electoral debates represented. Televised debates were proof that Spain had become a democracy. This dictatorial past determined a narrative, in which Spain was self-depicted as a backward democracy.

In 1993, Spanish journalists seemed to agree that the more televised debates a country was able to hold, the more democratic it was: "This debate has enriched Spanish citizens' judgment, it is a common instrument used by modern democracies" (*ABC*, 1993b, May 25), "It was the mother of all debates and it infused the atmosphere with democratic strength" (*El Mundo*, 1993f, June 1). Televised debates were perceived, first of all, as a stage on which political tensions could be displayed, and, second, as a form of accountability. No differences could be detected with regards to these two points among the three analyzed newspapers. All of them produced representations in which these two elements were identified. The political and historical context of Spain seemed to influence the perception of these first televised electoral debates to a large extent.

In the UK, on the other hand, the press media's representations of their first ever televised debates were detached from the concept of democracy. In fact, public arguments for the rejection of the debates were precisely based on democratic grounds: "the reluctant party leaders cited largely constitutional reasons – in particular, that debates are not appropriate for a non-presidential parliamentary system of government" (Bailey, 2012, p. 5). However, Bailey points out that the real reason for the lack of televised debates in the UK before 2010 was because of a political strategy; that is, party strategists thought candidates would run the risk of damaging their images in a televised debate. *Guardian*, for instance, did not judge British democracy based on the existence or non-existence of televised electoral debates.

On the contrary, it questioned the importance of televised debates, and criticized new political dynamics characterized by "frivolous" shows and the entertainment industry. *Guardian* associated televised debates with superficiality and sometimes also with a deterioration of democracy: "Their culture of spin has poisoned our political system" (2010f, April 30), "[televised debates] enhance the presidential character of elections [...] that's not healthy [...] [they are] ripe for abuse and manipulation" (2010b, April 16). Journalists from *Guardian* accepted the introduction of televised debates and depicted them as an unavoidable performance in contemporary politics, but they did not consider them the best political practice. The *Daily Express* and the *Daily Mail* did not observe a link between televised debates and democracy either, and depicted televised debates as an irrelevant political event with no impact on the British political system, and cut off from most voters: "Millions of voters will surely have thought something else: 'None of these parties speaks for me'" (*Daily Express*, 2010a, April 16), "Despite the publicity surrounding the debate, there appears not to have been a seismic change" (*Daily Mail*, 2010d, April 17), "Despite the two leaders' debates [...] remarkably few have any idea what the main parties stand for" (*Daily Mail*, 2010e, April 24).

In the US, a discussion about the democratic value of televised electoral debates did not occur, but their influence on politics was judged to be beneficial. The three examined newspapers seemed to have normalized televised debates as a custom during political campaigns, that is, there was not a discussion about why they should or should not exist, and they were thus taken for granted. In the articles from *The Wall Street Journal*, we could not find an explicit representation of either the role or the influence of televised debates on American politics. However, *New York Times* and *Washington Post* held them in high esteem. They considered televised debates the only place in a campaign where marketing or mediators cannot intervene. Both newspapers represented televised debates as useful opportunities for citizens to observe politics without interferences: "Tonight was the first opportunity for tens of millions of Americans to assess the contenders for more than a flash in a television commercial or on the evening news" ... "The debate gave viewers a chance to step beyond polls and media analysis" (*New York Times*, 2000b, October 4), "Debates, it is said, are the Super Bowls of politics" (*Washington Post*, 2000b, October 5), "But the debate was useful nonetheless. The candidates [...] revealed substantial differences" (*Washington Post*, 2000a, October 4).

Televised Debates as TV Shows

Spanish newspapers, however, displayed a very different representation of televised debates, as they were portrayed as entertainment programs rather than political events. The positive influence televised debates could have for a budding democracy did not prevent *El Mundo* from expressing critical judgments, as they portrayed televised debates as taking part in entertainment culture: "It did not matter if they transformed television into a stage of political debate, because television is still a frivolous, trivial, superficial and stupid mass media" (1993c, May 25). *El País*, in contrast, just evaluated that elements from entertainment culture were present, but opinionated comments on the role of television were not displayed. It paid more attention to the impact of the debates on TV stations: "Antena 3 Televisión was undoubtedly a winner" (1993b, May 25). *ABC* exhibited its admiration for television and described the televised debates as a positive and useful event: "This debate is worthier than the whole campaign" (1993a, May 25).

The staging, the meeting of the candidates, and the aesthetics of the event attracted extensive attention in the three analyzed Spanish newspapers. Every detail shown through this visual medium could be considered decisive for winning the debate: the height of the chairs, the color of the set, the way a candidate's tie was knotted, the position of the cameras, the color of the candidates' suits, the timing, etc. Even newspapers that criticized the debates because of television's superficiality included articles which analyzed audiovisual elements and aspects of the performances: "Aznar's makeup. Too bright [...] suits had to be in plain dark colors, without a brooch in the tie, and no distracting cufflinks" (*El Mundo*, 1993c, May 25). Full articles were dedicated to the rules, the body language, the negotiations, the aesthetics of the candidates, the television set, and other technical issues: "How was it possible that, having the most advanced technology, they were unable to divide the screen?" (*El País*, 1993d, June 1), "we were surprised by scenery, the lighting" (*ABC*, 1993d, June 1). Thus, all three newspapers devoted broad spaces to analyze the audiovisual and performative elements reminiscent of the entertainment business in the debates, though they differed in the degree to which they praised or criticized that the debates were such a TV spectacle.

Newspapers from the UK also tended to associate televised debates with entertainment, or with mere political machinations. The main argument used when judging televised debates as negative events was that they led to the mediatization of politics and to a fascination with maneuverings and performative elements that left little room for serious discussions of important policies. Nevertheless, despite being the most widespread perception, it was not unanimously shared among the three newspapers. The *Daily Mail* and *Guardian* were particularly critical, while the *Daily Express* did not express disapproval over the show business dimension of the televised debates.

The *Daily Mail* insistently condemned it: "Last night's TV debate [...] was a hyper-hyped media event [...] invested heavily in staff and resources [...] the scale of such waste" (2010a, April 16). To support the view that televised debates had a negative impact on politics, an article concluded that the greatest British leaders would have failed, should they have participated in televised debates, because "these debates provide no real guide to a politician's capacity to govern [...] superficial eloquence has nothing to do with the great leadership" (2010g, April 30). Critical reviews of the debates even extended to the *Daily Mail*'s cartoons. Nevertheless, despite the criticism, the *Daily Mail* paid close attention to some of the audiovisual elements, such as audience figures and polls (2010b, April 16; 2010d, April 17; 2010e, April 24), as well as the performance of the candidates: "Mr. Clegg looked straight at the camera, kept one hand in his pocket" (2010c, April 16), "Cameron wore so much make-up" (2010h, April 30). Even the debate moderator's outfit was commented upon: "Dimbleby was banned from wearing his favorite tie for the debate because it clashed with the set" (2010h, April 30).

The notion that televised electoral debates are closer to TV shows than to politics was also expressed by *Guardian*: "the debate now is primarily about means, not ends" (2010b, April 16). Journalists expressed their contempt for televised debates by comparing them to popular TV shows: "Let's be honest: the nearest analogy is actually The X Factor" (2010c, April 16). Although to a lesser extent than the *Daily Mail*, *Guardian* also dedicated pages to the performative aspects of the debates: "Brown, never able to fix the camera with his gaze" (2010g, April 30), "Check out the set. All red and blue and jagged [...] the floral tie of Sky moderator" (2010e, April 23).

The *Daily Express* barely mentioned topics in the debate's agenda and mostly focused on performative elements: "A much better show by the Tory leader" (2010d, April 23), "Mr. Clegg sweating profusely [...] relaxed hand gestures became wild and stabbing [...] the tone of his voice rose several notes higher [...] the aggressive and wooden performance" (2010e, April 30). Whole articles were dedicated to talking about the body language and acting mistakes of the candidates (2010b, April 16; 2010c, April 16).

Contrary to perceptions in the UK and in Spain, in the US, debates were expected to entertain the audience. The three American newspapers represented the televised debates as political spectacles and a good show from candidates was highly valued: "Mr. Bush once chastised Mr. Gore for breaking the rules and speaking out of turn, it was then when the candidates stepped outside the lines that the debate came to life" (*New York Times*, 2000g, October 19), "The audience was giggling, chuckling – even guffawing – at the theatrical exchanges that brought this debate to life in ways the first two encounters, for all their substance, never achieved" (*Washington Post*, 2000f, October 18), "Bush and Gore were so polite they were boring" (*Washington Post*, 2000d, October 13), "Candidates show their spirit in St. Louis. Last of presidential debates is marked by a return to confrontational tone" (*The Wall Street Journal*, 2000e, October 18).

In American newspapers, performance issues were also approached. However, no newspaper criticized these elements as a negative aspect of the televised debates. They focused on facial expressions, body language, and reactions to the opponent's speeches, and analyzed them as strategic elements for winning the debate: "They steered clear of personal criticisms" (*New York Times*, 2000b, October 4), "Gore ventured close to the borderline of the pedantic [...] his theatrical sighs" (*Washington Post*, 2000e, October 13), "their problems lie not on emotional ground, but in their communication skills (Mr. Gore) and cognitive abilities (Mr. Bush)" (*The Wall Street Journal*, 2000d, October 12). Despite the fact that these aspects were examined, American newspapers dedicated most of their articles to substance. *The Wall Street Journal*'s concern about economic issues should be noted. It studied in detail the effects of policies not only on the federal budget, but also on families' budgets (2000a, October 4; 2000b, October 12).

In Spain, the way that the televised debates were represented in fact also had to do with overall perceptions of US politics, at least partially. Newspapers mentioned the US as a reference concerning televised electoral debates, though not necessarily with a negative connotation: "It is an imitation. It looks like Clinton's stuff, but smaller. Our candidates are shorter, TV presenters are younger..." (*El Mundo*, 1993c, May 25), "Aznar was Kennedy and González Nixon" (*ABC*, 1993a, May 25). But, occasionally, it also led to a narrative on the erosion of the political system due to a dominant media culture, which implied disapproval over the spread of the North American model: "We gamble it all in the debate, in the TV show, the ludo, the sketch and the boxing ring set [...] no matter how decisive these kind of debates have been in America" (*El Mundo*, 1993c, May 25).

In the UK, perceptions of the US played a relevant role as well. As we have observed, British media expressed severe criticism against entertainment culture leading politics, which *Guardian* also linked to the US: "all anyone remembered from the American debates were the 'jokes and the gaffes'" (2010a, April 16), "Their [American] culture of spin has poisoned our political system" (2010f, April 30). When the BBC's chief political adviser, Ric Bailey, analyzed the reasons for the delay in bringing televised debates to the UK, he points out how critical their perception of American politics was. The US is depicted as having a rather inferior and shallow brand of democratic politics. It remains at the heart of the suspicion that holding television debates between those who aspire to lead us is peculiarly inappropriate to our parliamentary democracy – "un-British" and even a touch vulgar (Bailey, 2012, p. 46).

Effects of Newspaper Representations on Candidates' Televised Behavior

Beyond critiques, discussions, and controversies with regards to the televised debates, newspapers also displayed elements and points of views that revealed what they considered to be most relevant in winning an electoral debate. A remarkable consequence of the newspapers' representations is that they may have highly influenced candidates' behaviors during subsequent rounds of televised debates, especially in Spain and the US. In their representations of the second rounds, newspapers highlighted how candidates had modified their behavior. Most of them changed their performances according to previous newspapers' representations of their performances.

In the analyzed press articles, critical mistakes were typically attributed to language and a candidate's appearance or behavior, but not to policies or other issues of substance. Mistakes with regard to political content never appeared in the headlines, and they were scarcely mentioned overall. The media did not check whether figures mentioned were correct, with the exception of *The Wall Street Journal*. In most cases, the press put the weight of its critiques and praise on mistakes or victories of performative elements.

In the Spanish media, rhetorical belligerence was positively valued as a criterion in declaring a winner: "Aznar was good. [...] he was appropriate and even cruel" (*El Mundo*, 1993d, May 25). In addition, the impression that the candidates had been trained for the debate and had studied relevant details was considered praiseworthy from the point of view of the journalists: "the People's Party candidate had facts and numbers. He had practiced" (*El Mundo*, 1993e,

May 25), "Aznar went to the debate better trained, he provided a big quantity of numbers and facts" (*ABC*, 1993c, May 25). It is interesting to notice that the use of numbers was examined as a strategy, yet the information itself that the data provided was not remarked upon.

The Spanish socialist candidate, Felipe González, was considered a skillful politician, who stood out because of his communication skills. Newspapers expected him to train for the debate, to make use of facts and figures, and to show a more aggressive attitude. However, he did not do so, and thus his opponent, Aznar, who was not very skilled in communication, was proclaimed the winner: "Aznar was a surprise [...] Felipe was the favorite [...] but he was not able to reply" (*El Mundo*, 1993b, May 25), "Aznar worked harder, he was trained" (*El País*, 1993c, May 25), "As in the Bible, David-Aznar defeated Goliath-González" (*ABC*, 1993b, May 25).

Facing the second round of TV debates, González seemingly took the newspapers' reactions into consideration and applied their advice: "He [González] showed another character [...] looked to the camera [...] more aggressive and dynamic" (*El Mundo*, 1993g, June 1), "González was aggressive [...] Aznar was paralyzed [...] he went to the debate with facts and more aggression" (*El País*, 1993e, June 1), "González corrected his mistakes" (*ABC*, 1993e, June 1).

In the UK, rhetoric seemed to be important to *Guardian*. It observed candidates' communication skills, stylistic resources and their use of vocabulary: "He's a good orator [...] he laughed inappropriately from time to time [...] He had a creative, relatively popular piece of policy which, if presented well, could have made life difficult for the other two, but he botched the presentation" (2010d, April 16), "He spoke a technocratic language" (2010g, April 30). Both the *Daily Express* and the *Daily Mail* focused on body language as relevant details in declaring a winner: "Mr. Brown's aggressive stance [...] was a big turn-off for voters [...] The Tory leader [...] looked nervous" (*Daily Mail*, 2010c, April 16). In an article titled "Brown, Cameron and Clegg: What lies behind their smiles," the *Daily Express* declared a winner by pointing to the leaders' smiles: "It was Liberal Democrat leader Nick Clegg – winner of the live TV debate – whose smile was the most pleasing to see" (2010c, April 16). They even considered the influence of the prime minister's physical attributes: "Brown is heavily built with a square jaw and thick eyebrows – he comes across as much more powerful" (2010b, April 16).

In the UK's case, the impact of newspapers' representations on candidates' behavior was not as apparent as it was in the case of Spain. Contrary to Spanish newspapers, British ones did not criticize any particular element or point out serious mistakes in the first round of debates. However, we can assume that the fact that all the candidates were deemed as having done their best, according to the selected newspapers, had its own impact on their behavior during the following rounds. They barely modified their strategies and, indeed, newspapers noticed how candidates insisted on using the same strategies for all three rounds with minimal changes. David Cameron continued to display confidence and Nick Clegg kept the same attitude as in the previous debates. Although Gordon Brown's performance was not criticized, in the second round he appeared slightly more aggressive and determined, probably since the newspapers had praised these attitudes shown by Cameron and Clegg. "Brown's improved performance was notable [...] he was the first of the big party leaders to land a blow directly on Clegg" (*Daily Express*, 2010d, April 23), "The Prime Minister also yesterday launched a fresh attack" (*Daily Mail*, 2010f, April 24).

While communication skills were given a lot of importance in the British candidates' performances, for American newspapers these skills were not as big of a priority. Quite the contrary, at some moments they were judged as a negative quality, especially by *New York Times*, where candidates with communication mistakes or mispronunciations gained their support: "Vice President Al Gore [...] behaved in a similarly encyclopedic fashion [...] Mr. Bush less fluent than the vice president, [...] gave incomplete replies [...] Mr. Bush had done well enough" (*New York Times*, 2000d, October 4), "Some of his [Bush's] phrasing revealed him to be less articulate and less precise with language than Gore (though this may not really matter to voters)" (*Washington Post*, 2000d, October 13), "Mr. Bush accused Mr. Gore of using 'phony numbers' and 'fuzzy math' to oppose his tax cuts" (*The Wall Street Journal*, 2000e, October 18). The reasoning displayed by *New York Times* in their praise of Bush was that, because of his problems on stage, he looked more spontaneous and closer to the American citizens (*New York Times*, 2000b, October 4).

The US candidates appeared to pay attention to the newspaper representations. First of all, Al Gore's strategy, which focused on his political qualifications and knowledge, was abandoned in the second round, as he had been harshly criticized for this by journalists. As we have seen, he was depicted as pretentious. In the second round, he made an effort to show a humble attitude and to avoid using too many figures: "Mr. Gore, chastened by criticism over the last week, wanted to be less off-putting" (*New York Times*, 2000f, October 12), "A significant change in style and tone from the initial presidential debate, particularly for Mr. Gore" (*The Wall Street Journal*, 2000c, October 12), "Gore was clearly under more pressure tonight, given the post-debate criticism" (*Washington Post*, 2000c, October 12).

Despite having been declared victor by the newspapers in the first debate, Bush's advisors were also mindful that his seeming lack of knowledge, highlighted by these newspapers, could damage the candidate in the long run, and, therefore, their strategy was slightly modified. In the second round, Bush started to use references to laws and facts in order to show his political knowledge. He paid more attention to grammar and spelling as well: "Mr. Bush was rummaging through a trove of big words [...] He also went through a roll call of Middle Eastern countries [...] he even mentioned Viktor Chernomyrdin [...] and managed to pronounce his name correctly [...] Mr. Bush wanted to look smarter" (*New York Times*, 2000e, October 12), "Bush showed he was able to use big words like 'abrogate' and 'egregious'" (*Washington Post*, 2000d, October 13).

Discussion

Two of the three examined series of debates were the first ever televised electoral debates among prime ministerial candidates in their countries, i.e., in Spain and the UK. However, the overall representation of this first-time event was very different in each country. While Spanish newspapers assured their public that televised debates improved democracy, British newspapers showed doubts about whether these would have any positive impact, to the point that some of them even considered televised debates to be damaging to the British democratic system.

Unlike in the UK, the debates in Spain were not considered to be a means of political strategy but rather a democratic right. That Spanish newspapers should represent these televised debates as an improvement in the political system was an indication of the influence of previous long-standing experiences of dictatorship. Political debates in front of TV cameras were not only a political event, but a symbolic event that signified a departure from a legacy of political censorship and lack of freedom of expression. Televised debates were perceived "as a requirement for belonging to Western political culture" (Rospir Zabala, 1999, p. 78).

In the UK, the press stated that televised debates were more likely to damage its political system. This narrative was usually justified through a negative perception of the US and its dominating show business culture. On the one hand, some newspapers highlighted that televised debates strengthened candidates and, therefore, would tend to "presidentialize" the British system. On the other hand, televised debates were thought to transform politics into entertainment. The British press shared the view that television reduces politics into a gameshow and prioritizes image over substance.

In American newspapers, there was not an explicit debate about the impact of televised debates. Nevertheless, newspapers displayed an opinion when representing them. Televised debates were judged as positive, and what's more, newspapers considered them the purest political event, where candidates could communicate their proposals without the influence of advertising.

Spanish newspapers notably focused their attention on candidates' performances, writing about the candidates' clothes or the set lighting. If one takes into consideration that the debates were perceived favorably, this tendency might be explained as a result of fascination toward a new and unfamiliar political event.

Although British print media also faced a new political event, the newspapers' and tabloids' representations responded to a different reasoning. Considering that the televised debates were perceived so negatively, especially in

Guardian and the *Daily Mail*, this positioning might have become a self-fulfilling prophecy: As televised debates were considered superficial events and closer to TV shows, the coverage of the debates was not judged to be the proper place for deep discussion on political substance. Therefore, newspapers represented televised debates as superficial political events.

We can reach a similar, yet opposed explanation regarding the coverage of American newspapers. Since the American press widely claimed the televised debates to be the best moment to learn about candidates' proposals, they considered them to be the best opportunity to address significant discussions on substance.

A remarkable difference between UK and US newspaper representations could be seen in their assessments of candidates' behavior and rhetoric, revealing two different understandings of politics. Media from both countries, unlike Spanish newspapers, examined performance elements as political strategies. Nevertheless, while in the UK a candidate's outstanding communication skills were highly appreciated, in the US these were not particularly valued. Al Gore was able to prove he had profound knowledge of administration and policies; however, he was accused of being pedantic and even of bullying the other candidate. Despite the fact that descriptions of George W. Bush as lacking cognitive abilities were published in all newspapers, displaying doubt and making mistakes were not judged as negative qualities for a candidate for presidency since he appeared closer to the common citizen.

Finally, the potential influence of the media could be particularly observed in two of the studied cases. Spanish and American newspapers reflected behavioral changes that candidates put into practice during the second rounds of televised debates in accordance with critiques or praise expressed in previous media representations. In Spain, Felipe González presented facts and figures, showed that he had been trained for the debate, and displayed a more aggressive attitude. American candidates also changed their performances, especially Al Gore, who made an effort to appear less informed and categorical. In the case of the UK, the absence of relevant changes in candidates' behavior can be understood in a similar way; in view of the fact that newspapers did not report any relevant mistakes, candidates had no incentive to modify their behavior.

Conclusions

Televised debates from three different countries have been analyzed with the aim of disclosing whether similarities of newspaper representations, and therefore of meaning, exist. The second aim was to assess whether newspapers' representations had had an impact on candidate behavior and whether it was possible to detect any signs of their influence by analyzing subsequent newspaper representations.

Regarding the first research question, the results indicate that televised debates are not interpreted with a universal meaning, since very different representations were displayed. Although these three countries shared a similar approach to democratic values and procedures, newspapers' representations remarkably varied, and differences between the three countries ran deep. The Spanish and British cases are especially enlightening. Even though both Spanish and British journalists were facing a new political event, their assessments were diverging. Historical processes and the political context might explain the different perceptions. In the US, by contrast, the existence of televised debates is not a topic for discussion in newspapers as they have become part of the essential events in an election campaign. In fact, American press journalists judged televised debates to be the best chance for politicians to show their proposals without interference from outside opinions or advertising. Contrary to this perception, British newspapers evaluated televised debates to be superficial political events, where questions of substance could barely be discussed.

To reach the second aim, newspapers' representations of candidate performances were analyzed. Newspapers judged them based on different elements depending on the country and, sometimes, the newspaper. However, general patterns could be observed. In Spain, there was a general tendency to value rhetorical belligerence and the use of facts and figures. In the UK, rhetorical skills, attitudes, and the body language of candidates were discussed by newspapers. In the US, the ability of candidates to display humility and an identity similar to that of the typical American citizen was notably appreciated. In all three cases, newspaper representations of the second rounds of TV debates suggested that previous newspaper representations had influenced candidate behavior.

This research represents a preliminary approach to the representation of a particular political event in the media. On the one hand, the results indicate that the meaning of political events is not necessarily shared by relevant actors in democratic societies, such as newspapers. On the other hand, we can observe that newspapers have the potential to modify the behavior of candidates via their representations of debates.

Television is probably the mass medium that has had the greatest impact on the representation of political events and, therefore, on their significance. In this study, we could observe that, despite analyzing press documents, the ability of the candidates to project a positive image on television was critical in how the debates were represented.

Given the influence of mass media to shape public opinion, research into media's representations of political events, processes, or institutions can provide us with a better and more detailed understanding of their meaning in specific societies. Further comparative studies that analyze the evolution of the representation of different political events in different types of media would help us to better understand to what extent the media may shape reality.

Studies on the impact of new technologies will also shed light on possible changes in the representation of political events. There is no doubt that social networks are new channels of communication which affect our everyday habits.

However, it remains to be determined whether social networks can really provide possible alternative representations to those given by the media, or whether they are simply new ways for the media to maintain a high degree of power over the representation of reality.

Notes

1. The general election was held on June 6, 1993. The Socialist Party, led by Felipe González, obtained the largest number of votes.
2. The general election took place on May 6, 2010. The Conservative Party, with David Cameron as its leader, won the largest number of votes.
3. The presidential election was held on November 7, 2000. The Republican candidate, George W. Bush, obtained victory and was elected president of the United States.
4. According to information from audience databases: the Oficina de Justificación de la Difusión in Spain (Edo, 1995), the Audit Bureau of Circulations in the UK (*Guardian*, 2010h, May 14), and the Alliance for Audited Media in the US (*New York Times*, 2000a, May 2).
5. The list of primary sources for this chapter can be found in the online Appendix.

References

Bailey, R. (2012). *Squeezing out the oxygen – or reviving democracy? The history and future of TV election debates in the UK*. Oxford: Reuters Institute for the Study of Journalism.
Benoit, W. (2014). *Political election debates*. Plymouth: Lexington Books.
Benoit, W. L., & Currie, H. (2001). Inaccuracies in media coverage of the 1996 and 2000 presidential debates. *Argumentation & Advocacy*, 38, 28–39.
Benoit, W. L., McHale, J. P., Hansen, G. J., Pier, P. M., & McGuire, J. P. (2003). *Campaign 2000: A functional analysis of presidential campaign discourse*. Lanham, MD: Rowman & Littlefield.
Burton, M. J., Miller, W. J., & Shea, D. M. (2015). *Campaign craft. The strategies, tactics and art of political campaign management*. Santa Barbara, CA: Praeger.
Coleman, S. (2011). *Leaders in the living room: Prime ministerial debates of 2010: Evidence, evaluation and some recommendations*. Oxford: Reuters Institute for the Study of Journalism.
Drew, D., & Weaver, D. (1991). Voter learning in the 1988 presidential election: Did the debates and the media matter? *Journalism Quarterly*, 68(1/2), 27–37.
Edo, C. (1995). La prensa diaria de Madrid en la década de los 90. *Estudios sobre el mensaje periodístico*, 2, 127–139. [in Spanish].
Ericson, R. V., Baranek, P. M., & Chan, J. B. L. (1989). *Negotiating control: A study of news sources*. London: University of Toronto Press.
Fridkin, K. L., Kenney, P. J., Gershon, S. A., & Woodall, G. S. (2008). Spinning debates: The impact of the news media's coverage of the final 2004 presidential debate. *Harvard International Journal of Press Politics*, 13(1), 29–51.
Gallego Reguera, M. (2017). *El regreso del cara a cara en España: La organización profesional de los debates electorales televisados entre candidatos a la presidencia del gobierno en 2008*. (Doctoral thesis). Complutense University of Madrid. [in Spanish].
Gerbner, G. (1964). Ideological perspective and political tendencies in news reporting. *Journalism Quarterly*, 41, 495–508.
Goffman, E. (1974). *Frame analysis: An essay on the organization of experience*. New York: Harper & Row.

Graber, D. A., & Dunaway, J. (2015). *Mass media and American politics*. London: Sage/CQ Press.
Hellweg, S. A., Pfau, M., & Brydon, S. R. (1992). *Televised presidential debates*. New York: Praeger.
Herman, E. S. (2000). The propaganda model: A retrospective. *Journalism Studies*, 1(1), 101–112.
Herman, E. S., & Chomsky, N. (1988). *Manufacturing consent: The political economy of the mass media*. New York: Pantheon.
Hodgetts, D., & Chamberlain, K. (2014). Analysing news media. In U. Flick (Ed.), *The SAGE handbook of qualitative data analysis* (pp. 380–393). London: Sage Publications.
Kinder, D. R. (2003). Communication and politics in the age of information. In D. O. Sears, L. Huddy, & R. Jervis (Eds.), *Oxford handbook of political psychology* (pp. 357–393). New York: Oxford University Press.
Kraus, S. (2011). *Televised presidential debates and public policy*. New York: Routledge.
Krippendorff, K. (2004). *Content analysis: An introduction to its methodology*. Thousand Oaks, CA: Sage.
Lanoue, D. J. (1991). The turning point: Viewers' reactions to the second 1988 presidential debate. *American Politics Quarterly*, 19(1), 80–95.
McCombs, M. E., & Shaw, D. L. (1972). The agenda setting function of mass media. *Public Opinion Quarterly*, 36(2), 176–187.
McQuail, D., & Windahl, S. (1981). *Communication models for the study of mass communications*. London: Longman.
Noelle-Neumann, E. (2010). *La espiral del silencio: opinión pública*. Barcelona: Paidós. [in Spanish].
Patterson, T. E. (1980). *The mass media election: How Americans chose their president*. New York: Praeger.
Pinilla García, A. (2004). Historia y medios de comunicación: La reconstrucción periodística del 23F. In C. Forcadell (Ed.), *Usos de la historia y políticas de la memoria* (pp. 218–234). Zaragoza: Prensas Universitarias de Zaragoza. [in Spanish].
Robinson, P. (1999). The CNN effect: Can the news media drive foreign policy? *Review of International Studies*, 25(2), 301–309.
Rospir Zabala, J. I. (1999). La globalización en las campañas electorales. In A. Muñoz Alonso, & J. I. Rospir Zabala (Eds.), *Democracia mediática y campañas electorales* (pp. 55–88). Barcelona: Ariel. [in Spanish].
Ross, M. H. (1992). Television news and candidate fortunes in presidential nominating campaigns: The case of 1984. *American Politics Quarterly*, 20, 69–98.
Schreier, M. (2012). *Qualitative content analysis in practice*. London: Sage.
Schreier, M. (2014). Qualitative content analysis. In U. Flick (Ed.), *The SAGE handbook of qualitative data analysis* (pp. 170–183). London: Sage Publications.
Tuchman, G. (1977). The exception proves the rule: The study of routine news practices. In P. H. Hirsch (Ed.), *Strategies for communication research*, Vol. 6 (pp. 43–62). Beverly Hills, CA: Sage.
Van Dijk, T. A. (2009). News, discourse, and ideology. In K. Wahl-Jorgensen, & T. Hanitzsch (Eds.), *The handbook of journalism studies* (pp. 191–204). New York: Routledge.
Wiesner, C., Haapala, T., & Palonen, K. (2017). *Debates, rhetoric and political action*. London: Palgrave Macmillan.
Wolf, M. (1987). *La investigación de la comunicación de masas*. Barcelona: Paidós. [in Spanish].

ND# 9

NON-SYSTEMIC FACTORS UNDERLYING RAPID CHANGE IN GENDER-BIASED MEDIA FRAMING OF FEMALE POLITICIANS

2009 and 2013 Israeli Newspaper Election Coverage

Gilad Greenwald and Sam Lehman-Wilzig

Introduction

In her article based on qualitative analysis of popular television channels and print newspapers, Lachover (2015) noted the continuation of a journalistic trend over the past few years: Studies have found a moderate change in the traditional media's gender framing of female politicians. The elections for the Knesset (Israeli Parliament) in 2013 witnessed positive reportage of senior, female politicians – especially two who were running at the head of their respective major parties as candidates for prime minister: Shelly Yachimovich ("Labor") and Tzipi Livni ("*Ha'tnuah*"). Lachover (2015, pp. 451–452) found that during that election campaign these two female campaigners' visibility was higher than expected (most of the time they were at the center of the media's agenda), and were "framed" as serious political actors and not as "women" – a real electoral alternative to the (male) incumbent prime minister, Benjamin Netanyahu.

Conversely, four years earlier, Gedalya, Herzog, and Shamir (2011, pp. 238–239) used a similar qualitative methodology to study the journalistic framing of Tzipi Livni over the 2009 Knesset election campaign when she also was a candidate for prime minister, but they found deep gender bias here, portraying her as lacking experience, unable to make decisions, and in general framed stereotypically with "feminine traits," e.g., "young child," "puppet on a string," and "incessant talker."

Our present study is based on the belief that it is important to understand the reasons underlying the significant change in such a relatively short time frame. Intuitively, it would seem that deep social, historical, or journalistic change could not occur over a mere four years. Thus, it is possible that time-specific, particular, non-systemic elements – perhaps even "random" – brought about this transformation.

To that end, the present study undertakes a direct comparative analysis of these two elections and their leading female candidate(s) for the highest office.[1] The first part compares the journalistic output of these two campaigns statistically, to ensure the veracity of the above studies' findings. The second, main section analyzes and explains the significant differences between the two elections' coverage in light of *particular* political changes occurring before and during the 2013 election period.

Thus, this study contributes to the theoretical literature on journalistic gender framing that has tended to focus on large-scale, societal factors, to the detriment of localized/temporary changes that also might bring about more balanced gender-framing coverage. Moreover, if so, then practically this study could point the way to decreasing or eliminating media gender stereotyping without waiting for glacial, widespread societal changes to emerge.

Framing as a Function of Deep Social, Historical, and Professional Journalism Processes: The General and Gender-Related Contexts

Media Framing Theory: Reality Representation or Construction?

"Media framing" theory is one of the central theories in contemporary mass media studies, enabling us to investigate deep-rooted strata in the media's imagery of events, social groups, and personalities (Scheufele, 1999). Framing belongs to the tradition of "powerful media effects," claiming that the media have the power to *create* authoritative interpretations, based on narratives, enabling the consumer to read, identify, label, and process the news for long-term memory and future use (Entman, 2004; McQuail, 2005).

Nevertheless, scholars that belong to the "cultural" school of communication studies tend to emphasize the role of framing in *reflecting* and maintaining society's de facto, collective ideology and culture, and not only the media's design and (re)construction of social reality. Carey (1989), a doyen of the "cultural approach to communication," defined mass communication as a cultural ritual, its main task being preserving existing social order and meaning. This approach sees media framing as the use of generally accepted symbolic meaning in order to reinforce social reality as humans recognize and live it. The resulting collective convergence preserves society over time through common beliefs representing each culture in its era.

The General Context: Framing as an Expression of Deep-Rooted Processes in Society and the Media

Here are several examples of this based on Carey's approach. Socio-politically, Roeh and Cohen (1992, p. 46) found that Israeli television focused on the

Israeli viewpoint through premeditated framing of the Palestinians' First Intifada, e.g., in repeated interviews with Israeli army officials who described the fighting from their standpoint. American TV, on the other hand, systematically presented the Palestinian narrative, e.g., through quotes from Palestinian sources who called the fighting "slaughter by the Israeli conquest" (ibid., 1992, p. 47).

From a historical perspective, framing is described as a function of changes, developments, and long-term historical progress. Israeli and Rosman-Stollman (2014, pp. 205–207) analyzed the long-term changes in the image of Israel's soldiers within the Israeli press. They concluded that, in line with general historical trends in civil–military–media relations, the image of the Israeli soldier changed from the "manly fighter" in the 1980s (p. 200) to "mom's son" or a "sitting duck" in the 2000s.

Within a journalistic context, one can note how the newspaper's work processes/professional norms influence media framing, taking into account that numerous studies have found different frames between mass-popular and elite-quality newspapers. The former frame the news emotionally from an individual perspective, with lots of colorful pictures and large headlines. Their subject matter tends to be "soft news," often without the paper feeling any social responsibility to present constructive values but rather driven by the profit motive (what sells).

Conversely, elite papers' framing involves "harder" stories, from a societal perspective, accompanied by data and statistics to support their opinions. The headlines are more serious, with more restrained pictures and colors. These papers' interests are viewed as concomitant with society's interests: raising awareness of social problems and covering groups that are usually found on the margins of the public agenda. They perceive themselves as "democracy's watchdog," and in general tend to be found on the liberal side of the spectrum (Baum & Jamison, 2011; Bloch-Elkon & Lehman-Wilzig, 2007; Lehman-Wilzig & Seletzky, 2010).

The Gender Context: How News Framing of Female Politicians Serves as an Expression of Patriarchal Culture?

The general assumption that the media reflect social norms and widely held opinions among the public offers a possible explanation of journalists' tendency to project male hegemonic values. Thus, "gender bias" in the media against women in politics is widespread: Several studies have found that their news visibility is lower than their male counterparts. Additionally, it was found that when female politicians are covered they are then presented in stereotypical fashion, in many ways reflecting the public's attitudes regarding women (Kittilson & Fridkin, 2008; Lawrence & Rose, 2009).

For example, the media emphasize the externalities of female politicians unlike their male counterparts – appearance as reflected in women's dress, makeup, age, weight, and general sexuality. Indeed, many times they are portrayed as sex objects, something completely irrelevant to the job they are vying for (Gedalya et al., 2011; Heldman, 2009).

The traditional roles of women in the family arena, as mothers and wives, offer frequent examples of framing coverage as well. In general, female politicians are perceived as active in, and identified with, the two spheres of activity – the private-familial and the political-public. Therefore, the media's tendency is to emphasize personal relationships of female politicians and their competency in the private sphere, for example, vis-à-vis their children, their partner, and in the context of household chores (Lachover, 2015; Trimble & Gerrits, 2013). Sometimes even the woman's choice to serve as a public servant is framed in the media as a betrayal of her more "natural" emotional role, thus often portrayed as a "masculine woman" (Gedalya et al., 2011; Meeks, 2012).

Another trend found to be a significant feature of media framing of female politicians is their identification with what is called "feminine issues." When voters evaluate candidates for leadership positions, they tend to seriously consider the candidates' ability to deal with various political issues. A binary separation between "feminine issues" and "masculine issues" is a traditional social practice that assumes women may better address issues that are perceived as identifying with the emotional and "therapeutic" roles assigned to them in traditional society, such as welfare, education, the environment, health, and women's rights. Men, on the other hand, are perceived in tribal society as breadwinners and as providers of protection and security, and therefore today, too, political issues such as economics, security, and foreign policy are socially defined as "masculine topics" (Heldman, Carroll, & Olson, 2005; Meeks, 2012; Rudman & Kilianski, 2000).

Other studies have found that female politicians tend to be portrayed in the media as pioneers and as those who, by entering the public sphere, upend rigid, social norms. Such "novelty" labels are frames of coverage that present events or people as "historical," "new," or "different." Female politicians and leaders are defined as "breaking [or undermining] norms" in many countries, developed and developing alike, encouraging journalists to describe them, positively or negatively, as pioneers (Meeks, 2012).

Finally, studies have found that media framing also tends to reflect gender divisions regarding "character traits." In this context, it has been demonstrated that the media often identify female politicians with perceived "feminine character traits," such as empathy, sensitivity, sincerity, altruism, dependency, and passivity. Conversely, male politicians are identified with "masculine character traits," such as resilience, assertiveness, aggressiveness, independence, and self-confidence (Banwart & McKinney, 2005; Meeks, 2013). Not only do gender stereotypes and dichotomies express the mood of patriarchal society, but they can also strengthen, concretize, and regularize the idea that women are passive, dependent, indecisive, and therefore not "tough" enough to lead or win a political campaign (Kahn, 1994; Lawrence & Rose, 2009).

In light of the considerable differences in media framing of female politicians as a result of deep social or historical processes, several studies have focused on this question. For example, a study by Kittilson and Fridkin (2008) examined differences in media coverage of women based on political culture and governmental system. By comparing the framing of female politicians in the American, Australian, and Canadian media, the two researchers concluded that parliamentary democracies, in which citizens are required to vote for the party rather than directly for the candidate, witness a smaller, media gender bias than presidential democracies, where voting tends to be based on the candidates' personal traits.

Cohen-Avigdor (2000) examined historical differences in the coverage of Knesset members in 1959, 1977, and 1996 in Israeli women's magazines. Her main finding indicated that, in light of the overall improvement in the status of women in Israel, women's magazines framed politicians more stereotypically in the 1950s than in the 1990s, i.e., a positive historical trend was found. Elsewhere and conversely, the opposite trend emerged in an American study: Heldman (2009) found that media coverage of the candidates for US vice president (Geraldine Ferrero's 1984 case study compared with Sarah Palin in 2008) actually became more sexist as the years passed.

Despite different findings in these studies, the common denominator is that all found long-term factors, such as cultural and political differences or historical changes, also reflected in the gender differences within the media's framing of politicians.

Media Framing of Female Politicians as an Expression of Non-Systemic Factors

In contrast to the aforementioned studies, a few others have noted non-systemic, short-term, and sometimes "immediate" or "incidental" factors that might shape and fundamentally change the media's framing of female politicians. For example, several studies have examined the connection between stereotypical coverage and the *type of political position* that the politician holds or is a candidate for. They found that there is indeed a fundamental difference between the way in which the media report on a junior politician as opposed to a senior politician, with media practices such as "symbolic annihilation" more common in the coverage of junior politicians than other practices (such as undermining stereotypical social norms) that are more frequently found in coverage of senior politicians (e.g., Lachover, 2015; Meeks, 2012).

Other studies have dealt extensively with the question of how much coverage of women depends on the particular *gender of the journalist or the editor* in question. Various studies have found different trends on this issue, some inconclusive and others even contradictory (Limor & Lavie, 2004; Meeks, 2013).

Finally, Meeks and Domke (2016) argued that, while past studies examining female politicians in the media have focused on comparisons with male politicians, recent years have been characterized in the United States by accelerated entry of women into the political arena, providing an interesting new standpoint: election campaigns in which a *number of women face each other* ("woman-versus-woman" elections). Their findings indicate that, in such situations, along with some continuity of stereotypes, there are also more complex images of these politicians, i.e., balanced gender characteristics, and the topics that interest them – "male" as well as "female" issues that concern them.

The importance of the small number of these last studies stems from their indicating that even "local" elements (and not only long-term ones) – i.e., the position the female politician is vying for, the gender of the journalist, and the number of women candidates for the position – can influence media framing of politicians. The need to research this aspect at a deeper level constitutes the starting point of the present study.

The Study

Purpose

The purpose of this study is to demonstrate whether, and to what extent, media framing of candidates for political leadership roles depends on local, non-systemic, temporary, and even "accidental" factors. We examined the coverage of Tzipi Livni and Shelly Yachimovich, who competed at the head of their respective parties to become Israel's prime minister in the 19th Knesset (2013) election campaign, comparing that coverage to Livni's coverage during the previous 18th Knesset (2009) election campaign, then the only woman with any real chance of becoming prime minister. We assume that Yachimovich's 2013 candidacy, side by side with Livni, can explain at least some of the different findings regarding the gender-bias media framing in these two election campaigns.

Comparing the coverage of two female senior politicians in two political campaigns is particularly appropriate for our purpose. As past studies have shown, gender framing in Israel's 2013 elections was significantly different from that in the 2009 elections; moreover, there is an inherent assumption that differences between the reportage in two successive campaigns do not stem from significant, deep, historical and politico-cultural processes undergone by Israeli society or its media during such a short time frame.

Two main research expectations operationalize the general purpose of this study:

Expectation 1 (E1): Based on past qualitative research findings presented in this study's introduction (Gedalya et al., 2011; Lachover, 2015), it is expected that media framing of Tzipi Livni and Shelly Yachimovich in the 19th Knesset election campaign (2013) will be more realistic and less stereotypical than in the 18th Knesset campaign (2009), also on the quantitative-statistical level.

Expectation 2 (E2): Although "long-term" variables such as political culture and the status of women in Israel,[2] as well as the norms of journalistic work, will feature prominently in the framing of both campaigns, "specific" variables that depend on the transitory political-gender situation in the 2013 campaign – among them (according to Meeks & Domke, 2016) the fact that two women ran concurrently for the position of prime minister – will be prominent in this election campaign alone, thus constituting a significant factor behind the "normalization" of gender coverage, in that election campaign's media coverage specifically.

Research Design

This study examines the media's coverage of two candidates for the post of prime minister of Israel in two printed newspapers, one mass-popular and the other quality-elite, during the 2009 (Livni alone) and 2013 (Livni and Yachimovich) elections: Tzipi Livni was elected chairwoman of the *Kadima Party* in September 2008 and ran for the post of prime minister of Israel during the election campaign for the 18th Knesset (2009). After an eight-year ministerial career, she was serving at the time of the campaign as deputy prime minister and foreign minister (The Knesset, 2017).

In the run-up to the elections for the 19th Knesset (2013), Livni served as the head of a new centrist party called *Ha'tnuah* and re-declared her candidacy for prime minister in November 2012. Shelly Yachimovich, the chairwoman of the "Labor" party (its first woman candidate since Golda Meir 43 years earlier) and the head of the opposition in the Knesset, also declared her candidacy for the post of prime minister. This was the first election campaign in Israel's history in which two women announced their candidacy for the post (The Knesset, 2017).

In order to ensure comprehensive and reliable examination of the coverage, two newspapers were selected: the prestigious *Haaretz* and the popular *Yedioth Ahronoth*. From the 1970s until 2010, *Yedioth Ahronoth* was the largest circulation newspaper in Israel (today it is second in distribution, but its main rival, *Israel Hayom*, is free).

Haaretz has a much smaller readership (about 7.5% in 2009 and 6.5% in 2013), but it is the only paper in Israel with consistent high-quality journalism (Rivak, 2012). The decision to focus on these two specific newspapers stems mainly from the fact that both of them constitute a fairly reliable "prototype" of the two types of journalistic styles in the theoretical literature: popular versus quality journalism.[3] An examination of the differences in gender coverage between these two sources can serve as the basis for another discussion of "long-term variables" that shape media coverage of Israeli politicians (in addition to the cultural elements listed in note 1).

Content analysis was carried out on Livni's 2009 media coverage in *Yedioth Ahronoth* and *Haaretz*, as well as Livni's and Yachimovich's 2013 election coverage in those two newspapers – in both campaigns, over the last three months before election day. In this context, it is highly important to note that, when the elections in Israel are advanced (as happened in 2013), an accurate voting day's date is set exactly three months in advance.

The news items were selected using search words that included the full names of the politicians during the selected period, assuming that an article carrying the candidate's full name emphasized more direct and essential aspects of her political campaign. The final sample produced 1,572 items (including reports, articles, interviews, opinion pieces, pictures, and cartoons): 690 items in the case of Livni (2009); 408 items in the case of Livni (2013); and 474 items in the case of Yachimovich (2013).

Each item was analyzed and coded as an individual unit, scoring it "present" (= 1) or "absent" (= 0) for each of nine gender frameworks reviewed in the literature mentioned in the above theory section:

1. Relating to the *body or appearance* of the politician, including weight, age, ethnic/racial affiliation, and direct reference to appearance (clothing, haircut, makeup, etc.);
2. *Sexual innuendos* of any kind;
3. Reporting on the *family*, including: assigning the woman to the domestic sphere (e.g., the politician's photo in her kitchen), referring to her marital relationship or motherhood in a family context, and referring to the "price" the family pays because of her career;
4. Mention or hints regarding *character traits* that are perceived as "feminine," including emotional, passive, dependent, childish, silliness, frivolous, and manipulative;
5. Allusions to (or direct mention of) the woman politician's "loss of femininity" or "*masculinity*" due to choosing a public life: "aggressive," "tough," "bad," or "bitch";
6. Coverage of *issues* that are perceived as "feminine," because the candidate is a woman: health, education, environment, and nursing, (e.g., "as a mother, she is required to take care of our children's education"); questioning her ability to deal with issues that are perceived as "masculine," such as economics, security, and foreign policy;
7. Dealing with breaking/undermining social norms (*novelty labels*), by challenging/questioning the existing social order – for example: "first," "historical," or "pioneering";
8. Remarking on the candidate's inferiority, lack of experience, *incompetence* for political leadership, or her seemingly low chances of being elected, e.g., "amateur," "unfit," "beginner";
9. Covering her political activities promoting *women and their rights*, or her positions and activities regarding feminist issues.

Data coding reliability was tested using a random sample of 26% of the items ($n=413$) for two coders. Based on *Scott's pi* statistical test, the reliability of the coding ranged from pi = 0.91 in the coverage frames of "breaking social norms" and leadership "inexperience/competency," to pi = 0.74 for the frame of "feminine character traits."

In order to examine the significance of the differences between the coverage of the two election campaigns, we performed *logistic regression*. This statistical test is specifically suitable for examining significant differences where there is a two-level categorical dependent variable, i.e., binary (in this case, presence = 1 or absence = 0 of a gender element in the news item).

The comparison between Livni's test case (2009) and Livni's and Yachimovich's (2013) was made possible by summing up the number and percentage of reports that included gender coverage, and then separating the findings according to year of coverage (2009/2013) and name of the politician (Livni/Yachimovich).

Findings

E1 predicted that, in view of previous qualitative findings, significant gender bias would be found in the coverage of senior politicians in both of these elections, with the 2013 Livni vs. Yachimovich campaign displaying somewhat less stereotyping.

The findings were surprising in their intensity, especially in light of the close temporal proximity between the two elections. As detailed in Table 9.1, in almost all of the categories examined and codified – with the exception of the categories "sexual innuendo" and "dealing with women's rights" (in the case of Yachimovich only) – the coverage of Livni and Yachimovich (2013) in the two newspapers was far less stereotypical (in most frames, on the level of: $p < 0.01$) than Livni's (2009) campaign coverage.

E2 predicted that "long-term" variables, such as political culture and the status of women in Israel, as well as journalistic norms, would be reflected in the coverage of the two election campaigns, whereas "more specific" variables (e.g., the fact that in the 19th Knesset elections two female candidates were vying for the post of prime minister) would be reflected in this campaign alone with more realistic coverage of the candidates. The following two subsections offer a detailed explication of the findings in this regard.

Long-Term Variables: Political Culture and Type of Press

First, in the category of "feminine issues," in the election campaign for the 18th Knesset the newspapers offered constant skepticism and disdain for Livni's ability to deal with Israel's security issues. For example, from *Yedioth Ahronoth*: "Netanyahu is a strong leader, he will take better care [than her] of Israel's security and economy" (October 28, 2008); from *Haaretz*: "She cannot deal

174 Gilad Greenwald and Sam Lehman-Wilzig

TABLE 9.1 Percentage and number of news reports with gender coverage frames: Livni (2009) vs. Livni and Yachimovich (2013) in *Haaretz* and *Yedioth Ahronoth*

Gender coverage frame	Livni (2009)	Livni (2013)	Yachimovich (2013)
Appearance	38 (5.5%)	4 (0.9%)**	5 (1.0%)**
Sexually suggestive	13 (1.8%)	5 (1.2%)	7 (1.4%)
Family labels	45 (6.5%)	15 (3.6%)*	16 (3.4%)*
"Feminine" character traits	88 (12.7%)	28 (6.8%)**	13 (3.6%)**
Masculinity/loss of femininity	23 (3.3%)	2 (0.4%)**	1 (0.4%)**
"Feminine" issues	44 (6.3%)	9 (2.2%)**	17 (3.6%)*
Breaking social norms	70 (10.1%)	18 (4.4%)**	27 (5.7%)**
Lack of experience/competency	107 (15.5%)	16 (3.9%)**	9 (1.9%)**
Women's rights/feminism	28 (4.0%)	4 (0.9%)**	23 (4.9%)

Notes
For Livni's coverage (2009), $n=690$ (531 for *Haaretz*; 159 for *Yedioth*). For Livni's coverage (2013), $n=408$ (286 for *Haaretz*; 122 for *Yedioth*). For Yachimovich's coverage (2013), $n=474$ (345 for *Haaretz*; 129 for *Yedioth*). Significant gaps between coverage of Livni (2009) compared to coverage of Livni and Yachimovich (2013), as demonstrated by the logistic regression test: $*p < 0.05$. $**p < 0.01$ (marked on the side of the *low* findings).

with the Iranian nuclear program" (October 28, 2008). Figure 9.1 (*Haaretz*, January 2, 2009), for example, shows a caricature of Israel's defense minister, Ehud Barak, standing and confidently observing the fighting between Israel and Gaza, while Foreign Minister Livni remains behind, looking outside and trying to defend herself with an umbrella.

Despite significant differences between the two elections in this category (though less significant than for the other categories), the practice of disrespecting

FIGURE 9.1 Cartoon by Eran Wolkovsky, January 2, 2009
Source: © *Haaretz* Daily Newspaper Ltd. All Rights Reserved.

Media Framing of Female Politicians **175**

the political and security capabilities of female politicians in the foreign and security spheres was still found in the 19th Knesset election coverage. For example, in *Yedioth Ahronoth*: "Yachimovich is forced against her will to deal with the issue of national security, although she is in her element much more regarding the Institute for National *Social* Security." And also: "She is running away from the political issue because of her lack of understanding in this field" (January 15, 2013). *Yedioth Ahronoth* mocked Livni's talks and meetings with the Palestinians: "She was photographed with Condoleezza Rice and sent to idle talks, seminar talks with Abu Ala [Palestinian prime minister], while Olmert[4] [Israel's prime minister] secretly negotiates with [Palestinian president] Abu Mazen" (December 3, 2012).

Second, regarding the variable of "undermining social norms," in the 2009 elections, profound religion and state factors in Israel were evident in presenting and framing Livni as a "pioneer." This was due to the refusal of the ultra-Orthodox *SHAS Party* to form a government with Livni, and also because of the vandalizing of her campaign posters in Jerusalem. Some representative examples from *Yedioth Ahronoth*: "What disturbs Eli Yishai [*SHAS* leader] is that Livni is a woman"; "*SHAS* is not ready for a woman prime minister" (October 26, 2008); "The ultra-Orthodox community says her pictures [posters] will not be hung" (October 28, 2008).[5]

Although the effect of religion–state relations on the candidates' "pioneering" media frame experienced a decline during the subsequent election campaign, they were still present. For example, Figure 9.2 (*Haaretz*, January 10, 2013) shows the

FIGURE 9.2 Cartoon by Amos Biderman, January 10, 2013

Source: © *Haaretz* Daily Newspaper Ltd. All Rights Reserved.

ultra-Orthodox *SHAS Party* feeling satisfied with Yachimovich's TV campaign commercial in which she appears to be working in her kitchen.

In addition to these religion–state influences, certain differences were also found in terminology, journalistic language, and general framing between the two types of newspapers examined. These were expressed in the coverage of the two election campaigns in several respects. For example, regarding "sexual innuendo," in the 2013 campaign, the popular *Yedioth Ahronoth* newspaper described the political struggle between Livni and Yachimovich as "mud wrestling":

> It turns out that the (speculative) combination of these two women ignites the imagination, especially the masculine. I heard quite a few people mentioning the possibility that they would go together as a cool option, interesting female power, a sexy combo, as if they were talking about a pornographic movie and not a political potentiality.
> *(October 15, 2012)*

Similarly, in the 2009 elections *Yedioth Ahronoth* placed great emphasis on Livni's appearance. For example, in a series of articles, in main news headlines and supplements, the paper made intensive use of colorful images and sensational headlines "comparing" Livni's appearance to that of an anonymous "clone." This practice, or anything similar, was not found in any form in *Haaretz*.

Finally, the gaps in "journalistic language" were also reflected in Livni's consistent portrayal as being an inexperienced and unqualified leader, especially during the 2009 elections. *Yedioth Ahronoth*, for example: "She has no experience whatsoever" (December 19, 2008); "She is like a gymnast who was just ordered to work out from outside the school" (February 2, 2009). By comparison, although *Haaretz* also challenged Livni's qualifications, the paper generally displayed social responsibility in its descriptions, e.g., "She did not accumulate enough authority and political experience" (October 26, 2008).

Non-Systemic Variables: Candidate Multiplicity, Livni's Second Campaign, Political Collectivization

In contrast to the "long-term" elements reviewed to date, shaping the coverage of Livni and Yachimovich to a certain extent in the two election campaigns, there are three more "local" (non-systemic) elements specifically relevant to the 2013 politically gendered campaign, to a large extent contributing to the "normalization" of these women candidates' political framing.

First, regarding "undermining social norms," the significant gap of at least 5% between Livni's "breakthrough" in 2009 and her relatively minimal coverage in this category in 2013 can best be explained by the fact that now two women – Livni and Yachimovich – were running for prime minister, greatly reducing the "attribution of pioneering" to the phenomenon. For example, in 2009 the theme of Livni's "uniqueness" in comparison to her male colleagues, a motif that was "lost" in the 2013 elections, was very conspicuous: "The machos are not willing to have a woman lead them"[6] (*Haaretz*, December 4, 2008); "She is the only woman who heads a party in Israel" (*Haaretz*, February 3, 2009); "She is a woman in a manly world" (*Yedioth Ahronoth*, February 10, 2009). On the other hand, the few "undermining social norm" frame examples of the two candidates in 2013 underscored the fact that this was the first time in Israeli history that two women ran concurrently for the position, as can be seen in this quote: "This is the golden age of female leadership in Israeli politics" (*Haaretz*, November 29, 2012).

Second, regarding the variable "lack of experience/leadership (in)competency," large differences (12% or more) were found between the two elections. This finding is particularly surprising for Livni, because most of her ministerial experience came from the years 2001–2008 (i.e., before the 2009 elections), whereas in 2009–2012 she served mainly in parliamentary positions (in the opposition). Here, there is somewhat of a "mismatch" between objective reality and the media's framing. One of the explanations for this phenomenon is the specific fact that the 19th Knesset elections were the second consecutive election period in which Livni ran for the post of prime minister; this seems to have positioned her as a more naturally legitimate candidate for the post compared to the previous campaign. Moreover, in 2013 her two main rivals on the center-left, Yachimovich and Yair Lapid (who established a new, popular party), were competing for that position for the first time. Thus, *Haaretz* opined: "Of the three, she [Livni] has the most impressive experience" (January 14, 2013).

Third, the media's coverage of the 2009 election campaign was characterized by highly personalized discourse (which tends to be more "genderized"), mostly focusing on the two main candidates for the post of prime minister: Livni and Likud chairman Benjamin Netanyahu. As proof, the most prominent slogan of this election campaign, also expressed in media framing, was "Tzipi or Bibi." On the other hand, in the 2013 elections the severe split within the center-left camp on the Israeli political map and the inability of the three main leaders of this camp (Livni, Yachimovich, and Lapid) to create a bloc in order to block a right-wing government, led to collective, non-gender discourse regarding the three center-left politicians together, even occasionally relating to them as one unit. For example, *Yedioth Ahronoth* reported:

> The three met in order to coordinate positions ahead of the elections, and especially how to act if Benjamin Netanyahu formed the next government.
>
> (*January 7, 2013*)

> Lapid bit into *Kadima* and Livni bites Lapid, and if this whole chain of food would band together, it could attain something; together they are a power. If this entire food pyramid works together it will get places.

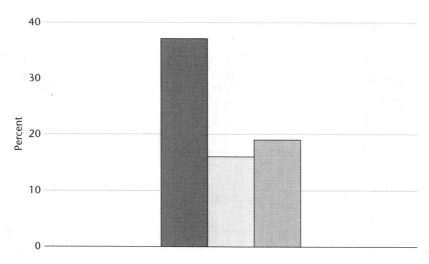

■ Livni's coverage (2009)   □ Livni's coverage (2013)   ▨ Yachimovich's coverage (2013)

FIGURE 9.3   Percentage of total reports with gender coverage: Livni (2009) compared to Livni and Yachimovich (2013) – *Yedioth Ahronoth* and *Haaretz*

Together they have strength; each separate are as the remnants of a cannibal meal on the platform of an inflated ego.

(December 2, 2012)

In short, as noted, the differences found between these three cases were surprising: 37% of items about Livni in 2009 included gender coverage, compared to only 16% of her items and 19% of Yachimovich's items in 2013 (Figure 9.3). Generally, Israeli newspapers clearly showed much lower gender bias toward both candidates in the latter campaign for three main reasons: The two women simultaneously vied with each other to serve as prime minister; it was Livni's second run for PM; and the political discourse as a whole was less personal and more collective.

Discussion and Conclusions

This study adds to the increasing recognition by political and gender communication scholars (e.g., Heldman, 2009; Raicheva-Stover & Ibroscheva, 2014) that media framing of female politicians is not dichotomous and binary, but depends in part on context and the ad hoc nature of various elements and variables, as well as the professional norms of media types. The particular novelty of the present study, as expressed in some of its findings, is that more local-specific – and even "random" – components related to a given political-gender situation can influence and shape these framing processes in a fundamental, even radical, manner.

Regarding these two elections, and in line with our first expectation based on similar findings in past studies, we found that Livni's media coverage in the 2009 elections was much more biased and gender-stereotypical than hers and Yachimovich's coverage four years later. Our second expectation was also validated: These differences were not a result of fewer (or changed) "long-term" variables, such as political culture/the status of women in Israel or journalistic work norms – clearly expressed in both election campaigns, and certainly not having undergone any significant change in the relatively short period of time between the two elections – but rather stemmed from "non-systemic" variables that were particularly relevant to the political situation surrounding the 2013 elections.

In the context of culture, Jerby (1996) pointed out that the dominance of military values and norms within Israeli society, as well as the security problems and the ongoing external conflict with which Israel copes, constitute a hindrance to the status of women in the country. This is because the military arena is traditionally considered a "domain for men only" and tends to emphasize dichotomies and gender separation. Indeed, in accordance with Carey's (1989) cultural approach, it is not surprising that the Israeli media reflected this sociopolitical ethos when covering the two female politicians in both campaigns, mainly through the frame of "feminine issues." A clear expression of this was the contempt for Livni's ability to deal with the Palestinian issue or the Iranian nuclear program, as well as the argument that Yachimovich is better suited to deal with National *Social* Security than with National Security. It is important to emphasize that, in this context, media frames not only reflected shared culture, but also (at least potentially) actively undermined the political electability of the two female politicians, especially in view of the fact that Israeli voters tend to relate to security issues as highly salient when evaluating political leaders (Izraeli, 1999).

Similarly, the relationship between religion and state in Israel, and its negative effects on the status of women in Israel (Samooha, 2000; Kimmerling, 2004), was another deep-rooted cultural aspect in framing the two election campaigns, especially regarding coverage of "undermining social norms." In the 2009 elections, for example, coverage of the ostensible refusal of the ultra-Orthodox parties to form a coalition with Livni (after many years in which these parties served as the fulcrum in Israeli politics), as well as the vandalizing of Livni's image in ultra-Orthodox neighborhoods, reflected continuing difficulties for women's status in Israel, more than in other liberal democracies. Indeed, Figure 9.2 shows that these difficulties continued to be a dominant feature of media framing even during the 2013 elections, indicating that political culture in Israel did not experience significant change between these two election campaigns. In other words, cultural issues like these did not constitute a mechanism that can explain the significant differences between the two campaigns.

A similar conclusion was reached in the context of journalistic work norms: The popular *Yedioth Ahronoth* used a far more sensational journalistic language, with stereotypical frames, than did the quality paper *Haaretz*. In 2009, *Yedioth Ahronoth* consistently emphasized Livni's appearance and used "graphic" terminology in describing her experience, whereas in 2013 it described the political struggle between Livni and Yachimovich as "mud wrestling," emphasizing sexist elements. Therefore, in both elections, *Yedioth Ahronoth* reflected the tendency of popular newspapers to include "soft news" and to use biased descriptions, even in covering substantive political issues (Baum & Jamison, 2011; Bloch-Elkon & Lehman-Wilzig, 2007), thus undermining the seriousness of these two women's candidacy.

In contrast to the "long-term" elements associated with political culture and the norms of journalistic work, it appears that "unstructured" elements and variables related to the particular political situation of the 2013 elections may explain, at least in part, the "normalization" of Livni's and Yachimovich's media coverage of this campaign (as shown in Table 9.1 and Figure 9.3) – in line with the second research expectation.

This accords with the findings of the Meeks and Domke (2016) study: In situations where there is a large number of women candidates for a senior political position, a certain gender balance tends to be created (mixing "feminine" content with "masculine"), along with continuity of some stereotypes. In other words, on the one hand it is possible to see a certain "adaptation" of previous gender-biased framing to the new and unique situation in which two senior politicians are candidates for the post of prime minister. For example, instead of framing the female politician as a pioneer, the new "pioneering" frame relates to the phenomenon of a multiplicity of women candidates. Perhaps to make up for such "framing moderation," there was even a certain radicalization in the stereotypical and sexist language regarding these two politicians. On the other hand, overall, the findings show that when two female candidates run for a senior position at the same time, media framing becomes increasingly balanced and in certain respects even "gender-blind."

Second, as noted in previous research (e.g., Kahn, 1994) and as this study reinforces, there is no essential connection between a candidate's experience or objective competence and the media's assessment of her (in)ability to lead as a woman. Again, in the 2009 elections, Livni was presented (sometimes sarcastically and disparagingly) as lacking basic experience and leadership skills, but not so in the ensuing election (despite Livni not having gained any more executive experience in the interim). The reason for this lies in the simple fact of her having already run for office, i.e., she became "regularized" in the eyes of the media. In this context, it is also important to note that in 2009 Livni's main rivals were Ehud Barak and Benjamin Netanyahu, two former prime ministers perceived by the Israeli public as candidates with bona fide political and security authority. In contrast, in 2013 Livni's main rivals were perceived to be

Yachimovich and Lapid: two first-time candidates for prime minister and leaders with no significant ministerial experience. In other words, although the (female) politician's frame as "inexperienced" is not always reality-based on concrete facts, in a political situation where the candidate vies against inexperienced rivals, her frame may well become fairer and more balanced without having really done anything in the political realm since the last election frame.

This study also offers an important caveat to findings in studies such as Kittilson and Fridkin (2008), who concluded that political systems and "personal" government systems (e.g., direct presidential elections) tend to create gender-biased media frames, whereas collective/parliamentary governance tends to be more party-oriented and therefore naturally more "gender blind." Such studies do not take into account the fact that personal or collective discourse may sometimes be a function not only of long-term bureaucratic-governmental elements, but also of a given "random" political situation. As shown above, the 2013 campaign – especially on the center-left – was characterized by more collective and less personalized discourse, compared with the 2009 election campaign ("Tzipi or Bibi") that constituted a clear example of the general personalization process Israeli politics had been undergoing (Rahat & Sheafer, 2007).

In other words, the temporary dominance of collective politics on the center-left side of the political map in the 2013 elections, stemming from the multiplicity of parties that competed for the same electorate, led to a significant reduction in gender elements in the media's discourse surrounding Livni and Yachimovich. Thus, although systemic factors continue to be important, these findings emphasize the converse element of a temporary political constellation that can neutralize personalization and concomitantly reduce a measure of typical stereotyping. It is important to note that these differences can also explain the large difference between the number of items collected in the coverage of these two campaigns: 690 items for Livni in the more "personal" 2009 elections, compared to "only" 408 and 474 for Livni and Yachimovich (respectively) in the 2013 more "collective" campaign.

Strong confirmation of this conclusion can be found in Lachover's (2015) study. As mentioned, she too found gender framing of Livni and Yachimovich in the 2013 elections to have improved. However, in the same study she also examined changes in media representation of more junior politicians, i.e., Knesset members who ran within the various party lists. In contrast to our two senior female politicians, her study concluded that the media frame during the 2013 elections continued to be biased and stereotyped for those junior (female) parliamentarians. Thus, it can be assumed that at least part of the "normalization" of Livni's and Yachimovich's framing can be explained by factors that were uniquely relevant to the political-gender situation created at the level of *senior* Israeli politics for that election, and not by any deeply rooted social, historical, and/or media changes over such a short four-year period.

In summation, from a social-scientific and a normative perspective, the conclusions of this study indicate that in addition to "long-term" elements, such as embedded political culture and long-standing journalistic norms that influence the media's gender-biased framing, there are also elements and variables that we tend to perceive as "superficial" but at times can have just as much impact on the degree of such framing: the number of women running simultaneously for a senior political position; the number of consecutive campaigns in which women run for top political posts, as well as the identity of their main political rivals; and the number of parties competing for the same electoral niche during a given political campaign. Therefore, in order to really understand media gender framing, any comprehensive future study of this subject will have to look closely at local, temporary elements – in addition to the usual systemic elements that have traditionally served as the only (or main) variables that were taken into account.

Notes

1. In the 2009 campaign, there was no additional female candidate for prime minister other than Livni.
2. Among the cultural difficulties and obstacles affecting women's status, and the perception of their roles and rights in Israel, Jerby (1996) detailed the following elements: (1) The influence of religion on politics and the resulting exclusion of women from the public-political sphere (see also Kimmerling, 2004; Samooha, 2000); (2) Militarism, and security problems, that tend to neutralize the capabilities of women in this masculine arena; (3) The difficulty of perceiving women as political representatives due to circumstances related to the dominance of traditional, Israeli patriarchal culture compared to other liberal democracies.
3. See an explanation of the differences between the two types of newspapers in the literature review section.
4. Ehud Olmert served as prime minister of Israel during Livni's tenure as deputy prime minister and minister of foreign affairs.
5. As mentioned in Jerby's (1996) book, the ultra-Orthodox parties believe in male exclusivity when it comes to political representation. These parties are often criticized in Israel for not having female representatives in their party lists. In 1955, for instance, the "Agudat Yisrael" and "Hapoel HaMizrachi" religious parties refused to support Golda Meir for Tel-Aviv mayor, and as a result Meir lost the campaign. Another type of example is no less relevant today: Pictures of women are never shown in the ultra-Orthodox press.
6. This refers to the two candidates for prime minister in the 2009 elections: former defense minister Ehud Barak and (then) opposition leader Benjamin Netanyahu.

References

Banwart, M. C., & McKinney, M. S. (2005). A gendered influence in campaign debates? Analysis of mixed-gender United States senate and gubernatorial debates. *Communication Studies*, 56, 353–373.

Baum, M. A., & Jamison, A. (2011). Soft news and the four Oprah effects. In R. Y. Shapiro, & L. R. Jacobs (Eds.), *Oxford handbook of American public opinion and the media* (pp. 121–137). New York: Oxford University Press.

Bloch-Elkon, Y., & Lehman-Wilzig, S. (2007). Media functioning during a violent international crisis: Differences between elite and popular press coverage of American policy in Bosnia (1992–1995). In H. Nossek (Ed.), *Media and political violence* (pp. 119–142). Creskill, NJ: Hampton Press.

Carey, J. (1989). A cultural approach to communication. In J. Carey (Ed.), *Communication as culture: Essay on media and society* (pp. 13–36). London: Routledge.

Cohen-Avigdor, N. (2000). Female politicians compared to male politicians in the Israeli women's journalism: Media framing in times of political campaigns, 1959, 1977, 1996. *Patuakh*, 4, 45–75. [In Hebrew].

Entman, R. (2004). *Projection of power: Framing news, public opinion and US foreign policy*. Chicago, IL: The University of Chicago Press.

Gedalya, E., Herzog, H., & Shamir, M. (2011). Tzip(p)ing through the elections: Gender in the 2009 elections. In A. Arian, & M. Shamir (Eds.), *The elections in Israel, 2009* (pp. 165–195). London: Transaction.

Heldman, C. (2009). From Ferraro to Palin: Sexism in media coverage of vice presidential candidates. *2009 American Political Science Association Annual Meeting*, Toronto, Canada, September 3–6.

Heldman, C., Carroll, S. J., & Olson, S. (2005). She brought only a skirt: Print media coverage of Elizabeth Dole's bid for the Republican presidential nomination. *Political Communication*, 22(3), 315–335.

Israeli, T., & Rosman-Stollman, E. (2014). From a "fighter" to "mom's little boy": The Israeli soldier in the eye of journalism. *Studies in Israeli and Modern Jewish Society*, 24, 185–209. [In Hebrew].

Izraeli, D. (1999). *Sex, gender, politics: Women in Israel*. Tel Aviv: Hakibbutz Hameuchad. [In Hebrew].

Jerby, I. (1996). *The double price: Women status and military service in Israel*. Tel Aviv: Ramot. [In Hebrew].

Kahn, K. F. (1994). The distorted mirror: Press coverage of women candidates for statewide office. *The Journal of Politics*, 56(1), 154–173.

Kimmerling, B. (2004). *Immigrants, settlers, natives: Israeli state and society between cultural pluralism and cultural wars*. Tel Aviv: Am Oved. [In Hebrew].

Kittilson, M. C., & Fridkin, K. (2008). Gender, candidates' portrayals and election campaigns: A comparative perspective. *Politics & Gender*, 4(3), 371–392.

Lachover, E. (2015). Signs of change in media representation of women in Israeli politics: Leading and peripheral women contenders. *Journalism*, 18(4), 446–463.

Lawrence, R. G., & Rose, M. (2009). *Hillary Clinton's race for the White House: Gender and the media on the campaign trail*. Boulder, CO: Lynne Rienner Publishers.

Lehman-Wilzig, S., & Seletzky, M. (2010). Hard news, soft news, "general" news: The necessity and utility of an intermediate classification. *Journalism*, 11(1), 56–97.

Limor, Y., & Lavie, A. (2004). Feminization of Israeli media: Recent updates. *2004 Israel Communication Association Annual Meeting*. [In Hebrew].

McQuail, D. (2005). *McQuail's mass communication theory*. London: Sage Publications.

Meeks, L. (2012). Women candidates for executive political offices and news coverage. *Journal of Communication*, 62, 175–193.

Meeks, L. (2013). All the gender that's fit to print: How *The New York Times* covered Hillary Clinton and Sarah Palin in 2008. *Journalism & Mass Communication Quarterly*, 90(3), 520–539.

Meeks, L., & Domke, D. (2016). When politics is a woman's game: Party and gender ownership in woman-versus-women elections. *Communication Research*, 43(7), 895–921.

Raicheva-Stover, M., & Ibroscheva, E. (2014). *Women in politics and media: Perspectives from nations in transition*. London: Bloomsbury.

Rahat, G., & Sheafer, T. (2007). The personalization(s) of politics: Israel, 1949–2003. *Political Communication*, 24(1), 65–80.

Rivak, H. (2012). *TGI: Israel Hayom is getting stronger, passing Yedioth Ahronoth*. Retrieved from *Walla News* website: https://b.walla.co.il/?w=/3050/1715485. [In Hebrew].

Roeh, I., & Cohen, A. (1992). One of the bloodiest days: A comparative analysis of open and closed television news. *Journal of Communication*, 42(2), 42–55.

Rudman, L. A., & Kilianski, S. E. (2000). Implicit and explicit attitudes towards female authority. *Personality and Social Psychological Bulletin*, 26(11), 1315–1328.

Samooha, S. (2000). Israel's regime: Civil democracy, non-democracy or ethnic democracy. *Israeli Sociology*, B(2), 565–630. [In Hebrew].

Scheufele, D. A. (1999). Framing as a theory of media effects. *Journal of Communication*, 49(1), 103–122.

The Knesset. (2017). *All past and present members of the Knesset*. Retrieved from https://knesset.gov.il/mk/eng/mkdetails_eng.asp. [In Hebrew].

Trimble, L., & Gerrits, B. (2013). Is it personal? Gendered mediation in newspaper coverage of Canadian national party leadership contests. *The International Journal of Press-Politics*, 18, 462–481.

10

OLD TRAPS AND NEW PROSPECTS

Gendered Media Images of Leading Female Politicians in Germany as Evidence for a Contested Modernization of Gender Knowledge

Dorothee Beck

Introduction

During the electoral campaign preceding the last general election in Germany on September 24, 2017, some news media outlets constructed a remarkable contrast between Chancellor Angela Merkel and two of her challengers. Merkel's proverbial sobriety and lack of excitement became the basis for a representation of the chancellor as a bored political leader weary of office. In contrast, Christian Lindner of the Liberal Party (Freie Demokratische Partei, FDP) and Cem Özdemir of the Green Party (Bündnis 90/Die Grünen) were depicted as ambitious, can-do men of action.

The Social Democrats (SPD) faced a crushing defeat in this election. Party chairman Martin Schulz did not have to resign, but in the election of the SPD-parliamentary group's chairperson, he had to defer to Andrea Nahles, former minister of labor and social affairs. Nahles had long been seen as an ambitious party leader-to-be. Now the media had begun to refer to her as the SPD-*Trümmerfrau*, the "rubble woman," who would have to sort out the mess the men had left behind.[1]

The media, through agenda-setting, have a considerable influence on what a society judges to be important issues and problems, as well as on its perception of public persons. Moreover, it does not simply reproduce reality, but constructs its own images of reality (Hall, 2000, 2004). In contemporary democracies, people tend to perceive politicians mainly through media. Thus, for women (and men) aspiring to power, media coverage is crucial (Jarren & Donges, 2011). Obviously the media still generates at least part of its informative power through gendered images. Essentialized images of what male or female politicians should or should not be circulate widely.

In the present contribution, I reflect upon the contested modernization of such media images, focusing on the metaphor of the "political mother" as well as on change and persistence in hegemonic political masculinity in media representation. My case studies are Chancellor Merkel, Defense Minister Ursula von der Leyen, Hannelore Kraft (prime minister in North Rhine-Westphalia from 2010 to 2017), and the two male 2017 general election candidates mentioned above. I will combine reflections upon these cases with the findings of my earlier study of media coverage of female candidates for prime minister in state-level German election campaigns between 1994 and 2012 (Beck, 2016b).

After some explanatory notes regarding the theoretical framework, basic research assumptions, and methodology, I will outline my findings about gendered media images of three groups of female political candidates: (1) the three early candidates, who did not have a realistic prospect of gaining office, (2) the first female German prime minister, Heide Simonis, and (3) the two more recent candidates, both of whom had at least an opportunity of winning office. This forms the basis for a discussion of the mother as the dominant metaphor for women in politics. The subsequent question of whether or not a modernization of political masculinity can be observed will refer to media coverage of the 2017 general election and give an outlook of useful further investigation.

Theoretical Framework and Previous Studies

Gender Knowledge: A Useful Concept for the Perception of Gendered Media Images

The concept of gender knowledge (Dölling, 2005) provides a useful framework to discuss both change and persistence in gendered media coverage. In my study, media representations are interpreted as a collective stock of social knowledge. Knowledge, according to the sociology of knowledge (Keller, Reichertz, & Knoblauch, 2013; Reichertz & Soeffner, 2004), "is anything that is recognized as knowledge in a society, including the totality of the symbolic order – from meaningful everyday practices to very specific scientific knowledge" (Moser, 2010, p. 13). Gender knowledge is one part of this shared body of knowledge; it establishes guidelines, for instance, regarding what women and men are, how they act, and what they look like. It includes discursive knowledge as well as incorporated knowledge. The latter can be defined as natural, unconscious attitudes that are not reflected upon but are visible in everyday practices (Dölling, 2005). Collective knowledge drives the social process of news production, publication, and reception (Hall, 2000, p. 133).

Dölling discusses the situations in which traditional gender images in the media are being affirmed, updated, or revised. She suggests that changes in collective gender knowledge depend on discursive stocks of knowledge, and occur as a result of the utility that these changes have in a specific social field. Because traditional gender relations are predominantly still the main knowledge basis in the media (as well as in society), modernized gender knowledge will be brought forward only when it corresponds with the specific media outlet's political stance or when the producers assume some other advantage, such as higher expanded audience, a personal career in the media, or something else (Beck, 2016a, p. 69).

Most studies of gendered images in the German media argue that femininity is still constructed as the second gender in the political field. Gender and femininity are equated and made visible, whereas masculinity is the unspoken norm, and thus does not have to be addressed explicitly in the media (e.g., Gnändiger, 2007; Holtz-Bacha & Koch, 2008; Lünenborg & Röser, 2012; Pfannes, 2004). This can be interpreted as an aspect of traditional collective gender knowledge. Starting in 2005, Merkel's chancellorship encouraged the production of multiple studies of gendered media representations in Germany. In contrast to other female political leaders, beginning with her candidacy for chancellorship, Merkel as a candidate, as well as in chancellorship, avoided the essentialized double bind between a "real" woman and a "true" political leader (Jamieson, 1995). During the 2005 general election, Holtz-Bacha and Koch (2008) identified this as the "Merkel-Faktor." This could have been due to Merkel's effort to avoid being labeled a *female* political leader; besides, the dignity of the office may simply have obscured the importance of gender.

Scholz focused on another aspect of gendered media images in the beginning of Merkel's chancellorship, and identified a change in political masculinities. She proclaimed the political alpha-male's[2] death, and stated that the era of political leaders who seek predominance and tend toward self-staging in the media had come to an end (Scholz, 2007, p. 110). This statement corresponds with Merkel's proverbial sobriety, pragmatism, and unpretentiousness (e.g., Brosda, 2013, p. 69). Lünenborg and Maier (2012) also focus on masculinities. They argue that masculinity has shifted from the unspoken norm in the political field to a visible gender that can be debated. These recent findings identify changes in gender knowledge.

Political Public and Private Spheres: From Dichotomy to Complementarity

In this chapter, the meaning and relevance of media representations for women's aspirations to power are being discussed within the theoretical framework of the relation of the public and private spheres. In classical conceptualizations (e.g., Arendt, 2010; Habermas, 1991), the two spheres are polar or dichotomous opposites. Feminist theories consider this to be a gendered hierarchy. Skills and attributes that, in classical conceptualizations, are expected in the public sphere, such as sobriety, objectivity, and reason, are regarded as masculine. Those attributes expected in the private sphere, such as empathy, care, and emotion, are regarded as feminine (Hausen, 1976). This dichotomy places women who aspire to political leadership into an essentialized double bind (Jamieson, 1995). They can be either "real" women or "true" political leaders, but not both.

Kutt (2010) and Absolu (2014) argue that Merkel's unwillingness to play the gender card added to her success. In contrast, Ségolène Royal, the socialist candidate for the French presidency in 2007, stressed her private experience as a mother of four. Most French and German media outlets did not approve of this strategy, and coverage had a largely negative tenor. In a comparison of Tarja Halonen, the president of Finland in 2006, and Angela Merkel in 2005, van Zoonen (2006) shows that both politicians avoided addressing private issues and instead held themselves to an androcentric[3] political code (List, 1986). Van Zoonen (2006) argues that, as opposed to male leaders, female politicians always risk being depreciated in media coverage of private situations. To avoid this, female leaders would have to observe the classical dichotomy of the political public and the private spheres, whereas male leaders are free to present a modern mix of political and private images.

In contrast, Lünenborg and Maier argue that personal traits attributed to the private sphere are being transferred into the political public sphere, and are thus increasingly being appreciated as indicators of political capability. For example, Gesine Schwan, the social democratic candidate for the federal presidency in 2004 and 2009, was depicted as empathetic and caring, which was seen as a positive trait for a political figure (Lünenborg & Maier, 2012, pp. 91–92).

Assumptions and Methodology

Gender, obviously, continues to be a relevant aspect of differentiation in political news media, although recent studies suggest that this is increasingly linked to specific contexts. The contextual basis of the gendering processes should verify the assumption of a contested modernization. This means that traditional gender images are replaced by more modern ones. However, the risk of a comeback to traditional gender images remains in certain contexts. There should also be more evidence for a shift in the relationship between the political public and private spheres. It should also be possible to find indications of a shift in masculinities, as described by Lünenborg and Maier.

The empirical framework used here is based in large part on my earlier study (Beck, 2016b), which includes all six of the leading social democratic state-level candidates in 11 campaigns from 1994 to 2012. Before the 2008 election in Hesse, the only party to run female candidates was the Social Democrats. It was only in 2009 that in Brandenburg the Christian Democrats nominated Johanna Wanka and the left-wing party Die Linke nominated Kerstin Kaiser. The Christian Democrat Julia Klöckner competed in Rhineland-Palatinate in 2011,[4] and Annegret Kramp-Karrenbauer, another Christian Democrat, in Saarland in 2012. The Green Party has always run with a mixed-gender duumvirate; but Renate Künast's campaign for Governing Mayor of Berlin in 2011 was the first time the Green Party ran a woman for a sole leadership position. Thus, within the time frame of the previous study (1994–2012), six Social Democrats were compared to five candidates from three other parties. The restriction of the previous study to the Social Democrats helped me to avoid any party bias in my analysis, as the media's political stance in relation to the candidates remained constant.

The study was organized around three main research questions:

1. How is female gender constructed in news media? In which contexts is female gender regarded as relevant?
2. With which patterns, attributions, framings, stereotypes, and narratives is female gender connected to political power?
3. What meaning and relevance do the findings have for women's aspirations to power?

The methods applied were qualitative content analysis (Mayring, 2010; Schreier, 2014) as well as an additional sequential analysis of selected passages following the hermeneutic sociology of knowledge (Kleemann, Krähnke, & Matuschek, 2013; Reichertz, 2013).

The analysis focused on print news media: the daily tabloid *Bild-Zeitung*, the daily quality newspapers *Frankfurter Allgemeine Zeitung* (FAZ, conservative) and *Süddeutsche Zeitung* (SZ, liberal), and the news magazine *Der Spiegel* and its web service *Spiegel Online*.[5] The database comprised approximately 400 articles published at the height of the election campaigns (about four weeks before the election), as well as an additional 50 articles about the efforts of three social democratic candidates to form a red and green minority government. The articles about the election campaigns were restricted to a maximum of ten per campaign and paper. The articles about the government-building phase were restricted to five per case and media outlet. The selection combined content-based and formal aspects (Beck, 2016b, pp. 84–85). (1) Articles of minor informative value regarding the research questions were canceled. (2) To restrict the text corpus to ten, the remaining articles were counted out (i.e., every second or third article was excluded.)

In order to include the general election in 2017 in the discussion, selected articles from several newspapers as well as from *Spiegel Online* were added. The reflection on the metaphor of the political mother is additionally based on a previously published essay (Beck, 2016a), which discussed the meaning and relevance of motherly metaphors for female politicians. I examined a variety of "political mothers." Only in Merkel's case was political leadership strengthened by this metaphor. In other cases, political power was contested.

Media Representations of Leading Female Candidates at the State Level in Germany

The Early Female Candidates: Exotic Outsiders, Poor Politicians

In addition to Germany's first female prime minister, Heide Simonis (1993 to 2005 in Schleswig-Holstein), the Social Democrats nominated three women to challenge the incumbent government leaders in general elections at the state level: Renate Schmidt (1994 and 1998) in Bavaria, Ingrid Stahmer (1995) in Berlin, and Ute Vogt (2001 and 2006) in Baden-Württemberg. But before the early years of the current century, news media did not take such female politicians' attempts to win political power seriously. Schmidt and Vogt were experienced politicians at the federal level, but they were nonetheless seen as newcomers at the state level. The media represented them as exotic, attractive, talented outsiders. Their political programs were hardly mentioned. For example, the daily *SZ* described Ute Vogt's street campaign in the city of Ulm as if a pop star like Britney Spears were to unexpectedly do her weekend shopping at Münsterplatz in Ulm:

> One or two people dare to approach and ask for an autograph. Women are startled, old ladies twitch at their husbands' sleeves. Fathers with children clap spontaneously. But it is only Ute Vogt, walking through the pedestrian streets of Ulm. She smiles and waves. And some youngsters shout: "Great! You're great!"
>
> *(SZ, March 13, 2001, p. 3)*

There is no suggestion here that Vogt's mission is an election campaign. She is compared to a pop star. The subtext is that other women are afraid that she will poach their husbands. Five years later, a similar situation was described very differently:

> At the marketplace in Kirchheim, Ute Vogt tries to get out of the defensive, arguing where there is space to argue. She talks intensely to a retired woman who is upset about Müntefering's proposal to change the legal retirement age to 67.[6] "That won't affect you anymore," she says. Listening but not bending or conceding to everybody, that is her strategy. [...] And the woman who was just shouting the loudest wishes Vogt all the best for her health and future when she says goodbye. A tiny battle in this election campaign that Ute Vogt has won.
>
> *(SZ, March 23, 2006, p. 3)*

Here, Vogt is being depicted in a political context, engaged in discussion about the legal retirement age. But she is on the defensive, and her party's prospects for the election are bad. She has to fight, and disputes with some voters. In the end, however, the woman with whom she has argued seems to feel for her.

This sequence is an example of a shift in the tenor of media coverage of a female candidate from the first to the second election, a shift that Greenwald and Lehman-Wilzig also discuss in this volume, in relation to Israeli politician Tzipi Livni. Now Vogt is no longer the exotic newcomer. Instead, she is part of the political system and is being assessed by the system's (androcentric) criteria. Prior to the first years of this century, female politicians were never seen as satisfying these standards. Ingrid Stahmer, for example, was not at all a newcomer when she became the SPD's candidate in Berlin in 1995. In fact, she was the capital's experienced senator of social affairs.[7] Thus, she did not even have the opportunity to benefit from the exotic status described above.

> At the hairdressers, the staff was already prepared to clock off. Suddenly she swept in, spontaneously but without invitation, unsophisticated and unpretentious but surrounded by cameras and scribbling reporters. "I am Ingrid Stahmer," the candidate begins, Pause. "The one on the posters. ... I thought, maybe you wanted to ask me something." The hairdressers try to smile. The silence is agonizing. "Not at the moment." ... The pharmacist also says "not at the moment," after Mrs. Stahmer has waited for a solid minute for him to sell some aspirin. When someone finally does ask something, Ingrid Stahmer displays competence without hesitation. She recites figures. She quotes clauses, paragraphs, and dashes, she interprets the constitution, she knows street names, rents, social statistics. She is patient, expert, and keen on details.
>
> (FAZ, October 20, 1995, p. 3)

In this passage, Stahmer is first portrayed as a nice, harmless woman. At the same time, the camera spotlights contradict the description of her behavior as unpretentious. When it comes to demonstrating competence, she seems to be a bureaucrat rather than a politician who presents visionary ideas for the capital.

According to the news media, it was powerful men who granted political leadership to these early candidates. Stahmer was said to be the SPD establishment's candidate. Renate Schmidt, in 1994, was presented as the Social Democrats' torch bearer in Bavaria. SZ cited a male party leader, "whose relationship with Renate Schmidt at the beginning of her career had hardly been spotless," praising her for being one of the best party leaders since World War II (SZ, September 21, 1994, p. 3). Four years later, on the eve of Gerhard Schröder's victory in the federal election in 1998, some media sources suggested that Schmidt, once again the leading candidate in Bavaria, was eager to enter the federal cabinet as a minister. But, according to these sources, Schröder did not want to appoint her to his shadow cabinet during his campaign. She had to disclaim her ambition publicly, and was depicted as a pretentious and overambitious woman. In contrast, Ute Vogt, in 2001, was represented as Chancellor Schröder's mentee and protégée, and the media predicted she would have a career in the federal government (Beck, 2016b, p. 125).

First Female Prime Minister: The Boss and the Eccentric Woman

"Women only become something when men spin out of control" (e.g., *SZ*, February 15, 2005, p. 3). This quote is ascribed to Heide Simonis, the first female state-level prime minister in Germany, in the state of Schleswig-Holstein. The statement refers to Simonis' own career. She gained office in 1993 in the middle of an electoral period when her predecessor, Björn Engholm, had to resign in the aftermath of a political scandal. This circumstance resulted in her being described as a political *Trümmerfrau*.

Simonis remained in office as prime minister until 2005 and ran in three general state-level elections (1995, 2000, and 2005). At first, the news media depicted her as the pragmatic, down-to-earth, and competent alternative to Engholm, the intellectual "high-flyer." But then they failed to find a narrative for a powerful woman. Instead they applied masculine descriptors when addressing the political leader, e.g., referring to her as "the boss," an expression which has a strongly masculine connotation in German (e.g., *SZ*, February 21, 2000, p. 3).

Feminine descriptors, by contrast, were applied when referring to the woman. Simonis was portrayed as chatty and eccentric. She spoke very fast and was said to be sharp-tongued and quick at repartee. But when it came to the woman, this competence for political debate turned into the notion of a cheeky tease in some media coverage. *Der Spiegel* described sympathetic brash behavior "on the sometimes narrow path between amusement and embarrassment" (*Der Spiegel*, 12/1996, p. 45). *FAZ*, by contrast, described her way of debating as churlishness. "The mouth, she would say, the muzzle, is her tool kit. [...] It is spluttering, grating, shavings are falling. Sometimes she slips. When she then apologizes, she is not afflicted by doubts about whether she has actually been excused" (*FAZ*, March 20, 1996, p. 3). There was also the eccentric woman wearing fancy hats and lots of finger rings, and collecting things at flea markets. In a profile, the tabloid *Bild* included a list of hobbies: "collecting! Knick-knacks, pictures, she has 80 sofa cushions, 30 hats, 380 towels..." (*Bild*, February 26, 2000, p. 2).

Strange to say, media representations of Simonis as an eccentric woman did not challenge images of her as a powerful boss. Yet Simonis' image as a powerful female political leader was contested by the construction of a gender hierarchy through bodily practices. For instance, according to *FAZ*, Chancellor Schröder embraced her whenever photographers wanted him to, "even when this gave the impression that the woman disappears behind the man" (*FAZ*, February 5, 2005, p. 3).

In 2000 and 2005, the Social Democrats focused their state-level election campaign entirely on Heide Simonis. In 2000, there was a campaign group wearing red hats, called "Heide hat's." This is a pun on words between "Heide's (fancy) hats" and the German expression "Heide hat es" (Heide has that certain something). In 2005, the SPD used posters with nothing but the logo "HE!DE" on them. Subsequently, the media reproached her and her party of using a "cult of personality" to hide the Social Democrats' lack of political vision.

In the 2005 election, the SPD, again with Simonis as leading candidate, lost votes. Yet Simonis succeeded in forming a red and green minority coalition, which should have been tolerated by the Danish minority party.[8] Yet when it came to the parliamentary election of the prime minister,[9] she lost by one vote in four ballots. This unexpected end to her career led to a backlash in media coverage. Now she was described as an old woman who would have to be helped up the stairs, who would cling to power not knowing when to step back. At home, she would have nothing to look forward to but bickering with her husband. And even worse, like other women, she would not be able to park the car, an allusion to a common stereotype about female drivers (Beck, 2016b, p. 198).

> The official car was more than a status symbol for her. "An official car with a driver means I don't have to search for a parking spot. Great – I enjoy that. Sometimes one is treated like a little queen, with a little daily attention." Soon, when she comes home from her vacation in Tuscany with her husband Udo, she will have to learn to park her Toyota herself.
> *(Bild, April 28, 2005, p. 2)*

More Recent Candidates: Femininity as a Political Trait

A remarkable change is apparent in media coverage of state-level candidates over the last ten years, including Andrea Ypsilanti in Hesse in 2008 and Hannelore Kraft in North Rhine-Westphalia in 2010 and 2012. The media represented these women as capable politicians, although their political skills at first were questioned (Beck, 2016b, pp. 164–166). In contrast to the earlier candidates, they were not "the first woman" (as leading candidate, prime minster, etc.). The explicit topic in the media was no longer female gender in the political field. However, in specific contexts, such as success or defeat, female gender in the political field was constructed through attributions of ambition, power-consciousness, or assertiveness. In addition, the notion of the *Trümmerfrau* remained. *FAZ* noted that, after the Social Democrats' defeat in North Rhine-Westphalia in 2005, Kraft had become the chairwoman of the party and their parliamentary group "without having had to prevail over male competitors" (*FAZ*, May 11, 2012, p. 3), which implied that only male competitors were real competitors.

In many depictions of success, there were gendered descriptors. *FAZ* described a situation in which Kraft was handed a bouquet of flowers after her election as prime minister of a minority government in parliament in 2010. At the same time, the paper commented that her defeated predecessor, Jürgen Rüttgers, was "puzzled when Mrs. Kraft presented him a big bouquet of flowers with ribbons in the state's colors" (*FAZ*, July 15, 2010, p. 3). The message between the lines was that, for a woman, a bouquet is appropriate, while to a man the same gift seems rather odd.

Two years later, Kraft was confirmed in office with a majority. Now *Spiegel Online* declared her the SPD's "new star" and the model for the three Social Democrats competing for the candidacy for chancellor at the federal level.[10] As a woman, Kraft would show the three how to win an election and would be more popular than any of them. But she did not want to throw her hat in the ring. "Any other candidate will thus have to live with the drawback of being second choice for many party members" (*Spiegel Online*, May 13, 2012). In the media, Kraft was seen as a qualified candidate for chancellor. At the same time, her refusal to run for office was highlighted, and interpreted as analogous to a mother staying at home with the kids and not following a career of her own.

When female politicians are criticized in the media, traditional stereotypical attributions are often used. The election in North Rhine-Westphalia in 2010 left the parliament without clear majorities. Kraft first hesitated to take the risk of a minority government. In response, some media outlets evoked the notion of a "woman who doesn't trust herself" (*SZ*, June 14, 2010, p. 4), conjuring the common image of a frightened, overcautious woman.

Andrea Ypsilanti, by contrast, had taken this risk in Hesse two years earlier. For more than seven months, she negotiated a red and green minority coalition government tolerated by the left-wing party Die Linke. In the media, this was unanimously criticized as a scandalous breach of promise, as Ypsilanti had excluded this option during the election campaign. In her case, the stereotype was not the overcautious woman, but the vain woman who is greedy for power and impervious to advice. In this perspective, being ambitious, assertive, and power-conscious is only appropriate for men, whereas women in the same situation are said to be vain, egomaniacal, and greedy. Ypsilanti's efforts to form a government made her fair game for sharp media criticism, and led to sexist coverage. For instance, *Spiegel Online* (September 2, 2008) published a commentary based on a completely fictitious story, insinuating that female politicians like Ypsilanti would soon be undressing in public.

In the end, Ypsilanti had to give up her intention of forming a minority cabinet, as four members of her own parliamentary group refused to support her. In any case, her effort to form a minority government tolerated by Die Linke was a breach of taboo for the Social Democrats. According to *Der Spiegel*, breaching taboos is a woman's job.

Once again, it's a woman who does the radical cut. First, Angela Merkel finished the "Kohl" system and became the first female federal chancellor.[11] Now Andrea Ypsilanti is opening the SPD to the political left. Women were outsiders in German politics, generally speaking; and they have learned that opportunities to achieve power are rare. This makes them act radically whenever a chance appears.

(Der Spiegel, 10/2008, p. 24)

The media no longer necessarily constructs a double bind between gendered expectations in the political and private spheres, within which female politicians would inevitably get trapped. Yet women's credibility in the political sphere continues to be debated in private contexts. The media discussed Ypsilanti's working class origins, which they also did in the case of Gerhard Schröder. But in contrast to Schröder's case, they referenced her private life when evaluating her political program. Some of the media referred to the Social Democrats' reform of the public educational system in Germany in the 1960s and 1970s. *Bild* and *FAZ* stressed that it was as a result of these reforms that Ypsilanti had been able to attain a high school degree. In her election program, she promised further school reforms, but her own son attended a private school (*Bild*, January 23, 2008, p. 2; *FAZ*, January 24, 2008, p. 2). Although her rationale for this was a lack of public full-time schools nearby, there were doubts about her neglecting her own political beliefs.

In contrast, in the case of Hannelore Kraft, *SZ* wrote that she "succeeded in achieving something where most Social Democrats fail: she pleases her party, the voters, and her son" (*SZ*, May 11, 2012, p. 6). That is to say, Kraft was a good politician *and* a good mother. Her style of leadership was depicted similarly. She was perceived as having an easygoing charm that helped her to hold the minority government together for far longer than anybody expected. "In Düsseldorf, she warmed everybody by talking, [...] like she chatted to other people offhandedly in her annual sports trip" (*Der Spiegel*, 18/2012, p. 30).

Ypsilanti's political profile was portrayed as "left-wing, soft, feminine" (*Spiegel Online*, January 17, 2008). Femininity turned into a trait that contrasted with those of the alpha-male. On the one hand, there was the down-to-earth woman, a worker's daughter who had climbed the social ladder, a mother with a 12-year-old son who knew everyday life and struggle; and on the other, there was the incumbent prime minister, Roland Koch, a privileged son of a minister, a lawyer who had climbed straight to the top, and a heavy-weight power broker.

Summary: From Exotic Outsiders to Feminine Political Players

Media representations of the earliest female candidates were appreciative when they evoked the notion of an exotic, attractive, and talented newcomer. As established politicians, the candidates could not meet the media's androcentric standards for a political leader. Their attempts to aspire and wield power were, according to the media, legitimate mainly when approved by a "strong" man.

In the case of the first female prime minister in Germany, Heide Simonis, the media had to consider the power of her office. Simonis, as a political leader, was represented with masculine descriptors. At the same time, she was depicted as a chatty and eccentric woman. Due to her unquestionable political power and competence, these media images did not challenge her image as political leader. Yet in criticism ("cult of personality") and after a defeat, media representations generally returned to more traditional images. This dynamic was also observed in other contexts.

In the course of the current century, the media has begun to represent women as having arrived in the political field as competent players. Yet appreciation is still constructed in terms of an essentialized femininity, in contrast to political masculinity. In specific contexts and by way of attributions, an essential contrast between masculine and feminine politicians was constructed. To a large extent, female leaders' traits, profile, and credibility were represented and debated in private contexts, predominantly by way of images of motherhood and parental care. This establishes a perfect contrast to political masculinity. This contrast explains why the dominant metaphor for female political leadership is the mother. This metaphor still bears the risk of relapsing into traditional constructions of gender hierarchies. Male politicians, in contrast, are described using a variety of figures of speech, including the man of action, the intellectual, the workers' leader, the paper shuffler, and the *Landesvater* (father of the state) (Beck, 2016a).[12]

The Mother of the Nation, the State, and the Company

An odd aspect of Chancellor Merkel's media coverage is that, despite her sober and cool image, she has been depicted as a mother. Even stranger is the fact that the media have been representing different types of motherhood. At first there was *Mutti Merkel* (Mommy Merkel), referring to Merkel scolding one of her ministers for not wearing a coat on a cold winter day. Subsequently, *Mutti* was the only person allowed to call to order the gang of little rascals in her cabinet. In this sense, the title *Mutti* can be interpreted as a warm, feminine-coded alternative to the masculine figure of the undisputable boss. In an earlier political age, according to the media, Merkel would have killed any rivals in her own party like a "black widow." The term *Mutti* shrank the alpha-males in her cabinet as well as in her party to pubescent, misbehaving boys (Beck, 2016a, pp. 75–77).

Merkel's second motherly image is the *Mutter der Nation* (the mother of the nation). The nation's mother performs a female presidential habitus, floating above everyone, especially above the parties, bestowing upon them their national identification. In the media, this was represented in her famous statement, as Germany faced the refugee crisis in the summer of 2015: "We will make it!"

The nation's mother is closely connected with the image of the *schwäbische Hausfrau* (Swabian housewife).[13] Untiring, the Swabian housewife worries about her children. She is keen on economizing and does not live on credit. This figure of speech connects neoliberal and austerity policies to everyday experience.

Media images representing Hannelore Kraft as *Landesmutter* (mother of the state) were very different. On the one hand, she was the hearty, unpretentious, and down-to-earth politician, in contrast to her cold and wooden predecessor, Jürgen Rüttgers, and to the intellectual "high-flyer" Norbert Röttgen, her challenger in 2012. Kraft herself carefully set up this image, especially during election campaigns, and the media took it. But on the other hand, Kraft's motherly image was linked to criticism on deficit spending (Beck, 2016a, pp. 77–78). In blind motherly love, Kraft would throw money down the drain in an attempt to solve every problem faced by her *Landeskinder* (children of the state), establishing programs to help degree holders find apprenticeships, programs for young delinquents, and programs for pregnant women facing difficulties (*Der Spiegel*, 18/2012, p. 31).

The true political mother in Germany is Ursula von der Leyen, minister of defense from 2013 and on. In her first federal office as minister of family affairs (2005–2009), she had made her status as a mother of seven central to her self-portrayal. As in the case of Ségolène Royal, many voices in the news media considered this to be intrusive. In the course of von der Leyen's political career, the motherly image faded.[14] But it came back with her surprise appointment as minister of defense in 2013, the first woman to hold this office in Germany. Now she became the *Mutter der Kompanie* (mother of the company). This was traditionally the first sergeant's nickname; he was said to be the soldiers' fatherly confidante. Today, this term is used figuratively to refer to a person who leads an undisciplined group with empathy and strength.

On the one hand, the company's mother established the frame for media discussions of one of von der Leyen's first actions as defense minister. She acknowledged that work–life balance in the army had to be improved. Even though the soldiers' families would surely agree with that, the media instead linked this issue to the minister's own family background. On the other hand, media used family and household terms to comment on von der Leyen's decisions. For example, they referred to an under-secretary of state's dismissal as "spring-cleaning."[15]

Due to her self-portrayal, von der Leyen's media image as a politician was closely linked to her family role. In her case, references to motherly care resulted in dismissive media coverage. Similarly, Kraft's defeat in the state election in 2017 was represented as a voting out on mother's day. In the case of Merkel, by contrast, motherly characteristics did not result in a return to traditionally gendered images. Merkel's power went largely unquestioned. Motherly figures of speech did nothing but warm up and gender the public image of a successful but reserved and cold female leader. Dülcke and Futh argue that, in accentuating this side of her image, the media aided in optimizing and securing her popularity (Dülcke & Futh, 2015, p. 269).

General Election in 2017: Comeback of the Modernized Alpha-Male

In the 2005 and 2009 general elections, Merkel's proverbial sobriety, pragmatism, and unpretentiousness (e.g., Brosda, 2013, p. 69) had been set in a positive contrast to hegemonic political masculinity depicted as an alpha-male (Scholz, 2007). Merkel's predecessor, Chancellor Gerhard Schröder, had been a perfect prototype for this dominating, if not authoritarian, self-staging behavior, which earned Schröder the title *Basta-Kanzler*, which means that he made decisions and stopped discussions in a very authoritarian way. In the 2017 election, this contrast was turned on its head, as some media voices began to judge Merkel's performance during the election campaign as "boring." Her sobriety was interpreted as weariness and lack of vision. By contrast, the leading Liberal Party and Green Party candidates were represented as dynamic and ambitious can-do men.

The two candidates, the Liberal Party's Christian Lindner and the Green Party's Cem Özdemir, were obviously trying to copy the campaign strategies of French President Emmanuel Macron, as well as those of Sebastian Kurz, the young, newly elected Austrian chancellor. Both Macron and Kurz represented themselves as young and innovative newcomers who challenge the political establishment, although this anti-establishment strategy was nothing but self-representation, as both had previously been part of the political elite; Macron, before becoming president, was well settled in the center of political power, and Kurz had been minister for foreign affairs (*Zeit Online*, October 22, 2017).

The Liberal Party's entire campaign was focused on Christian Lindner, the party's chairman. Lindner's presentation on campaign posters showed the iconography of fashion photography (*Stuttgarter Nachrichten* online, August 25, 2017). Most media addressed this in an at least neutral, and often positive, tone. They did not criticize this staging as an (obvious) attempt to foster a cult of personality. Instead, Lindner was acknowledged as the renewer of the Liberal Party (*Spiegel Online*, April 28, 2017). Yet the election program mainly consisted of well-known liberal positions, including low taxes, cuts in public expenses, and the privatization of social insurances. Moreover, Lindner himself was not at all a newcomer. In 2000, aged 21, he had already gained a seat in the state parliament of North Rhine-Westphalia. In 2009, he became the Liberal Party's general secretary. In the same year, he won a seat in the federal parliament. Since 2013, he has been party chairman.

Cem Özdemir, the Green Party's leading candidate, is also an experienced politician. Since 1994 he has been a member of both the federal parliament and the European parliament by turns. His self-representation, accordingly, was not as a newcomer but as a dynamic and unconventional "Anatolian Swabian."[16] This term combines his Turkish roots with his home and birthplace in the southwest of Germany. In some media voices, he was pictured in his shirt-sleeves, as down to earth, keen on power, and with a can do-attitude. For instance, the media eagerly picked up on his statement that the Greens, a party critical of reliance on the internal combustion engine, would have to save the German automotive industry from the "diesel crisis" because no one else was willing to do so (*Stuttgarter Nachrichten* online, September 11, 2017).

He served perfectly to fulfill the longing in some mainstream media outlets for new political constellations, which they mainly anticipated in a so-called Jamaica coalition (e.g., *Handelsblatt* online, September 17, 2017). This is the term used to describe the cooperation of the Christian Democrats (black), Liberal Party (yellow), and Greens, referring to the colors of the Jamaican flag.

These media images contrast perfectly with a female chancellor whom the media imputed had no more new ideas for Germany and the European Union. The online service of the *Tagesspiegel*, one of the dailies in the capital of Berlin, asked in a headline: "Merkel, a chancellor of boredom?" (August 29, 2017). Lindner's and Özdemir's media coverage, by contrast, gave the idea of the comeback of hegemonic masculinity in a modernized form. For instance, both were often represented in the media with female politicians at their sides, because presenting women in leadership positions nowadays is a must in the German political field. The Green Party's chair is always a mixed duumvirate, but in media representations it is mostly the male leaders who perform power. They are in the media, thus recreating a dominating attitude and self-staging. Still, there are modernized aspects, such as the anti-establishment habitus, the willingness to engage in unconventional cooperation (instead of "Basta-politics").

Conclusion and Outlook: Change and Persistence

The simultaneity of change and persistence in gendered media images of female politicians can be understood as a contested modernization of gender knowledge. The early candidates were depicted as exotic outsiders in the political field whose aspirations to power were legitimate only under certain circumstances or when approved by a strong man. Often, they had to face an essential double bind between the office which they sought and expectations regarding their female gender. This reflects traditional gender knowledge, which excludes women from public affairs. The more recent candidates were no longer caught in this trap. Instead, the media saw them as competent players in the political field. In this respect, gender knowledge was being modernized. Yet the women's attempts to achieve and exercise political power, as well as their traits and abilities, are still essentially and stereotypically coded as feminine. In these attributions, traditional gender knowledge persists. This tension bears the constant risk of a return to traditional media images. Figuratively speaking, the risk remains: The mother can still be thrown out of parliament and taken back home.

At the same time, hegemonic political masculinity shifted from the unspoken norm in media representations to a gender, which can be described, debated, and questioned. Although the general elections in 2017 give the impression of the comeback of the political alpha-male, there are some aspects of modernization. The alpha-males have to have female co-leaders at their side. Moreover, their habitus is being debated in the media. Masculinity, in most contexts, might still be the norm in the political field but it is no longer unspoken. This also shows both change and persistence in media images of political masculinity, and adds to the evidence of a contested modernization of gender knowledge.

Political traits and abilities that are coded feminine are largely based on the private role traditionally attributed to women. But, in contrast to an earlier moment in political history, this is no longer seen as a lack of qualification. Instead, it is regarded as a specific feminine approach to political office. This can be seen as evidence for a change in the relationship between the political public sphere and the private sphere in media representations. In the news media, both spheres are no longer (or not only) polar opposites. Rather, the private sphere takes on a complementary function for the public sphere. Traits and characteristics attributed to this sphere as well as to the women who are traditionally allocated to it become a factor in interpretations of female political personalities (Beck, 2016b, pp. 235–236). Yet the question of to what extent this could also be the case for male politicians, who have always been part of the political public sphere, requires further investigation.

A contested modernization can also be observed in media representations of private contexts. These representations not only construct a female model of leadership, but can also result in a return to traditionally coded gender stereotypes in media coverage, especially in contexts of criticism or defeat. Thus, female politicians still have to consider both the traditional and the modernized effects of gendered media images when campaigning for political power. But this increasingly seems to also be the case for hegemonic political masculinity, in both its traditional appearance and its modernized version.

Notes

1. The metaphor *Trümmerfrau*, widely used in German media, refers to those women who cleared away the debris, especially in Berlin, after World War II. According to this metaphor, female political leaders are not "normal" politicians in their own capacity, but are represented as "others," i.e., as a loophole in the case of male failure.
2. The alpha-male is a figure of speech for a hegemonial type of political masculinity (Connell, 2005). It combines assertiveness, unwillingness to compromise, an authoritarian leadership, aplomb, successful use of male insider relations, as well as a strongly masculine behavior.

3. Androcentrism is defined as the hypostasis of masculinity as the general model for humanity (Müller, 1991, p. 74).
4. In 2016, for a second time, Klöckner ran for office. In this election, she competed with the incumbent prime minister, the Social Democrat Malu Dreyer. Dreyer had come into office in 2013 in the middle of an election period. A comparative analysis of this election would be especially worthy. As Greenwald and Lehman-Wilzig argue in this volume, two women competing can produce very specific media images and can reduce the phenomenon of women pioneering or being unique.
5. Both publications have editorial boards of their own.
6. Franz Müntefering, at that time, was federal minister for labor and social affairs and the Social Democrats' chairman.
7. In Germany, in the city states of Berlin, Bremen, and Hamburg, the ministers are named senator.
8. Political toleration means that a party supports the government in specific issues instead of entering a coalition. This model is quite common in Scandinavian countries and often a loophole in parliaments with unclear majorities to form a government.
9. In Germany, the head of government (chancellor at the federal level, prime minister at the state level) is elected by the parliament, and not by popular vote.
10. Sigmar Gabriel, Peer Steinbrück, Frank-Walter Steinmeier.
11. The Christian Democrat Helmut Kohl was German chancellor from 1982 to 1998.
12. The metaphors *Landesvater* and *Landesmutter* derive from the scattered regionalism in German history. With the notion *Landesvater*, paternalistic characteristics were attributed to a sovereign. His wife, the *Landesmutter*, took care of her *Landeskinder* in a charitable commitment.
13. The Swabians, in the southwest of Germany, are said to be not only thrifty, but even niggard. And they would work without rest.
14. She also was minister of labor and social affairs from 2009 to 2013.
15. https://startthinkingnow.wordpress.com/gender-in-den-medien/presse/ursula-von-der-leyen-die-putzfrau-der-bundeswehr (last viewed October 23, 2017).
16. www.oezdemir.de/cem/anatolischer-schwabe/ (last viewed January 9, 2018).

References

Absolu, F. (2014). *Politikerinnen in der Presse: Mytheme, Biographeme und Archetyp. Die genderbetonte Darstellung von Angela Merkel und Ségolène Royal in den deutschen und französischen Printmedien während ihrer Wahlkampagnen*. Würzburg: Königshausen & Neumann. [in German].

Arendt, H. (2010). *Vita activa oder vom tätigen Leben* (8th ed.). München: Piper. [in German].

Beck, D. (2016a). Mutti ist die Beste: Die Mutter-Metapher als politische Kategorie in den Medien. In M. Dolderer, H. Holme, C. Jerzak, & M. Tietke (Eds.), *O mother, where art thou? – (Queer-)feministische Perspektiven auf Mutterschaft und Mütterlichkeit* (pp. 71–83). Münster: Westfälisches Dampfboot. [in German].

Beck, D. (2016b). *Politikerinnen und ihr Griff zur Macht: Mediale Repräsentationen von SPD-Spitzenkandidatinnen bei Landtagswahlen*. Bielefeld: transcript. [in German].

Brosda, C. (2013). Wenn der Rahmen nicht zum Bild passt: Politische und mediale Deutungsangebote im Wahlkampf. In *Macht ohne Verantwortung: Medien im Wahlkampf 2013* (pp. 59–71). Berlin: Heinrich-Böll-Stiftung, Hans-Böckler-Stiftung. [in German].

Connell, R. (2005). *Masculinities* (2nd ed.). Cambridge, UK: Polity Press.

Dölling, I. (2005). "Geschlechter-wissen" – ein nützlicher Begriff für die "verstehende" Analyse von Vergeschlechtlichungsprozessen? *Zeitschrift für Frauenforschung und Geschlechterstudien*, (1+2), 44–62. [in German].

Dülcke, D., & Futh, S. K. (2015). Die "Mutter der Nation" gegen den "Panzerkandidaten" – Geschlechterbilder in der Berichterstattung der Printmedien zum Bundestagswahlkampf 2013. In C. Holtz-Bacha (Ed.), *Die Massenmedien im Wahlkampf: Die Bundestagswahl 2013* (pp. 249–273). Wiesbaden: Springer VS. [in German].
Gnändiger, C. (2007). *Politikerinnen in deutschen Printmedien: Vorurteile und Klischees in der Berichterstattung*. Saarbrücken: VDM, Müller. [in German].
Habermas, J. (1991). *Strukturwandel der Öffentlichkeit: Untersuchungen zu einer Kategorie der bürgerlichen Gesellschaft* (2nd ed.). Frankfurt/Main: Suhrkamp. [in German].
Hall, S. (2000). Die strukturierte Vermittlung von Ereignissen. In *Ideologie Kultur Rassismus: Ausgewählte Schriften 1* (3rd ed.) (pp. 126–149). Hamburg: Argument. [in German].
Hall, S. (2004). Kodieren/Dekodieren. In *Ideologie Identität Repräsentation: Ausgewählte Schriften 4* (pp. 66–80). Hamburg: Argument. [in German].
Hausen, K. (1976). Die Polarisierung der "Geschlechtscharaktere" – eine Spiegelung der Dissoziation von Erwerbs- und Familienleben. In W. Conze (Ed.), *Sozialgeschichte der Familie in der Neuzeit Europas* (pp. 363–393). Stuttgart: Klett. [in German].
Holtz-Bacha, C., & Koch, T. (2008). Der Merkel-Faktor: Die Berichterstattung der Printmedien über Merkel und Schröder im Bundestagswahlkampf 2005. In C. Holtz-Bacha (Ed.), *Frauen, Politik und Medien* (pp. 49–70). Wiesbaden: VS. [in German].
Jamieson, K. H. (1995). *Beyond the double bind: Women and leadership*. New York: Oxford University Press.
Jarren, O., & Donges, P. (2011). *Politische Kommunikation in der Mediengesellschaft. Eine Einführung* (3rd ed.). Wiesbaden: VS. [in German].
Keller, R., Reichertz, J., & Knoblauch, H. (Eds.). (2013). *Kommunikativer Konstruktivismus: Theoretische und empirische Arbeiten zu einem neuen wissenssoziologischen Ansatz*. Wiesbaden: Springer Fachmedien. [in German].
Kleemann, F., Krähnke, U., & Matuschek, I. (2013). *Interpretative Sozialforschung. Eine Einführung in die Praxis des Interpretierens* (2nd ed.). Wiesbaden: Springer VS. [in German].
Kutt, M. (2010). *Auf dem Weg zur Macht: Politische Kommunikation in Deutschland und Frankreich. Die Darstellung von Angela Merkel und Ségolène Royal in der Wahlkampfberichterstattung überregionaler Tageszeitungen*. Duisburg Köln: WiKu. [in German].
List, E. (1986). Homo politicus – Femina privata? Thesen zur Kritik der politischen Anthropologie. In J. Conrad, & U. Konnertz (Eds.), *Weiblichkeit in der Moderne* (pp. 75–95). Tübingen: Ed. diskord. [in German].
Lünenborg, M., & Maier, T. (2012). "Kann der das überhaupt?" Eine qualitative Textanalyse zum Wandel medialer Geschlechterrepräsentationen. In M. Lünenborg, & J. Röser, (Eds.), *Ungleich mächtig: Das Gendering von Führungspersonen aus Politik, Wirtschaft und Wissenschaft in der Medienkommunikation* (pp. 65–126). Bielefeld: transcript. [in German].
Lünenborg, M., & Röser, J. (Eds.). (2012). *Ungleich mächtig: Das Gendering von Führungspersonen aus Politik, Wirtschaft und Wissenschaft in der Medienkommunikation*. Bielefeld: transcript. [in German].
Mayring, P. (2010). *Qualitative Inhaltsanalyse: Grundlagen und Techniken* (11th ed.). Weinheim: Beltz. [in German].
Moser, A. (2010). *Kampfzone Geschlechterwissen: Kritische Analyse populärwissenschaftlicher Konzepte von Männlichkeit und Weiblichkeit*. Wiesbaden: VS. [in German].
Müller, U. (1991). Gleichheit im Zeitalter der Differenz: Einige methodologische Erwägungen zur Frauenforschung. *Psychologie und Gesellschaftskritik*, 15, 3–4. [in German].
Pfannes, P. (2004). *"Powerfrau", "Quotenfrau", "Ausnahmefrau"...? Die Darstellung von Politikerinnen in der deutschen Tagespresse*. Marburg: Tectum. [in German].

Reichertz, J. (2013). *Gemeinsam interpretieren: Die Gruppeninterpretation als kommunikativer Prozess*. Wiesbaden: Springer VS. [in German].

Reichertz, J., & Soeffner, H.-G. (2004). Hans-Georg Soeffner: Expanding the action repertoire of societies: Hans-Georg Soeffner im Gespräch mit Jo Reichertz. *Forum: Qualitative Sozialforschung*, 5(3), Art. 29. [in German].

Scholz, S. (2007). Männer reden Merkel klein: Männlichkeitskritiken im Bundestagswahlkampf 2005. In S. Scholz (Ed.), *Kann die das? Angela Merkels Kampf um die Macht* (pp. 103–116). Berlin: Dietz. [in German].

Schreier, M. (2014). Varianten qualitativer Inhaltsanalyse: Ein Wegweiser im Dickicht der Begrifflichkeiten. *Forum: Qualitative Sozialforschung*, 15(1), Art. 18. [in German].

Van Zoonen, L. (2006). The personal, the political and the popular: A woman's guide to celebrity politics. *European Journal of Cultural Studies*, 9(3), 287–301

11

"MEN PREFER REDHEADS"

Media Framing of Polls and its Effect on Trust in Media

Pazit Ben-Nun Bloom and Marie Courtemanche

Introduction

Following Festinger's (1954) seminal social comparison theory, abundant research in psychology suggests that people strive to evaluate their attitudes. This is especially so when the public relies heavily upon external sources in forming and updating political attitudes due to a lack of political sophistication (Converse, 1964; Delli Carpini & Keeter, 1996) and increasing social alienation (Putnam, 2000). Public opinion surveys act to satisfy this motivation for self-evaluation, encouraging the media to publish such polls and explaining the audience's interest in them.

How are polls presented in the media, and how does this presentation affect trust in the media? Whereas publishing surveys and translating scientific results can advance an image of precision and neutrality, the media distribute polls of varying methodological quality. The same newspaper can publish rigorous ("objective" seeming) studies, as well as unrepresentative polls regarding sexual habits conducted by condom companies ("subjective" polls). The current literature typically focuses on surveys of pre-election preferences, such as "Poll: Hillary Has Twenty-Point Lead on Trump," and is often silent on the distinction between them and other types of polls, particularly the less professional ones, such as "Survey Concludes: Men Prefer Redheads." Yet, the latter headline demonstrates that media surveys are characterized by varying levels of professionalism and by a wide range of subjects with presentation methods not necessarily reflecting the rhetoric of objectivity. The publication of articles with low-quality polls is often attributed to the media's unprofessional handling of surveys.

This study examines the different manners of presenting polls in the Israeli press, and their effect on audience trust in the media. It first argues that the inconsistent quality of polls published by the popular media is not indicative of media persons' inability to distinguish between surveys on methodological grounds, and claims instead that different types of surveys are published to fulfill different functions (e.g., to ensure an image of objectivity, but also to entertain and to demonstrate investigative journalism). In order to differentiate the surveys they publish, however, the media create various frames for their presentation, where *framing* is defined as "the process by which a communication source, such as a news organization, defines and constructs a political issue or public controversy" (Nelson, Clawson, & Oxley, 1997, p. 567). We believe that frames dictate key elements of how the survey is handled, like the extent of methodological elucidation, the size and placement of the article within the newspaper, the tone and language of the text, and the inclusion of charts which allow media persons to convey their insights about the survey (i.e., signal their type) to media consumers.

Given this understanding, four meta-frames for surveys were derived deductively from different perceptions of the role of the popular media (Caspi, 1995; Weaver & Wilhoit, 1996). The hypothesized frames were then combined into two types: frames that present a survey as an "objective" and "neutral" tool (the survey as a "camera" that corresponds to the perception of the media as a mirror, and the survey as a "watchdog" that derives from the perception of the media as an overseer of democracy), and those that highlight the survey as "subjective" (the survey as an "entertainer" that stems from the perception of the media as a provider of diversion, and as a "confidential advisor," based on the critical perception of the media as a revealer of conspiracies).

To validate the existence of these frames in the media environment, a content analysis was conducted, confirming their use. Supporting the argument that the different frames enable journalists to signal the type of the survey to media consumers, an experiential validity test, in which the subjects matched metaphors with survey frames and identified their functions, confirmed that media consumers are able to differentiate between the frames.

Next, we suggest that subjective polls reinforce perceptions that the media are unprofessional and inaccurate, which manifests in cynicism and distrust. Cynicism activated by subjective poll frames may extend beyond the trust in the poll to affect trust in media in general (Cappella & Jamieson, 1997). Indeed, our experimental test reveals that individuals who were exposed to subjective surveys were more likely to express diminished trust in the media, as compared with those who read about objective surveys. These findings suggest that, even though individuals may be able to draw distinctions between different types of polls, certain surveys have deleterious effects nevertheless. Moreover, in an era of increased reliance on subjective news reporting, the media may be contributing to their own discredit, and perhaps demise, as people come to trust it less, slowly attributing it with fabricating "fake news."

Functions of Mass Opinion Surveys

While the media's first published survey appeared in 1824 (see Herbst, 1993, for a historical review), frequent use of surveys as a media tool did not begin until the 1970s. At that time, the widespread use of telephones considerably lowered the costs of executing surveys, and precision journalism – a genre of journalism that initiates surveys and produces news based on poll interpretation and analysis – was developed.

While election polls have been conducted over the years, it was not until the 1969 elections for the seventh *Knesset* (the Israeli Parliament) that surveys first appeared in the media in Israel (see Fuchs & Bar-Lev, 1998). The use of surveys has increased significantly since this time. Between 1969 and 1996, for example, the amount of space dedicated to reporting surveys in newspapers has multiplied 56 times over, and their prominence on the front page has also risen substantially (Weiman, 1998).

Where does the media's interest in publishing surveys originate? This question is especially interesting in light of research indicating that both the public and journalists are quite skeptical about political polls (e.g., Herbst, 1998, p. 49; Weiman, 1998, pp. 137–139). The survey is also not an appropriate tool for the many types of stories the media seek – it is somewhat tedious and dry, and decreases the flexibility of presentation (Shamir & Shamir, 2000, p. 90).

There may be several reasons for the media to take an interest in polls, however, from which various survey functions may be derived. First, the survey, as an objective scientific product, may contribute to the media's image as a producer of neutral factual information, as survey findings are supposedly accurate and independent of the reporter, or at least more difficult for the elites to manipulate. Survey findings also represent the reality that the media are eager to portray (Herbst, 1998).

However, in a world where the media themselves initiate and interpret survey findings, they also assist the media in shaping and influencing reality. Media coverage, for instance, influences political attitude formation and creates standards according to which people judge events and politicians (Iyengar, 1994; Iyengar & Kinder, 2010). Accordingly, polls present rules of thumb for understanding and judging reality through criteria selected by the media. They may also be used to predict election outcomes – a goal unto itself for every political journalist (Herbst, 1998, p. 99).

Publishing surveys not only contributes to the media's strength, image, and effectiveness, it is also in keeping with the objectives of the media in a democracy. The survey offers citizens information relevant to decision-making, helping to map and simplify the issues at hand, as well as the range of opinions (Faas, Mackenrodt, & Schmitt-Beck, 2008; Moy & Rinke, 2012). Poll results may encourage an individual to formulate a stance regarding political issues through self-comparison (Ben-Nun Bloom & Levitan, 2011). The poll also links the masses and the elite by presenting public needs without the show of force that the masses can utilize to convey their wishes (Della Porta, 2008).

That being the case, there are numerous reasons for publishing surveys in the media. However, the manner of presenting surveys, as derived from the various functions they may serve, is not necessarily uniform. A survey that serves as an easy or interesting story will not be presented in the same manner as a survey meant to contribute to a newspaper's objective image, and a survey designed to reflect reality will be presented differently than one meant to mold it. Surveys that serve different media role perceptions will each have their own distinct frames.

Why Frame Surveys?

The hypothesis regarding multiple survey frames is based upon the assumption that media persons are able to differentiate among surveys according to their level of professionalism. Academics sometimes doubt this assumption. For instance, Miller (1995, p. 119) claims that survey consumers, including media persons, do not possess clear standards of survey quality. Yet an empirical study based on interviews demonstrates that journalists express ambivalence regarding the use of surveys – on the one hand, they are professionally dependent on them, and on the other hand, they are wary of surveys that were not produced by their media employer (Herbst, 1998). Most importantly, journalists are skeptical of non-scientific surveys but they choose to utilize them nonetheless, attributing the problems they find in surveys to the manner in which interest holders use them. Because most non-election related surveys are not produced by the newspaper itself, journalists find the process of differentiating professional quality difficult and requiring a significant amount of time.

This study suggests that this ambivalence toward surveys manifests in the creation of frames for different types of articles featuring surveys in three different ways. First, media persons do not eschew publishing pseudo-surveys but are tempted to include these items for the spice they add to their publications. However, they are intuitively aware of the difference between a pseudo-survey and one which is more methodically professional, and they project that distinction via the frames they employ. Surveys published for diversionary purposes are accompanied by a humorous or cynical tone, thus blurring their research context, referred to here as the "the entertainer." Other surveys, though, may be published to guard against inimical government actions, performing a "watchdog" function for society and exhibiting a more serious tone.

Media persons are aware that survey results may be diverted in different directions; thus, they are wary of surveys initiated by others and frame them differently, by emphasizing the possible interests behind them, thus mimicking a "confidential advisor." On the other hand, surveys initiated by the media and others perceived by media persons as credible, such as those in fields considered "neutral" (like demographics and economics) or those whose results are presented by entities considered to be reliable, such as the Central Bureau of Statistics, are highlighted as objective and neutral, which we call the "camera."

Third, media persons become dependent upon surveys in order to learn about reality, as do other members of society. But while they tend to explain away their dependence as a sincere attempt to study society (framing self-initiated surveys as objective), they tend to emphasize the dependence of others on them (via frames presenting survey findings as subjective).

How is the Survey Concept Framed?

Different perceptions of the journalist's responsibility, as well as a separate set of values, stand behind each of these role perceptions, as do different views regarding the role and characteristics of the survey (Sheafer, Ben-Nun Bloom, Shenhav, & Segev, 2013). These role perceptions may certainly co-exist within the same person, and are suited to different needs of the media system.

According to the perception of the media as a reflection of reality or mirror, absolute truth does exist, and the media must report it objectively and neutrally. The survey is expected to serve as an auxiliary tool in this task. An appropriate frame for a survey presented from the viewpoint of this role perception is the camera, which emphasizes a survey's objectivity and neutrality.

Several key features may be hypothesized to emerge in an article in which the survey is framed as "a camera." First, there is no interpretation of the findings, as the facts speak for themselves. Diagrams, graphs, and other seemingly mathematical figures receive central visual expression. The word survey (or poll) or quantitative findings appear in the headline, along with elements enforcing the media's objective image, such as numbers and percentages. The accompanying text mostly cites the findings and avoids any critical tone toward the survey, without acknowledging any methodological limitations. The poll is presented as active (described as: examining, finding, seeking, discovering) and objective. Such articles may appear in the economics supplement and hard news sections of the newspaper.

The second perception of the media as democracy's protector means the media must wade through various opinions, caution against social gaps and deficiencies, and function as a check and balance. The survey is perceived as an objective tool that furthers this task, but it may be executed and presented in more than one manner, and thus, it is liable to be exploited by interest holders. Thus, external surveys are viewed ambivalently by the newspaper, respected but also suspected, while exclusive newspaper surveys are considered trustworthy because the interests behind their execution are transparent to the media people handling them.

The survey frame in such cases may be "the watchdog" emphasizing the survey's efficiency as a tool for uncovering dysfunctions for safeguarding purposes.

This metaphor suggests that polls are mostly objective, employed to investigate and expose problems in various realms of society to ensure that problems do not arise. This type of survey may facilitate the understanding of a complex reality and be used to judge among alternatives.

While the survey is presented as relatively objective in this case, it is less objective than in the "camera" frame because, unlike a photograph, findings by a watchdog may be interpreted, disagreed with, and compared with other results. Further, the watchdog exposes problematic circumstances, and the findings are not presented as episodic, but are broadened into a general phenomenon. Accordingly, an article presenting these survey frames will be of an investigative nature, critical of the state of affairs, and will point to a negative societal phenomenon.

This frame is expected to differentiate between surveys initiated by the media and by external sources. While the former will stress the investigative objectivity of the tool, the latter will be treated with greater suspicion, for example, by presenting various reservations, comparative surveys, etc. Findings from external surveys resemble a report by a new watchdog. This frame may be utilized in investigative magazine reports and in hard news, and it may suit investigative subjects such as social gaps.

In the perceived media role as a supplier of entertainment, from which the third frame is derived, the center of attention is the gimmick, rather than the presentation of reality. Accordingly, the survey is perceived as adding color to the newspaper, as a soft and spicy subjective item meant to break up the sequence of hard news. Therefore, the survey is not to be judged by the criteria of a real piece, but as something intended to amuse. The heart of such a survey presents a headline as an interesting punch line. A suitable frame for these kinds of surveys is the "entertainer," the features of which may be a humorous tone, colorful subjects such as sex, and an eye-catching headline.

Little effort is expected in specifying or interpreting the findings of a survey that is framed as entertainment, or in supplying methodological details regarding its execution because it is not judged based upon objectivity. Visually, one might expect colorful pictures that are not necessarily directly connected to the survey. This frame may suit relatively small reports, which usually appear as filler in daily magazines and in soft supplements.

Fourth is the critical media perception, according to which the media hold the normative role of revealing conspiracies, opening the eyes of the public, and pointing out inequalities in society. This reference to the media's role is based on a conflictual perception of reality asserting that there are constant societal struggles. Accordingly, the survey will be suspected as being a device by which the elite manipulates public opinion, thus facilitating the current hegemony. The frame fitting this perception is that of the survey as a "confidential advisor."

Articles presenting surveys in this frame will emphasize the power of the survey, its subjectivity, the dependency of decision-makers on this tool, and the manipulative use they make of it. As a part of the emphasis on the survey's subjectivity and power, it will be presented as active, because a confidential advisor is powerful and may determine developments by whispering in decision-makers' ears. Accordingly, a critical tone will be used toward the survey. At the same time, a reverse process of presenting the survey as passive and emphasizing its weaknesses as a subjective product is also possible, with people behind the survey using it to further their interests. One would expect to find this type of frame in relatively long reports in daily or weekly supplements regarding political or economic issues.

Table 11.1 summarizes the hypotheses concerning the frames' characteristics. See the Method section for the codes for each characteristic.

The Effect of Survey Frame on Trust in the Media

The effect of exposure to polls on socio-political attitudes has been examined extensively, albeit with inconclusive findings. Much of the work that has been done typically investigates the political bandwagon and underdog effects, trying to establish that exposure to polls affects public opinion in the direction of the majority vs. the minority. One recent study using an experimental design found that participants were more likely to demonstrate support for an issue when told that others had done similarly. Conversely, those who were given information suggesting low levels of issue backing were less willing to evince support themselves (Rothschild & Malhotra, 2014). In the realm of voting, research on exit polling indicates that individuals are more likely to turn out and vote for the person in the lead as suggested by the day's polling results (Morton, Muller, Page, & Torgler, 2015).

While the bandwagon effect may be larger for those who are not as politically savvy, some have found that polls can assist the less knowledgeable to make decisions in their best interests (Schmitt-Beck, 1996; Sinclair & Plott, 2012). Not all effects are positive, though, as overall turnout may be affected negatively when someone is projected to win (Morton et al., 2015). Moreover, individuals may not be conscious of the fact that they have adapted their attitudes to conform to the majority opinion (Ragozzino & Hartmann, 2014). Yet others have found no influence of feedback loops, or the reporting of polls, on the opinions of those reading them (Arnesen, Johannesson, Linde, & Dahlberg, 2017; Sonck & Loosveldt, 2010).

Whereas the lion's share of the literature examining the effects of poll exposure typically focuses on voters' preferences for candidates (e.g., Christenson & Smidt, 2012; Steger, 2013), more recent work examines the influence of polls that do not overtly depict election results but rather present public opinion on some other political issue (e.g., Ragozzino & Hartman, 2014; Rothschild & Malhotra, 2014). Likewise, in this work, we focus on the effect of the mere exposure to polls, regardless of their content, on trust in the media, expecting that different frames will have divergent effects.

TABLE 11.1 Frames' characteristics hypotheses

		Objective frames		Subjective frames	
		Camera	Watchdog	Confidential advisor	Entertainer
Visual presentation		Diagrams	Diagrams	–	Pictures
Space allocation	Size	Medium	Large	Large	Small
	Placement	Economics, headline	Magazines, headline	Magazines, supplements	Light magazines
Article's subject	Subject	Economics, politics	Social issues	Politics	"Color," piquant
	Subject's negativity	–	Negative subjects	Negative subjects	–
Criticism of the survey	Confrontation	No confrontation among survey results		Confrontation	–
	Critical tone	No critical tone toward survey		Critical tone	–
Manner of reporting the survey	Number of details reported	Many	Many	Few	Few
	Amount of interpretation	No interpretation	Interpretation	Interpretation	No interpretation

Trust in media is viewed to be particularly important due to its potential ties to confidence in democracy, as "without trust in the conduit of political information, trust in the fairness of collective decision-making is likely to be undermined" (Tsfati & Cohen, 2005, p. 32). It is also of great significance given that the media serve as a linkage institution, connecting citizens to those who serve them. If confidence in media deteriorates, with the media being regarded as irrelevant or, worse, inimical, individuals may discount relayed communications or seek information using other means. Indeed, research has demonstrated that trusted sources are more persuasive and likely to influence attitudes and that the skeptical are less likely to tune into mainstream media broadcasts (Eagly & Chaiken, 1993; Miller & Krosnick, 2000; Tsfati & Cappella, 2003).

An important source of distrust may in fact stem from the media themselves. As suggested by Cappella and Jamieson (1997) in their influential book *Spiral of Cynicism*, cynicism due to news content may be contagious, spilling over to trust in the media and additional social institutions. Indeed, both experimental and correlational research suggest that certain media content may translate to decreased trust in the media in general, as well as cynical attitudes toward politics and decreased trust in democracy (de Vreese & Elenbaas, 2008; Schuck, Boomgaarden, & de Vreese, 2013; Shehata, 2014).

Along these lines, cynicism activated by subjective poll frames may extend beyond the trust in the poll to affect confidence in media in general. Distrust in the media is often based on perceptions that the media are inaccurate, unprofessional, and imbalanced (Cappella & Jamieson, 1997). Consequently, frames that present surveys as subjective tools, underscoring the role of the media as a supplier of entertainment, may increase cynicism about the media's handling of news, and raise doubts about their competence. Indeed, it was found that the media's tendency to frame politics as a game was related to the recollection of strategic information rather than material of greater substance as well as increased cynicism for those exposed to the former type of information (Shehata, 2014; Valentino, Beckmann, & Buhr, 2001). If this is the case, then decisions regarding how information is presented to mass publics could ultimately be undermining the trust that individuals have for those doing the presenting. By giving its audience salacious style polls, the media may be contributing to their own discredit as cynicism for the instrument spills over to its distributer.

Method

Study 1: Content Analysis

The Newspaper and the Sampling List

The newspaper selected was *Yedioth Ahronoth*, the most popular Israeli daily at the time, which presents "story-telling journalism" in a tabloid format (much like *The New York Post*, *France-Soir* and *Bild Zeitung*). The sample included all the articles in all of *Yedioth Ahronoth*'s supplements (except for advertisements and letters to the editor, which are not framed by the editorial board) that mention the word "poll" (in Hebrew, the words "poll" and "survey" are synonyms) and its inflections during a period of seven years (1998–2004). The sampling list included 5,578 articles, with a mean of 797 articles per year. On average, 67 articles presenting the word "survey" were published each month, which yields an average of approximately 2.7 articles per issue. The list was then split into two: 200 articles were randomly sampled from 1998–2000 and analyzed using grounded theory where a preliminary version of the codebook was applied and articles were read as "openly" as possible to raise additional ideas for framing, and 100 articles were randomly sampled from 2001–2004 and analyzed using a quantitative content analysis (see codes below) (see Hertog & McLeod, 2001, for a similar analytical approach). A random sample of 20% of the articles was analyzed by a second reader, and inter-coder reliability tests were executed.

Codes for Confirmatory Content Analysis (2001–2004)

Visual presentation: *Size of diagram/graph.* 1 – there is no diagram or graph, to 6 – no text, only a diagram; *Size of picture/illustration that is not a diagram.* 1 – no picture, to 5 – larger than text.

Space allocation: *Article size.* 1 – up to 1/8 of a page, to 5 – more than one page; *Article placement within the newspaper.* "light" supplements (24 Hours, Yours, Modern Times, Seven Nights, holiday supplements and sports), "deeper" supplements (Seven Days, Weekend Supplement), headlines, economics.

Article's subject: *Subject of survey.* 11 options: political, economic, sports, culture and education, spicy ("color"), legal and criminal, criticism, ecology, communications, and society surveys; *Negativity.* 1 – negative subject, 2 – neutral, 3 – positive, 4 – N/A.

Criticism of the survey: *Criticism.* Does the article raise criticism or reservations and mention uncertainties and possible errors, or does it treat the survey as fully objective? 1 – harsh criticism, to 4 – no criticism, 5 N/A; *Confrontation.* comparing different surveys or contradicting conclusions. 1 – confrontation, 2 – no confrontation, 3 – N/A.

Reporting: *Number of methodological details.* e.g., sample size, sampling error, executing research institute, representativeness, comparison to other surveys, time of execution, distinction between populations, etc. (a count scale, where 99 – N/A). *Degree of survey interpretation.* 1 – much interpretation of the findings, to 4 – no interpretation, only findings, 5 – N/A.

The survey's frame was determined by the coder's impression. Each article was designated a metaphor from a list of eight (camera, confidential advisor, crystal ball, prophecy, court jester, state comptroller, magnifying glass, weapon), and accordingly was classified as (1) one of four meta-frames (camera, advisor, watchdog, entertainer), and (2) objective (camera and watchdog) or subjective (advisor and entertainer).

Inter-coder reliability: The inter-coder reliability for an article was very high both for determining one of the four meta-frames ($\kappa = 0.867$) and the objective vs. subjective frame ($\kappa = 0.828$). Inter-coder reliability was very high for seven of the specific characteristics (diagrams: $\kappa = 1$; pictures: K'r = 0.924; placement: $\kappa = 1$; size: $\kappa = 0.933$; article subject: $\kappa = 0.868$; number of details: K'r = 0.985; degree of findings' interpretation: K'r = 0.826), medium for the subject's negativity (K'r = 0.624) and for the measure of critical tone toward the survey (K'r = 0.672), and low for the measure of confrontation among various survey results (K'r = 0.338).

Study 2: The Experiment

One hundred and ninety-eight participants (mostly BA and MA political science students at Tel Aviv University) were randomly assigned to one of five conditions – four treatment groups, each presenting two original articles classified in a particular meta-frame, and a control: (1) camera ("*Yedioth Ahronoth* Survey: 62% – Sharon Submitting to Americans"; "Survey: Israel Leads the Worldwide Homeowners Rate – 80% of the Public"), (2) watchdog ("Health in Israel – Doctors Plentiful, Beds Lacking"; "Surprise: Israelis Happy with Life"), (3) confidential advisor ("Barak Startled by Public Opinion, Retreats from Golan Heights Retreat"; "Labor Party's Secret Survey: 1.5 Parliament Seats have been Lost to Shinui"), (4) entertainer ("Survey Reveals: Female Bosses Like to Fool Around with Male Employees"; "All Is Well if Hair Is Well"), or (5) no-poll control group. The treatments were two original articles from *Yedioth Ahronoth* which were classified in the content analysis as presenting surveys framed in one of the four meta-frames. After reading the articles, participants answered about trust in the media and trust in polls, and were given a frame recognition task by which they were asked to classify the articles they had read by frames, followed by background variables.

Trust in the media: The degree of agreement (1–4) with the statements: "I generally trust the Israeli media"; "I do not trust the Israeli press at all" (reversed); "You cannot believe what you read in the newspaper" (reversed) ($\alpha = 0.760$; $\bar{x} = 2.728$).

Trust in polls: The degree of agreement (1–7) with the statements: "You can rely on polls published in the media"; "I believe the surveys that appear in the press"; "The amount of use of polls used in the media should be reduced" (reversed); "Behind most surveys there is an economic or political interest" (reversed); "Polls reflect reality" ($\alpha = 0.823$; $\bar{x} = 3.609$).

Frame identification: "In your opinion, what is the role of the survey in the press based on the two articles you read? Presents facts in order to understand reality; an elitist means that aids the elite's deception of the public and internal struggles; exposes shortcomings and social phenomena; breaks monotony by adding 'color' to the newspaper; other."

Results

Study 1: Content Analysis

Throughout the analysis, the frames were grouped in two ways: (1) four meta-frames derived from the four media perceptions; of the sampled articles, 60% were classified in the "camera" meta-frame, 12% – "watchdog," 15% – "confidential advisor," and 13% – "entertainer," which may be conceived as a surprisingly low figure for a tabloid; (2) a dichotomous split into two groups of frames that presented the survey as either objective (camera and watchdog: 72%) or subjective (entertainer and advisor: 28%).

Table 11.2 summarizes the content analysis findings. Overall, the hypotheses regarding the existence of multiple framing of surveys and most of the meta-frames' characteristics were confirmed. Nine characteristics were found to be significantly related to the framing: diagram size, article size, placement, article subject, subject negativity, existence of confrontation between surveys, critical tone toward the survey, number of details reported on the survey, and the degree of interpretation of the findings. When grouped (except the article subject index, due to measurement level), a highly accurate prediction of the frame's objectivity or subjectivity was achieved ($R^2_{Nagelkerke} = 77.5\%$).

In particular, Figure 11.1 presents the frames by article placement. As hypothesized, the camera appears in the economics sections, the entertainer in light magazines, and the watchdog in the headlines ($\lambda = 0.24$, $p = 0.04$). In total, 61% of the objective condition articles were placed in the more serious supplements, which rely on the rhetoric of objectivity – the headlines and economics sections, while 75% of the subjective condition articles appeared in the magazines.

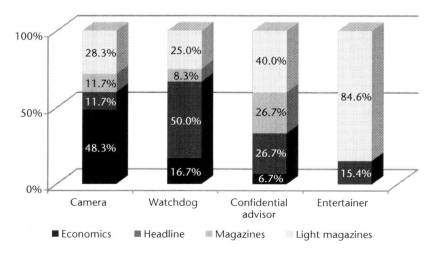

FIGURE 11.1 Article placement by meta-frame

TABLE 11.2 Summary of content analysis findings

		Objective frames		Subjective frames	
		Camera	Watchdog	Confidential Advisor	Entertainer
Visual presentation	Diagrams	39%	58%	0%	0%
Space allocation	Size	Varies	Large	Varies	Small
	Placement	48% economics	50% headlines	67% magazines	85% light magazines
Article's subject	Subject	50% economics, 17% politics	67% social issues	67% politics	100% "color"
	Subject is negative	38%	92%	47%	0%
Criticism of the survey	Confrontation	14%	8%	80%	0%
	Critical tone	7%	8%	92%	0%
Manner of reporting the survey	Methodological details reported	42% over 4	50% over 4	0% over 4	23% over 4
	Interpretation	63%	58%	0%	15%

Next, the expected significant correlation emerged between article size and meta-frame ($V_{Cramer's} = 0.30$, p = 0.01). The distribution of article size by frames is presented in Figure 11.2. The most prominent finding is that the spicy entertainer frame tends to appear in shorter articles, while the investigative watchdog appears in longer articles. The model including newspaper placement and article size as explaining the variance in an objective vs. subjective article frame nicely fits the data ($R^2_{Nagelkerke} = 35\%$).

It was hypothesized that objective frames will be more likely to depict the survey results in figures and diagrams. As per this expectation, diagrams of any sort appeared in 41% of the articles that were classified as objective, but in none of the articles in the subjective category ($\gamma = 1$, p < 0.001). Nonetheless, no significant relationship was found between the presence of pictures in an article and the conceptual frame of the survey. It appears that pictures were simply added when articles were longer.

The types of polls significantly differed by article subject ($\lambda = 0.47$, p < 0.001). As hypothesized, the articles framed as "confidential advisor" dealt more with politics, the "camera" with economic subjects (50%; additional 17% political subjects, and 12% society), the "entertainer" with colorful subjects (67%), and the "watchdog" with social issues (67%; an additional 25% with culture and education, 8% politics).

As anticipated, most of the articles in the objective frames, as well as all the entertaining articles, did not exhibit any criticism toward the poll they reported or pitted conflicting poll results against each other. Articles in the "confidential advisor" frame, however, revealed much more of both. Thus, confrontation

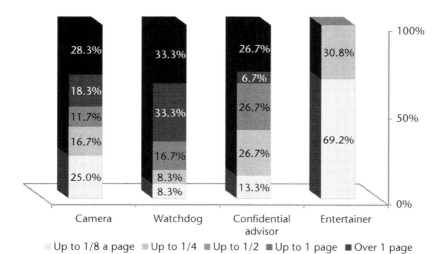

FIGURE 11.2 Article size by meta-frame

among different and contradictory survey findings were present in 80% of the "confidential advisor" articles, as opposed to 14% in the camera frame, 8% in the watchdog frame, and 0% in the entertainer frame (presence of a critical tone toward the survey: $\lambda = 0.41$, $p = 0.02$; presence of confrontation: $V_{Cramer's} = 0.56$, $p < 0.001$).

As hypothesized, objective frames offered more interpretation of the survey findings ($\gamma = 0.48$, $p = 0.04$) and more detailed information on the execution of the survey ($\gamma = 0.48$, $p < 0.001$). Thus, 42% of the articles in the camera frame and 50% of the articles in the watchdog frame provided more than four methodological details on the presented survey, as opposed to 23% in the entertainer frame, and none of the articles in the confidential advisor frame. However, interpretation and methodological detail were irrelevant in the vast majority of the confidential advisor articles (87% and 80%, accordingly), which dramatically reduced the sample for this frame in this part of the analysis.

Study 2: Experiment

Table 11.3 presents the regression coefficients for the effect on trust in the media (models I–IIIa) and trust in polls (models I–IIIb) of exposure to: (1) conditions in which the survey is presented as a subjective tool (compared to conditions that present articles in which the survey is presented as objective) (models Ia–b); (2) each of the subjective and objective conditions vs. the control (no-poll) group (models IIa–b); (3) each of the four meta-frames vs. the control (no-poll) group (models IIIa–b), all controlling for gender, age, and education. Across the various specifications, exposure to subjective polls reduces both trust in media and trust in polls (compared to both exposures to objective polls and to the no-poll control group), whereas trust in the media and truth in polls are unaffected by exposure to the objective polls.

Starting with models Ia–b, exposure to the two frames presenting the survey as subjective (entertainer and advisor) decreases trust in the media ($p_{Ia} = 0.001$) and trust in polls ($p_{Ia} = 0.011$) compared to the two frames presenting the survey as objective (camera and watchdog).

Next, when specified against the baseline of the control (no-poll) condition, exposure to the subjective polls decreases both trust in media ($p_{IIa} = 0.000$) and trust in polls ($p_{IIb} = 0.014$) in the treatment-only and in the controlled models, whereas trust in the media and trust in polls did not significantly differ in the objective polls compared to the control group ($p_{IIa} = 0.548$; $p_{IIb} = 0.767$).

In the same vein, the level of trust in the media and trust in polls upon exposure to a "camera" poll and a "watchdog" poll – the two frames presenting the survey as objective – did not significantly differ from the control group ($p_{IIIa} = 0.833$, 0.403; $p_{IIIb} = 0.626$, 0.291). Yet, exposure to the subjective "advisor" and "entertaining" polls each decreased trust in the media and in the polls compared to the control group ($p_{IIIa} = 0.000$, 0.009; $p_{IIIb} = 0.057$, 0.020).

TABLE 11.3 Trust in media and trust in poll by experimental condition

	Trust in media			Trust in polls		
	Ia	IIa	IIIa	Ib	IIb	IIIb
Frame type:						
Objective		−0.079			−0.072	
		(0.131)			(0.243)	
Subjective	−0.395**	−0.482**		−0.520*	−0.587*	
	(0.111)	(0.128)		(0.203)	(0.237)	
Camera			−0.032			0.136
			(0.149)			(0.279)
Watchdog			−0.130			−0.302
			(0.155)			(0.285)
Advisor			−0.589**			−0.531+
			(0.150)			(0.278)
Entertainer			−0.385**			−0.639*
			(0.147)			(0.273)
Male	−0.036	−0.015	−0.009	−0.103	−0.155	−0.168
	(0.117)	(0.101)	(0.101)	(0.213)	(0.186)	(0.186)
Age	−0.012	−0.008	−0.008	0.011	0.008	0.006
	(0.012)	(0.008)	(0.008)	(0.020)	(0.015)	(0.015)
Education	0.003	0.010	0.007	−0.125	−0.107	−0.087
	(0.051)	(0.039)	(0.040)	(0.093)	(0.072)	(0.074)
Constant	3.124**	3.030**	3.047**	5.230**	5.133**	4.934**
	(0.648)	(0.522)	(0.526)	(1.177)	(0.962)	(0.971)
N	149	190	190	148	188	188
R^2	0.099	0.105	0.116	0.060	0.062	0.075

Notes
Entries are unstandardized coefficients, standard errors in parentheses; ** $p < 0.01$, * $p < 0.05$, + $p < 0.1$.

Finally, to validate the results of the content analysis, we examined the extent to which participants can recognize the frame of the poll to which they were exposed. Results suggest that the frames were generally well identified by participants (p = 0.000). The entertaining poll was the easiest to identify (78% of the participants in this condition identified the frame by role), followed by the camera (63%), advisor (62%), and watchdog (35%). Overall, 63% of the subjects chose an image that fit the frame of the articles they received, suggesting that the frames were readily distinguishable by media consumers.

Discussion

Literature on political behavior and political communication habitually refers to news reports of mass opinion as surveys with considerable attention being given to their potential effects on subsequent mass opinion. However, little research is devoted to the distinction between meticulous surveys of pre-election preferences on the one hand, and surveys of other mass preferences, such as "64% of Israelis prefer pizza to burgers," on the other. This chapter aims to explicate this ambiguity and show that the media choose to publish several types of survey reports, and that these types have varying characteristics, such as article length, article placement in supplements or other non-headline sections, the use of visuals, and readers' interpretation of their function.

This study confirms the existence of "objective" and "subjective" framing for media surveys, as well as the four meta-frames that were derived from the role perceptions of the media – "camera," "watchdog," "confidential advisor," and "entertainer." As hypothesized, the objective frames work better than the subjective ones to increase a sense of neutrality and preciseness via diagrams and graphs. The camera frame is frequently presented in the various economic sections, the entertainer in short magazine articles, the confidential advisor in supplements, and the watchdog in the main news section. The last two frames, attempting to expose phenomena, describe developments, and understand the complexity of the social and political world, tend to present them on a broader scale. The articles that were framed as confidential advisor dealt more with politics, camera with economic issues, entertainer with colorful spicy stories, and watchdog with social issues. A survey framed as the latter is appropriate for articles with negative subjects, while a survey framed as entertaining is not appropriate for that type of article at all. Articles in the confidential advisor frame frequently present confrontations among different surveys and take on a critical tone toward the survey. More details regarding the survey's execution appear in the objective conditions, and more room is given to interpretation of the findings it raises.

The study also finds that frames have the ability to affect socio-political attitudes. Individuals who received survey narratives that were more subjective in nature were more likely to express lower levels of trust in the media than those who were exposed to those that were more objective. The results are in line with research that suggests that certain framing choices increase cynicism in general and cynicism toward the framing agency in particular (de Vreese & Elenbaas, 2008; Valentino et al., 2001).

This research indicates that individuals respond negatively toward the media when they report surveys in a particular fashion, a finding that may extend to other related areas. For instance, research describes a change in how information is presented, from a more neutral position to a more adversarial, judgmental tone (Fink & Schudson, 2014; Plasser, 2005). If our findings are suggestive of general trends, they would indicate that the media should experience a backlash for this change in reporting style. Specifically, by focusing on more subjective and mediated elements of coverage the media may be undermining the level of trust that people have for it.

While illuminative, the findings also hint at additional future research opportunities. Our study explored media frames within one specific outlet, *Yedioth*

Ahronoth, and one specific context, Israel. Interesting questions abound, however, regarding their implications for diverse settings and places. For instance, future research may examine changes over time in survey frames and compare the use of frames among the media. One could investigate the extent to which different types of media use the various survey frames. Could it be expected, for example, that an elite newspaper like *The New York Times* would use the same frames in the same proportions as a newspaper like *The New York Post*. Comparing the use of frames for surveys over time, place, and media type is especially interesting insofar as the manner of survey framing is a measure of the role perceptions of media persons.

Similarly, one could explore the extent to which the findings pertain to different socio-political contexts. Across democracies, for instance, does survey reporting take the same general form, or do differences exist? The media may exhibit diverse traditions depending upon individual customs specific to environment (Sheafer et al., 2013). Thus, countries where the media are held in high esteem may have different expectations for framing than one in which the media are more poorly regarded. Along the same line, do the media in esteemed democracies report surveys in markedly different ways than the media in developing democracies and in more autocratic environments?

Another possible area of exploration would be the examination of diverse media platforms. This study used a newspaper for its investigation, but there are other applications. Indeed, the past 20 years have seen many changes within the media environment, including the rise of the internet, citizen journalism, and the 24-hour news cycle. Given these new contexts, do the effects hold? One could imagine that the incessant search for audiences and consequent need to pander to base instincts has further eroded trust in media as an institution. Particularly, it is important to examine whether the use of subjective survey frames affects perceptions of truth and objectivity in a world of "fake news" and postmodernism.

Overall, this study reveals the full impact of role perception on framing. It appears that role perception is what allows flexibility in choosing a frame for the survey, and it is used as a means of justification for using subjective frames, especially the "entertainer." In the world of today's media, various principles – to create a "story" or a "headline" from the survey on the one hand, and to maintain the appearance of objectivity and neutrality on the other hand – contradict each other on occasion. Seemingly, the usual placement of each frame in a separate section of the newspaper (camera in economics, entertainment in the magazine, etc.) constitutes somewhat of a solution to the dissonance, because the executers of each section could formulate relatively independent perceptions and concentrate on a certain type of framing. However, the media consumer sees the newspaper as a whole, and the role of the press is transferred to them with no division between editors and sections.

Prudent use of surveys may assist the media in creating an open and democratic atmosphere, in which the public receives the most reliable information about events in the social, economic, and political world, and in turn, influences decision-making. Nevertheless, the frequent use of surveys and shallow reporting, and their use to create sensationalist headlines, are liable to lead to undesirable results that are manifested in decreased public trust in surveys, in the media, in academia, and in democracy as a whole. Hopefully, raising consciousness regarding the issue of surveys in the media, reflecting upon its implications, and further studying the role of framing surveys in attenuating this decline in trust will ultimately lead to a more responsible use of this tool.

Acknowledgments

For invaluable advice and support at different stages of the project, the first author is grateful to Michal Shamir and Gadi Bloom. All remaining errors are our own.

References

Arnesen, S., Johannesson, M. P., Linde, J., & Dahlberg, S. (2017). Do polls influence opinions? Investigating poll feedback loops using the novel dynamic response feedback experimental procedure. *Social Science Computer Review*, 1–9.

Ben-Nun Bloom, P., & Levitan, L. (2011). We're closer than I thought: Heterogeneity of social networks, source morality and political persuasion. *Political Psychology*, 32(4), 643–665.

Cappella, J. N., & Jamieson, K. H. (1997). *Spiral of cynicism: The press and the public good*. New York: Oxford University Press.

Caspi, D. (1995). *Mass communication: An introduction*. Tel Aviv: Open University. [in Hebrew].

Christenson, D. P., & Smidt, C. D. (2012). Polls and elections: Still part of the conversation: Iowa and New Hampshire's say within the invisible primary. *Presidential Studies Quarterly*, 42, 597–621.

Converse, P. E. (1964). The nature of belief systems in mass publics. In D. E. Apter (Ed.), *Ideology and discontent* (pp. 206–261). New York: Free Press.

Della Porta, D. (2008). Research on social movements and political violence. *Qualitative Sociology*, 31(3), 221–230.

Delli Carpini, M., & Keeter, S. (1996). *What Americans know about politics and why it matters*. New Haven, CT: Yale.

De Vreese, C. H., & Elenbaas, M. (2008). Media in the game of politics: Effects of strategic metacoverage on political cynicism. *International Journal of Press/Politics*, 13, 285–309.

Eagly, A. H., & Chaiken, S. (1993). *The psychology of attitudes*. Orlando, FL: Harcourt Brace Jovanovich College Publishers.

Faas, T., Mackenrodt, C., & Schmitt-Beck, R. (2008). Polls that mattered: Effects of media polls on voters' coalition expectations and party preferences in the 2005 German parliamentary election. *International Journal of Public Opinion Research*, 20(3), 299–325.

Festinger, L. (1954). A theory of social comparison processes. *Human Relations*, 7, 117–140.

Fink, K., & Schudson, M. (2014). The rise of contextual journalism, 1950s–2000s. *Journalism*, 15(1), 3–20.

Fuchs, C., & Bar-Lev, S. K. (1998). Polls – but how? In C. Fuchs, & S. K. Bar-Lev (Eds.), *Truth and polls*. Tel Aviv: The United Kibbutz. [in Hebrew].
Herbst, S. (1993). *Numbered voices: How opinion polling has shaped American politics*. Chicago, IL: University of Chicago.
Herbst, S. (1998). *Reading public opinion: Political actors view the democratic process*. Chicago, IL: University of Chicago.
Hertog, J. K., & McLeod, D. M. (2001). A multiperspectival approach to framing analysis: A field guide. In S. D. Reese, O. H. Gandy, & A. E. Grant (Eds.), *Framing public life* (pp. 139–162). Mahwah, NJ: Lawrence Erlbaum.
Iyengar, S. (1994). *Is anyone responsible? How television frames political issues*. Chicago, IL: University of Chicago.
Iyengar, S., & Kinder, D. (2010). *News that matters: Television and American public opinion, updated edition*. Chicago, IL: University of Chicago.
Miller, J. M., & Krosnick, J. A. (2000). News media impact on the ingredients of presidential evaluations: Politically knowledgeable citizens are guided by a trusted source. *American Journal of Political Science*, 44(2), 295–309.
Miller, P. V. (1995). The industry of public opinion. In T. L. Glaser, & C. T. Salmon (Eds.), *Public opinion and the communication of consent* (pp 105–131). New York: Guilford.
Morton, R. B, Muller, D., Page, L., & Torgler, B. (2015). Exit polls, turnout, and bandwagon voting: Evidence from a natural experiment. *European Economic Review*, 77, 65–81.
Moy, P., & Rinke, E. M. (2012). Attitudinal and behavioral consequences of published opinion polls. In C. Holtz-Bacha, & J. Strömbäck (Eds.), *Opinion polls and the media: Reflecting and shaping public opinion* (pp. 225–245). London: Palgrave Macmillan.
Nelson, T. E., Clawson, R. A., & Oxley, Z. M. (1997). Media framing of a civil liberties conflict and its effect on tolerance. *American Political Science Review*, 91, 567–583.
Plasser, F. (2005). From hard to soft news standards? How political journalists in different media systems evaluate the shifting quality of news. *Harvard International Journal of Press/Politics*, 10(2), 47–68.
Putnam, R. D. (2000). *Bowling alone: The collapse and revival of American community*. New York: Simon and Schuster.
Ragozzino, M., & Hartman, T. (2014). The influence of public opinion polls on issue preferences. doi: 10.2139/ssrn.2532324. Retrieved August 27, 2016 from http://ssrn.com/abstract=2532324 (27.08.2016).
Rothschild, D., & Malhotra, N. (2014). Are public opinion polls self-fulfilling prophecies? *Research & Politics*, 1(2), 1–10.
Schmitt-Beck, R. (1996). Mass media, the electorate, and the bandwagon: A study of communication effects on vote choice in Germany. *International Journal of Public Opinion Research*, 8(3), 266–291.
Schuck, A. R. T., Boomgaarden, H. G., & de Vreese, C. H. (2013). Cynics all around? The impact of election news on political cynicism in comparative perspective. *Journal of Communication*, 63, 287–311.
Shamir, J., & Shamir, M. (2000). *The anatomy of public opinion*. Ann Arbor, MI: University of Michigan.
Sheafer, T., Ben-Nun Bloom, P., Shenhav, S., & Segev, E. (2013). The conditional nature of value-based proximity between countries: Strategic implications for mediated public diplomacy. *American Behavioral Scientist*, 57(9), 1256–1276.
Shehata, A. (2014). Game frames, issue frames, and mobilization: Disentangling the effects of frame exposure and motivated news attention on political cynicism and engagement. *International Journal of Public Opinion Research*, 26, 157–177.

Sinclair, B. & Plott, C. (2012). Informing the uninformed: Do voters learn from pre-election polls? *Electoral Studies*, 31(1), 83–95.

Sonck, N., & Loosveldt, G. (2010). Impact of poll results on personal opinions and perceptions of collective opinion. *International Journal of Public Opinion Research*, 22(2), 230–255.

Steger, W. (2013). Polls and elections: Two paradigms of presidential nominations. *Presidential Studies Quarterly*, 43, 377–387.

Tsfati, Y., & Cappella, J. N. (2003). Do people watch what they do not trust? Exploring the association between news media skepticism and exposure. *Communication Research*, 30, 504–529.

Tsfati, Y., & Cohen, J. (2005). Democratic consequences of hostile media perceptions: The case of Gaza settlers. *The Harvard International Journal of Press/Politics*, 10, 28–51.

Valentino, N. A., Beckmann, M. N., & Buhr, T. A. (2001). A spiral of cynicism for some: The contingent effects of campaign news frames on participation and confidence in government. *Political Communication*, 18(4), 347–367.

Weaver, D. H., & Wilhoit, G. C. (1996). *The American journalist in the 1990s: US news people at the end of an era*. Mahwah, NJ: Lawrence Erlbaum.

Weiman, G. (1998). Beware of surveys? Coverage of pre-election polls in the Israeli media. In C. Fuchs, & S. K. Bar-Lev (Eds.), *Surveys: Some good, some less* (pp. 123–146). Tel Aviv: Hakibbutz Hameuchad. [in Hebrew].

12
MEDIA OWNERSHIP
Propositions for an Extended Research Agenda

Sonja Zmerli

Insights Gained

Assessing the psychology of political communicators and how their rhetoric, frames, representations, and agenda-setting impact on public discourse lay at the heart of this collection of empirical studies. With a major focus on the recent disruptive political and societal trends in liberal democracies, the contributions provide valuable insight into the interplay between politicians and the media in various cultural contexts.

For instance, they help us to understand how Donald J. Trump's electoral victory might partly be attributed to the rules of the game of Reality TV, which he mastered with aplomb. They inform us about the way Japanese cultural particularities determine the scope and the style of interactions between politicians and journalists during televised interviews and Japan's self-positioning on the world political stage. They greatly advance our knowledge of different types of populist communicators, their motivations, the means at their disposal, and their impact on political behavior. We are offered cross-national accounts of how and why the representations of female politicians in the media have changed over time and we learn under which circumstances the media may gain or lose people's trust, their most valuable currency. Simultaneously, this selection of studies clearly reminds us of the substantial complexity of interrelationships and significant cultural limitations of generalizability, with each contribution sketching various paths for related future research.

And yet, in light of the presented empirical evidence and currently observable developments related to the media landscape, additional research avenues are obviously open for in-depth scholarly inquiry. More specifically, the chapter discusses whether and to what avail a systematic assessment of power exercised through media owners in news organizations may elucidate the research field even further.

Propositions for an Extended Research Agenda

Media Ownership

Despite the encompassing perspective adopted by this volume, further research would open avenues toward fine-grained understanding of the causes of the recent developments in public discourse. In times of increasingly liberalized and deregulated media markets, the concentration of media owners, their own economic or political agenda, and the ensuing impact on the diversity and civility of public discourse have come to the fore. To be sure, ever since Silvio Berlusconi took office as Italian prime minister in 1994, the nature of the links between concentrated media ownership and (access to) political power have been under academic scrutiny. But only recently have there been attempts to develop a theoretical framework which allows us to identify, categorize, and evaluate news media owners' sources of power. Benson, Hessérus, and Sedel's theoretical proposition (forthcoming, cited in Scott, Bunce, & Wright, 2017) appears to be particularly fruitful in this regard.

Drawing on Scott et al.'s depiction (2017, p. 166) of Benson et al.'s theoretical framework of media owners' exercise of power within a news organization, four principal forms can be distinguished. First, there is the owner's aim to shape "journalists' conceptualization of their target audiences and audience-related objectives, as well as the ways in which they pursue them" (Scott et al., 2017, p. 166), which they label "market adjustment." One way of achieving this goal is by adapting formats of news stories to speak to specific segments of the audience who are of interest to advertisers (Scott et al., 2017, p. 166). Political and business instrumentalism, according to Benson et al. (forthcoming), are the second and third forms of ownership power. The main aim of both forms is to promote the media owner's political or economic interests, which may be exercised either through direct control of the editorial board or through journalistic self-censorship. Regardless of the channel of influence, the owner's ultimate goal is to affect journalists' selection of publicized events and topics in accordance with her concerns (Scott et al., 2017, p. 166). The fourth form of ownership power revolves around the interplay between profit expectations and resource allocations within a news organization which inevitably ends up affecting "the nature and level of [its] commitment to public service values" (Scott et al., 2017, p. 166). High demands on return, for instance, may lead to a shortage of resources for expensive reporting, such as reporting at the international level.

In practice, these four distinct modes of ownership power are usually intertwined and might be exercised simultaneously. Drawing on Bourdieu's sociological premises, Benson attributes to each form of power a "field-linked logic" of operation (Benson, 2016a, cited in Scott et al., 2017, p. 166) with "ownership power [being] mediated primarily by (1) the logics of the field that the media owner comes from and (2) the logics of the journalistic field" (Scott et al., 2017, p. 166).

Being equipped with this promising theoretical tool, further investigations into media owners' power pertaining to political and business instrumentalism seem particularly promising in order to extend the research field this volume is concerned with.

Over time, most empirical studies on the exercise of political and economic power have been conducted on Rupert Murdoch, until recently CEO of News Corporation, the world's second largest media company (Freedman, 2012, p. 3), some of which will be reported hereafter.

Benson's (2012) assessment of Murdoch as a "kingmaker or ringmaster" in American politics provides compelling insight into the political influence his conservative news outlets, e.g., the Fox News Channel, exert. They are clearly substantively more sensationalistic in both style and topic than other comparable news outlets, are definitely conservative, and are clearly linked to Murdoch's political and business interests. As Benson summarizes, "Murdoch media are among the most sensationalist and partisan media currently operating in the United States. They have done more than their share to lower the level of civility in American public discourse" (2012, p. 6). In-depth studies focusing on changes in reporting styles and topics covered before and after news outlets were purchased by Rupert Murdoch, such as the *New York Post* or the *San Antonio Daily*, add further empirical evidence to these general findings (Pasadeos & Renfro, 1988).

By the same token, McKnight underscores the importance of systematically studying the power wielded through news media ownership, particularly in light of Murdoch's role in English-speaking countries as one of the "key promoters of neo-liberal ideology of small government and deregulation over the past 30 years" (2012, p. 5). These assumptions are further corroborated by Dominguez and Pineda Cachero's investigation into Murdoch's ties "with the American conservative movement and the Republican Party" (2011, p. 195) and how these ties have been transforming the ideological landscape of the American media. As a paradigmatic mass medium, the Fox News Channel can be considered as one of the most effective amplifiers of his right-wing political leanings.

Rowinski's (2016) comparative study into the effects of media representations of Euroskepticism in Italy and Great Britain lends even more credence to Rupert Murdoch's perceived estimation of his own ability to influence European integration. In a BBC television interview in 2003 on the drafting procedures of a European Constitution, for example, he said "he would wait to see what was in the final EU Constitution, but that if it was anything like the draft, 'then *we'll* (his newspapers, author's italics) oppose it'" (BBC, 2003, cited in Rowinski, 2016, p. 984, text in parentheses in original).

Murdoch's propensity to intervene in politics by determining the political content of his media is furthermore corroborated by Shawcross' in-depth study (1992). In fact, as Berry (2016) puts it in his account of the so-called Leveson inquiry into the British press following the scandal and closure of Murdoch's *News of the World*:

> [i]ndeed, a point was reached where few British politicians or journalists dreamed of criticizing Murdoch, many among the latter group being mindful that even if they were not currently dependent on him for a livelihood, circumstances could easily arise in which they might be.
>
> (p. 285)

While Rupert Murdoch's political and economic ambitions seem to be most effectively put into place in the US, the UK, or Australia, media ownership in Central and Eastern European countries (CEE) reveals different, yet no less consequential, traits of political and business instrumentalism. The news media have only rarely achieved full autonomy from politics and the economy and this results in lower levels of structural differentiation of news media from the viewpoint of neo-functionalist sociology (Stetka, 2012, pp. 434–435). As a matter of fact, the composition of media ownership has experienced several phases in CEE countries after the fall of the Iron Curtain. The first phase began with the internationalization of the CEE media landscape with predominantly European and privately owned media corporations attempting to get a hold of, until then, uncharted media territory and to modernize all branches of news media production. In the aftermath of the Great Recession, though, patterns of media ownership changed substantially, which can be perceived as the de-westernization of CEE media markets (Stetka, 2012, p. 438). In light of substantial losses in advertising revenues, particularly in the print media, many foreign investors withdrew from this region. However, as Bodo Hombach, CEO of a German media corporation, put it in an interview, it was another major and locally-rooted obstacle that discouraged many foreign investors from further involvement: "Oligarchs in the Balkans are buying ever more often newspapers and magazines in order to exert political influence, not in order to win money. We cannot stand up to such market-destroying competition."[1] In fact, Hombach's personal account of the Balkans situation has frequently been confirmed by practitioners and academics from other CEE regions as well and can thus be conceived of as a general characteristic of "many of the Central and Eastern European media systems of today" (Stetka, 2012, p. 441). Basically, this trend is the second phase, and reflects the increasing commitment of local business elites to invest in news media outlets as amplifiers of their own political or business interests. Since their primary sources of profit predominantly lie outside of the media sector, they do not necessarily seek monetary profit. What they are really after is effective channels through which their political ambitions may operate. On a rather pessimistic note, Stetka posits that certain CEE countries might be on the path of "oligarization" (2012, p. 449), "where the concentration of media, business, and political power in the hands of significant individuals – colloquially known as oligarchs – has been omnipresent ever since the fall of communism" (ibid., p. 449). Moreover, most CEE countries' worsening Press Freedom Index scores objectively testify to these disturbing developments (ibid., p. 449).

Andrej Babiš' victory at the Czech parliamentary elections in December 2017, which subsequently led to his election as prime minister of the Czech Republic, forcefully illustrates the close relationship between business, media, and political power. As the founder and sole owner of Agrofert,[2] a holding company doing business in chemistry, food processing, agriculture, forestry, energy, and the media, and which is the largest employer in the Czech Republic, Babiš has become one of the richest people in his country and the leader of the protest movement ANO, whose stated purpose is the fight against corruption.[3] Ironically, shortly after he took office, Babiš himself lost his immunity in a parliamentary vote based on accusations of fraud related to EU subsidies.[4]

At the time this chapter was written, yet more evidence of political and business instrumentalism of media ownership occurred in the US. During the Easter weekend of 2018, the Sinclair Broadcast Group, the biggest owner of local television stations in the United States, owning or operating 173 of them, mandated a "must-run commentary" by all of its anchors in a promotional spin that echoed Donald Trump's anti-media rhetoric.

> The company's conservative-leaning politics have come down to Sinclair's stations through "must runs" – stories local producers are told to air during their newscasts. The "Terrorism Alert Desk" is a recurring segment. Pro-Trump commentaries by former Trump campaign adviser Boris Epshteyn are another "must-run" feature.[5]

Similar trends in political instrumentalism are observable for some online news sites. During the American presidential election campaign, for instance, Breitbart News, an American right-wing news site, gained substantive prominence and political leverage. Its co-owner at that time, Robert Mercer, an American billionaire, has long been known for his continuous substantial financial support of conservative politicians (Green, 2017; Wolff, 2018),[6] and Breitbart's executive chairman, Steve Bannon, became the White House chief strategist right after Trump's inauguration as American president.

The Israeli media ownership landscape offers further insight into the consequential presence of political and business instrumentalism. In what is currently known as the investigative case 2,000, the publisher of a leading Israeli newspaper was allegedly requested to publish supportive coverage of the Israeli prime minister, Netanyahu, by the prime minister himself in exchange for damaging a competitor, the pro-Netanyahu freesheet *Israel Hayom*. In the so-called case 4,000, by contrast, the owners of *Bezeq Israel Telecom* have been charged by prosecutors with having provided positive coverage of the Netanyahus on a news website in return for regulatory changes worth hundreds of millions of dollars.[7]

These and similar developments have led scholars to reflect on whether other, non-profit-seeking types of media ownership or financing through donors or foundations could be an effective remedy. Although recent empirical studies suggest that some of the key problems might be mitigated by these alternative ownership configurations, we are far from seeing the back of them (Benson, 2016b; Scott et al., 2017).

Some Examples of the "Fox News" Effect

So far, a multitude of studies have accumulated a large stock of empirical evidence which underscores to what extent the advent of opinionated news outlets as well as the presence of political and business instrumentalism, exercised by media owners, may affect public discourse, citizens' political involvement, and politicians' decision-making. Many of these analyses focus on recent significant changes in the US media landscape, some of which are reported below.

Examining the effects of structural changes to the media system, brought about by the Telecommunications Act of 1996 and the setting up of the Fox News Channel, Hmielowski, Beam, and Hutchens (2016) demonstrate that affective polarization increased more strongly after 1996 and that TV news usage contributed to this trend. Boukes, Boomgaarden, Moorman, and de Vreese (2014) use an experimental design to substantiate how opinionated news may provoke anger, via hostile media perceptions, particularly in people with incongruent political preferences.

Taking on a generally more pessimistic perspective, Lazitski (2014) argues that different forms of so-called media endarkenment, "including the construction of a false reality, intimidation, and simplification" (p. 898), were traceable during the 2012 US national TV channels' presidential election coverage. Media endarkenment is thus conceived of as a process of media influence that ultimately impedes the vibrancy of public discourse and citizens' level of information.

Turning the focus toward studies that specifically investigate the variegated effects of Fox News on its viewers, there seem to be several important factors. There is, first, evidence that Fox News bolsters pro-Republican voting intentions for Republicans and pure independents (Hopkins & Ladd, 2014), and beliefs are affected by the cultivation of conservative ideology (Hindman & Yan, 2015). The second factor is people's racial attitudes. Qualitative as well as quantitative and experimental studies suggest that the Fox News Channel perpetuates racist discourse, based on the TV channel's coverage of the shooting of an unarmed African American in Ferguson in 2016 (Mills, 2017), or promotes anti-Muslim attitudes, which have been spreading in the aftermath of 9/11 (Calfano, Djupe, Cox, & Jones, 2016). The third factor reflects attitude changes which can be attributed to business instrumentalism.

Particularly during the Great Recession, Fox News pundits appeared to be siding with the working class by advocating traditional moral-economic principles, framing the wealthy and the business class as job creators and thus including them in the moral community of "producers" (Peck, 2014, 2017). Indeed, Hochschild's (2016) in-depth study into the belief systems of conservative citizens from Louisiana provides ample evidence of the vibrancy of these moral-economic convictions. Finally, the fourth factor discloses to what extent the Fox News Channel has been affecting political elites' strategic responsiveness and legislative behavior irrespective of their party affiliation. For instance, both Republican and Democratic Members of Congress who represent districts with a sizable proportion of Republican voters are more inclined to support the Republican Party's position on divisive votes (Arceneaux, Johnson, Lindstadt, & Van der Wielen, 2016). Similarly, Jacobs and Townsley (2014) demonstrate that President Clinton lost support from representatives in districts where Fox News had started to broadcast compared with other districts where it was not yet present at that time.

In Conclusion

Public discourse, an indispensable pillar of liberal democracy, is a multi-faceted concept which never stops inspiring scholarly research. Its implications are far-reaching and perspectives that lend themselves to in-depth analyses manifold. As a consequence, the empirical studies collected in this volume address a delimited yet highly topical scope of research questions, ranging from Reality TV communication styles penetrating the sphere of public discourse to rhetoric and framing techniques used by populist communicators and changing representations of women in politics, to name but a few. These contributions provide valuable cross-cultural and cross-national insight into the causes and consequences of the destabilizing factors many liberal democracies are facing today.

Similarly, the volume's contributors have convincingly demonstrated how closely politicians and the media interact with each other, while embedded in a shared cultural context, to construct and shape public discourse.

Notwithstanding, an ever increasing share of public discourse is evolving on social media platforms, which were only marginally the subject of the analysis included in this volume. Undoubtedly, future research into the psychology of political communicators and their impact on public discourse would also have to take these new forms of direct communication between politicians and citizens into account. In the age of the Trump presidency, for instance, politics through Twitter feeds has become commonplace. Concomitantly, social media platforms seem to encourage people to use hate speech or defamatory language as their personal identities can remain concealed if they wish. In this vein, citizens might equally be partially responsible for making public discourse more uncivil and polarized. As the public has learnt in the wake of the US presidential campaign of 2016, though, foreign powers might also be tempted to misuse social media platforms in order to manipulate public discourse to their political advantage.

Having said this, it needs to be emphasized that, although democratic societies' recently emerging vulnerability and instability may be reflected in uncivil and polarized public discourse, the latter should not be mistaken as the cause thereof. Rather, the point is that pre-existing and steadily worsening conflicts over political, economic, and societal issues may offer fertile ground for fundamental public discord to build up, spread, and reinforce already existing conflicts. Thus, adopting an interdisciplinary research strategy, encompassing social psychology, sociology, political science, economics, or cultural studies, seems to be a necessary step toward a better understanding of the underlying causal complexities.

Notes

1. According to www.handelsblatt.com/unternehmen/it-medien/konzernchefhombach-sagt-dem-balkan-ade/3505254.html (accessed October 30, 2011, cited in Stetka, 2012, p. 441).
2. In order to comply with Czech legal requirements, Babiš had to formally abandon his ownership of Agrofert when he took office as prime minister.
3. www.anobudelip.cz/cs/volby/program/ (accessed April 2, 2018).
4. https://derstandard.at/2000072387330/Tschechiens-Parlament-koennte-Premier-Babis-wegen-Storchennest-Affaereausliefern (accessed April 2, 2018).
5. http://money.cnn.com/2018/04/01/media/sinclair-anchor-promos/index.html (accessed April 2, 2018).
6. www.washingtonpost.com/politics/pro-trump-megadonor-is-part-owner-of-breitbart-news-empire-ceo-reveals/2017/02/24/9f16eea4-fad8-11e6-9845-576c69081518_story.html?utm_term=.40b64d85b2d2 (accessed April 2, 2018).
7. www.theguardian.com/world/2018/mar/02/police-question-benjamin-netanyahu-over-third-corruption-case (accessed April 2, 2018).

References

Arceneaux, K., Johnson, M., Lindstadt, R., & Van der Wielen, R. J. (2016). The influence of news media on political elites: Investigating strategic responsiveness in Congress. *American Journal of Political Science*, 60(1), 5–29.

BBC, (2003). Murdoch paper may back Tories. BBC, 15 November. Retrieved July 25, 2013 from http://news.bbc.co.uk/1/hi/uk_politics/3272023.stm.

Benson, R. (2012). Murdoch in the United States: Kingmaker or ringmaster? *Global Media and Communication*, 8(1), 4–7.

Benson, R. (2016a). Institutional forms of media ownership and their modes of power. In M. Eide, H. Sjøvaag, & L. Larsen (Eds.), *Journalism reexamined* (pp. 29–47). Bristol: Intellect.

Benson, R. (2016b). Are foundations the solution to the American journalistic crisis? *Media Ownership Project Working Paper 2016–001*. New York: NYU Department of Media, Culture, and Communication.

Benson, R., Hessérus, M., & Sedel, J. (forthcoming). *How media ownership matters*. Oxford: Oxford University Press.

Berry, N. (2016). Afterword: Lessons of the Leveson inquiry into the British press. In L. Brake, C. Kaul, & M. W. Turner (Eds.), *The News of the World and the British press, 1843–2011: Journalism for the rich, journalism for the poor* (pp. 280–286). London: Palgrave.

Boukes, M., Boomgaarden, H. G., Moorman, M., & de Vreese, C. H. (2014). News with an attitude: Assessing the mechanisms underlying the effects of opinionated news. *Mass Communication and Society*, 17(3), 354–378.

Calfano, B. R., Djupe, P. A., Cox, D., & Jones, R. (2016). Muslim mistrust: The resilience of negative public attitudes after complimentary information. *Journal of Media and Religion*, 15(1), 29–42.

Dominguez, L. R., & Pineda Cachero, A. (2011). Media structure and neoconservatism: Rupert Murdoch and his media arrival in the USA. *Estudios Sobre El Mensaje Periodístico*, 17(1), 195–214.

Freedman, D. (2012). A round-table on the international dimensions of News Corp in the light of the UK phone hacking scandal. *Global Media and Communication*, 8(1), 3–25.

Green, J. (2017). *Devil's bargain. Steve Bannon, Donald Trump, and the storming of the presidency*. New York: Penguin Press.

Hindman, D. B., & Yan, C. M. (2015). The knowledge gap versus the belief gap and abstinence-only sex education. *Journal of Health Communication*, 20(8), 949–957.

Hmielowski, J. D., Beam, M. A., & Hutchens, M. J. (2016). Structural changes in media and attitude polarization: Examining the contributions of TV news before and after the Telecommunications Act of 1996. *International Journal of Public Opinion Research*, 28(2), 153–172.

Hochschild, A. (2016). *Strangers in their own land*. New York: The New Press.

Hopkins, D. J., & Ladd, J. M. (2014). The consequences of broader media choice: Evidence from the expansion of Fox News. *Quarterly Journal of Political Science*, 9(1), 115–135.

Jacobs, R., & Townsley, E. (2014). The hermeneutics of Hannity: Format innovation in the space of opinion after September 11. *Cultural Sociology*, 8(3), 240–257.

Lazitski, O. (2014). Media endarkenment: A comparative analysis of 2012 election coverage in the United States and Russia. *American Behavioral Scientist*, 58(7), 898–927.

McKnight, D. (2012). Henry Mayer Lecture 2012: The market populism of Rupert Murdoch. *Media International Australia*, 144(1), 5–12.

Mills, C. E. (2017). Framing Ferguson: Fox News and the construction of US racism. *Race & Class*, 58(4), 39–56.

Pasadeos, Y., & Renfro, P. (1988). Rupert Murdoch's style: The New York Post. *Newspaper Research Journal*, 9(4), 25–33.

Peck, R. (2014). "You say rich, I say job creator": How Fox News framed the Great Recession through the moral discourse of producerism. *Media Culture & Society*, 36(4), 526–535.

Peck, R. (2017). Usurping the usable past: How Fox News remembered the Great Depression during the Great Recession. *Journalism*, 18(6), 680–699.

Rowinski, P. (2016). Euroscepticism in the Berlusconi and Murdoch press. *Journalism*, 17(8), 979–1000.

Scott, M., Bunce, M., & Wright, K. (2017). Donor power and the news: The influence of foundation funding on international public service journalism. *The International Journal of Press/Politics*, 22(2), 163–184.

Shawcross, W. (1992). *Murdoch*. New York: Simon & Schuster.

Stetka, V. (2012). From multinationals to business tycoons: Media ownership and journalistic autonomy in Central and Eastern Europe. *The International Journal of Press/Politics*, 17(4), 433–456.

Wolff, M. (2018). *Fire and fury. Inside the Trump White House*. London: Little, Brown.

INDEX

Abe, Shinzō 50, 61, 65
affective polarization 230
agenda bias 129, 140
agenda-setting 185
androcentrism 201
anxiety 5, 15
attachment 94
attack 13, 18, 20, 22–23, 48, 51–52, 68, 83, 116, 119, 123–142, 148, 159

belonging 81, 96, 160
blame attribution 83, 85–86, 90–91, 93–94, 97
broadcast political interviews 5, 32; *see also* televised political interviews
Bush, George W. 61, 65–71, 73, 147, 150, 156, 159–161, 163

campaign tone 130, 139–140
Carpini, Delli 204
Clinton, Hillary 13, 21–22
CNN effect 146
collocations or collocates 59, 60, 63, 67, 70, 72
communication, political 8, 58, 67, 219
communication strategy 52, 80, 118
concordance(s) 59–60, 65, 67–68, 72
construction of meaning 5, 58
content analysis 7, 8, 85, 88, 89, 97, 107, 130, 146, 148–149, 171, 189, 205, 212–216
Corriere della Sera 105, 106, 112–116, 118

coverage bias 129, 138–139
cultural approach to communication 5, 54, 58, 71, 88, 101, 166
culture 1, 5, 8, 17, 31–32, 34, 50, 52–54, 56, 64–65, 70–71, 126, 153–154, 157, 160, 166, 167, 169, 171, 173, 179–180, 213, 217
cynicism 8, 51, 92, 205, 212, 220

democracy 27, 66, 68, 95, 101, 107–108, 110, 112–113, 116–119, 124, 145, 152, 153–154, 157, 160, 167, 205, 208, 212, 222, 231
democracy's watchdog 40, 103, 205, 207, 208, 209, 211, 214–220
Democratic Party of Japan 32, 53, 55
Diplomacy 56–57, 69, 71
discourse 1–6, 31, 58–60, 66, 71, 72, 79–83, 88, 91, 96, 107, 118, 145, 147, 177, 178, 181, 225–227, 230–232; *see also* political discourse
discourse analysis 4, 5, 9, 60
Dölling, Irene 186
double bind 187, 188, 195, 199
drama 17, 22–24

"easy" news story 207
election campaigns 6, 7, 14, 25, 26, 27, 123–125, 128–142, 150–151, 185–186, 188–191, 193–194, 198, 200
elections 68, 79, 97, 106, 118–119, 125, 128–131, 134, 139, 148, 153, 162–163,

165–166, 170–173, 175–177, 179–182, 190, 198, 200, 206, 229
elite/popular press 167, 176, 206, 228, 231, 101–102, 107, 110, 112, 114, 116–119
elites 24, 27, 80–85, 87–91, 94–96, 100–102, 107–108, 110, 112–114, 116–119, 206, 228, 231
emotions 2, 21, 101, 109, 114
entertainment provider 209, 212, 221
equivocation (during interviews) 3, 35–36, 49–53
equivocation theory 35–36
experiment 8, 80, 91, 93, 214, 218

face-damaging responses 34
"fake news" 2, 205, 221
female: characteristics 70; political leadership 7, 177, 188, 189, 191, 195–196, 199–200; politicians 7, 165–170, 173, 175–182, 185–196, 198–200, 225
Festinger, Leon 204
filter bubbles 96
frames 2, 3, 5, 6, 8, 58, 59, 65, 67–72, 80, 84, 85, 91, 95, 103, 128, 150, 165, 167–169, 173–175, 177, 179–181, 197, 205, 207–221, 225
framing theory 147, 166
Freedom Party 79, 81, 83–84, 89

gender: bias 7, 165, 167, 169–170, 178, 180–182; coverage 171, 173–174, 178; equality 70; framing 166, 170, 181; knowledge 7, 185–187, 199–200
gendered media images 7, 185–187, 197, 199–200
Goffman, Erving 147
Grillo, Beppe 6, 99–100, 104, 106, 114, 116, 119; and blog 105–106; speeches 104, 106, 110–111

Habermas, Jürgen 187
Hochschild, Arlie Russell 18–21, 231

identity framing 182
Il Fatto Quotidiano 105, 106, 112–119
Il Giornale 105, 106, 112–116, 118
"insurgent phase" 6, 99, 102, 104, 117, 119
interviewees 31–54
interviewers 31–54
invited behavior 5, 13, 26

Israel 4, 7, 8, 65, 165–182, 191, 204, 206, 212, 214, 220–221
Israeli media 165–182, 204, 212, 229
issue: "feminine" ("female") 168, 170, 173, 174, 179; policy 31, 34; political 3, 168, 180, 206, 210, 232; social 211, 216–217; societal 95, 232
Italian: elections 118–119; newspapers 99–100, 103–105, 107, 112, 114, 117–118; political class 114, 117, 118, 119; press 100, 104, 105, 107, 112, 117–119
Italy 4, 6, 103–105, 119

Japan 4, 5, 31–34, 37–38, 40–42, 46, 48, 50–55, 57, 59–67, 69–73, 225
Japanese National Parliament (Diet) 32
journalism 171, 205–206, 212, 221
journalistic work/ethics 54, 84–86, 88, 167, 171, 173, 176, 179–180, 182
journalists 4, 14, 25, 31, 33, 46, 52, 54, 84–88, 95–97, 129, 130, 147, 153, 155, 157, 159, 162, 167–168, 205–207, 225–226, 228
journalist's responsibility 167, 208

La Repubblica 105, 106, 112, 113, 114, 115, 116, 118
leadership: media 25; political 3, 15, 16, 17, 70, 101, 123, 168, 170, 172–173, 177, 180, 191; *see also* female, political leadership
Liberal Democratic Party (Japan) 32, 53, 55
Liberal Democratic Party (UK) 125, 129

mass market media 102–105, 118
mass media 1, 2, 145, 148, 154, 162, 164, 166
McCombs, Maxwell 146
meaning, construction of 5, 56–59
media: amplification 128; (communication) channels 8, 104, 107, 110–112, 118, 162, 165, 230; coverage 4, 6, 7, 13, 24–25, 97, 99–100, 102–105, 107, 112, 114, 116, 118, 124, 129, 131, 133, 136–140, 146–148, 161, 169–181, 185–186, 188, 191–194, 196–197, 199–200, 206; effects 13, 24, 58, 79–80, 91, 93, 97–98, 124, 128, 148, 152, 157, 166, 179, 205, 210, 221; gender dichotomies 168, 179; gender stereotypes 168, 170, 180; objectivity

media *continued*
    204–205, 208, 215, 221; representation 7, 146, 147–150, 152–153, 175, 160–163, 185–187, 190, 192, 195, 198–200; and role perceptions 205, 207, 208, 220, 221
mediated communication 6, 99, 104–107, 119, 145
Merkel, Angela 185, 188, 195
message: political 3, 49, 57, 58, 64, 112, 116, 127; political parties' 107; populist 79, 84, 85, 86, 90–97, 111, 118
mother, as a metaphor 186, 188, 189, 194–195, 196–197, 200
motivated reasoning 93

negative campaigning 4, 6, 123–129, 131–133, 136–139
Netherlands, the 4, 6, 32, 37, 38, 40, 41, 46, 48, 50–52, 70, 80–82, 84, 87–89, 91, 94–95
news: coverage 24, 84, 128, 133, 139, 147; frame 128, 167; as reflection 2, 146; value 102, 128, 140, 226
Noelle-Neumann, Elisabeth 146

Obama, Barack 61, 65

partisanship 105, 127, 139
perception(s) 2, 4, 6, 8, 44, 59, 80–81, 88–96, 124, 138–139, 146–147, 155–157, 162, 185–186, 205, 207–209, 212, 215, 220–221, 230
persona 17
personal: attacks 18; career 187; communication 104; conflict 20, 24; connection 5; experience 145; ideas 50; information 35; opinion 44; perspective 35; relationship 15, 168; traits 169, 188
personality (personalities) 16–17, 23, 26, 166, 193, 196, 198, 200
personalization 128, 181
polarization, societal 8, 96, 230
political: campaign 2, 6, 7, 16, 104, 124–130, 139, 152, 154, 170–173, 176–182, 188–190, 193, 198, 229; cynicism 8, 92, 205, 212, 220; discourse 1, 3, 58, 59, 71–72, 178; femininity 172, 187, 193, 195–196; incivility 126; information 40, 212; masculinity 7, 172, 186–187, 196, 198–201; party (parties) 32–34, 42, 44–45, 53, 81, 83–84, 105, 118, 124–127; political issues *see* issues

polls 8, 128, 154–155, 204–206, 209, 210, 212, 214, 217–219
popular media 205
populism 2, 6, 8, 24, 79–96, 99–104, 107–119; as communication style 100–102, 107, 109, 111–112, 114–116, 118; ideological elements of 100–103, 112, 116; "laboratory of" 104
populist: communication 6, 79–80, 83–84, 87, 90–96, 101–102, 117–118; message 6, 79, 84–86, 90–96, 107, 111–112, 114, 116–119; party 6, 79, 81, 83, 84, 89, 90, 99, 102–104, 107, 110–111, 114, 117–119
positive campaigning 6, 125–129, 131–133, 136–139
press–party parallelism 129, 139
prime minister 5, 7, 42, 48–49, 50, 52, 55, 61, 123, 150–151, 158–160, 163, 165, 170, 171, 173, 175–178, 180–182, 186, 190, 192–196, 201, 226, 229, 232
public and private spheres 168, 187–188, 195, 200
public opinion 6, 72, 94, 96, 146, 204, 210, 214

qualitative content analysis 7, 60, 61, 67, 88, 89, 146, 148–149, 165, 189

Reality TV 5, 13–17, 20–27, 225, 231
relative deprivation 89, 90, 93, 95, 96
rhetoric 1–3, 8, 21, 27, 80, 81, 84, 107, 127, 132, 136, 138, 158, 161, 204, 215, 225, 229, 231

Sanders, Bernie 19, 21
second gender 7, 187
selection bias 95–96, 124, 129, 139, 140
selective exposure 93–94
self-directed communication 99–100, 102, 104, 107, 116–118
sequential analysis 189
Shaw, Donald 146
social comparison theory 204
social identity perspective 88, 90; theory 95
social networks 162–163
sociology of knowledge 186, 189
statement bias 129, 140
Swabian housewife 197, 201

televised debates 7, 22, 128, 154–163
televised political interviews 31–32, 40, 50, 51, 53–55, 225

television 3, 5, 15, 25, 31, 119, 124, 140, 145, 148, 152, 154, 155, 157, 160, 162, 165–166, 227
The Apprentice 15–17, 25
threat to "face" 34, 40, 44–45, 51, 53–55
Trump, Donald J. 2, 5, 13–17, 20, 23, 25–26, 225, 229
trust in media 204–205, 208, 210, 212, 214, 218, 219–222

United Kingdom (UK) 4, 6, 7, 32, 37–38, 40–41, 46, 48, 50–52, 123–126, 128–129, 131–136, 138, 140, 145–146, 148, 150–151, 153, 155–158, 160–163, 228

United Nations (UN) 5, 57, 61, 63–68, 71, 72
United Nations General Assembly (UNGA) 5, 56–61, 64–65, 67–69, 71–72
United States of America (US) 2, 4, 5, 7, 13, 17, 19, 56–57, 59–73, 124, 128, 138, 145–148, 150–151, 154, 156–157, 159–163, 227–230

Wilders, Geert 81, 83

Yedioth Ahronot 8, 171, 173–178, 180, 212–214

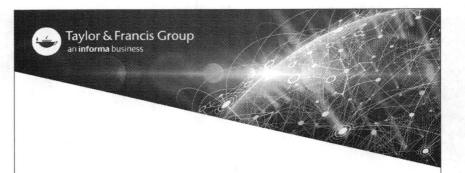

Printed in the United States
by Baker & Taylor Publisher Services